MW00897749

From The

CRADLE

To The

CROSS

Series of Sermons
for
Advent and Lent

by

Robert L. Tasler

" Preach the Word" 2 Tim 4:2

Tasler 2015

BOOKS BY THE AUTHOR

Daily Walk With Jesus
Daily Word From Jesus
Day By Day With Jesus
Spreading The Word
Fun And Games At Palm Creek
Reflections
Bobby Was A Farmer Boy
From The Cradle To The Cross
Discipleship Bible Study Series (six studies)
    Old Testament Prophets, Matthew
    James, First and Second Peter
    Philippians, Colossians (coming soon)

(E-Book only)

Country Preacher
Small Town Preacher
Immigrant Son

PERMISSION FOR USE

The author grants permission for pastors to use any or all parts of these sermons, revised or in entirety, without copyright infringement. The author does, however, request his readers to recommend this book to friends and colleagues if they have found it useful.

The author is an Emeritus Pastor of the Lutheran Church – Missouri Synod, a graduate of Concordia Seminary, St. Louis, Missouri, ordained in 1971. All of his published works, including Daily Devotionals and Bible Studies, may be found online at his website: www.bobtasler.com.

TABLE OF CONTENTS

ADVENT

ADVENT Series One............................ Page 1
"The Prophets Speak"

ADVENT Series Two........................... Page 17
"Advent Questions"

ADVENT Series Three........................ .Page 35
"Prophet, Priest and King"

ADVENT Series Four.......................... Page 53
"Women of Advent"

ADVENT Series Five.......................... Page 65
"Getting Ready"

ADVENT Series Six .... Page 83
"What to do In Advent?"

LENT

LENT Series One.............................. .Page 97
"Certainty For Uncertain Times"

LENT Series Two.............................. .Page 131
"Were You There?"

LENT Series Three........................... Page 165
"Seven Last Words"

LENT Series Four............................ Page 197
"Miracles of Good Friday"

LENT Series Five............................ Page 223
"Living for the Lord"

LENT Series Six .... .Page 251
"The Lord's Prayer" (Eight sermons)

AUTHOR .... Page 283

PREFACE

Most pastors who observe the Church Year seasons of Advent or Lent seek new ideas each year for sermons and themes from which they may help their members understand the meaning of Advent or Lent.

Advent points us to the Lord's first coming into the world and prepares us for a proper celebration of Christmas. Lent is a unique time that reminds us of the great love shown us through the suffering and death of our Messiah Jesus and prepares us for a joyful celebration of His resurrection at Easter.

These sermons were written and delivered during various years by the author, a retired Lutheran Pastor of the Lutheran Church – Missouri Synod. While a theme may sound familiar, the contents of these sermons are mostly original. Except for minor corrections, they are printed here as originally presented from the pulpit. Accordingly, the author asks forgiveness for the occasional typo or misplaced word.

Writing manuscripts meant to be spoken can be different from those meant to be read. Hence, there will be occasional sentence fragments and questionable grammar. These are a part of the author's speaking style.

If you see a familiar theme, don't assume the sermons will be what you have seen before. The author has presented his own thoughts on the theme. The illustrative stories within the sermons are either original or adaptations. The author gives credit to stories if their origin is known.

May the Lord of the Church bless your efforts as you inspire people with Christ-centered thoughts and messages during Advent and Lent.

Rev. Robert L. Tasler, 2015
Castle Rock, CO
Casa Grande, AZ

DEDICATION

To all shepherds who struggle each Church Year to find new and fresh messages to feed to their flock during Advent and Lent.

(These Advent sermon series were written for a specific congregation and time)

Sermons For Advent

ADVENT SERIES ONE
"The Prophets Speak"
Week One

Jeremiah 33:14-16   *"Looking for Righteousness"*
"The days are coming, declares the LORD, when I will fulfill the gracious promise I made to the house of Israel and to the house of Judah. In those days and at that time I will make a righteous Branch sprout from David's line; he will do what is just and right in the land. In those days Judah will be saved and Jerusalem will live in safety. This is the name by which it will be called: 'The Lord Our Righteousness'." (Yahweh Tsidkenu)

✛ ✛ ✛

Once again we are in the midweek services of Advent, the beginning of the Church Year which started last Sunday. The Church Year is divided into two halves, the Lord's Half, beginning with Advent, and the Church's Half, beginning with Trinity Sunday. The Lord's Half Year is all about events in the life of our Lord Jesus - His birth, ministry, suffering, death, resurrection and ascension back to heaven.

The Church's Half Year concentrates on the teachings of Jesus, His parables, His miracles, His teachings given to his disciples about salvation, His substitutionary sacrifice for the sins of all people. Advent is the time to recall Christ's coming into the world and how it changed everything.

Advent is a penitential time, a time to change something in our life for the better. *Ole and Sven were Norwegian bachelor farmers from Minnesota, so they were also Lutheran. One day in December Ole reminded Sven it was Advent, a time to repent. "I guess ve gots to change sumting!" he said. Hopefully Sven changed into a new pair of overalls.*

Now, is that the kind of change we need in Advent? Or should we act differently than we normally do, maybe get

1

penitential, or try harder to be good?

Advent, we know, means "arrival." On Christmas Eve, our household will celebrate the arrival of son Brian who flies down to Arizona each year to join us and his brother's family for Christmas. This year we also celebrate the arrival of our third grandchild, an infant baby girl who arrived just a month from African Congo to be adopted by our other son Chuck and his family.

Together we will celebrate the first arrival of the infant Jesus, recalling how He came as a human child from heaven to earth, born of the virgin Mary, to live with sinful humans and pay the price for our sins. Most of us will probably place more emphasis on the arrival of family and festivities than on the arrival of baby Jesus, but this time of year we can be glad about both. Advent brings us together.

The Church has made Advent a penitential season. As we prepare to celebrate Christ's first coming to earth, we are encouraged to reflect on how we can live better lives and serve Christ and His people better, as we await His second coming. We take time to confess our sins and ask God's grace to improve our behavior. With thoughtful and caring hearts we reflect on His first Advent at Bethlehem, and with expectant hearts we await His second Advent in Judgment. Though Judgment Day seems off in the future, it also should be for Christians a present reality. The older we become, the closer and more real Judgment Day becomes.

Our Advent theme this year is: "The Prophets Speak," and this week Jeremiah speaks. The prophet Jeremiah spoke these words 600 years Before Christ, speaking on behalf of God, saying, **"Behold, the days are coming when I will fulfill the gracious promise I made."** Through the prophet Jeremiah God reminds His people of the promised Savior who would come to rescue them. In reminding them, God is calling them back to Him in repentance.

At the time Jeremiah spoke these words, the Chosen People of Israel and Judah had strayed far from God. They were living wicked and godless lives. It had been four hundred years since King David, and nine hundred years since the Exodus. The people had forgotten the Covenant, and turned to other gods,

2

like so many people are doing today.

This is one of our sinful human traits – we forget. We forget birthdays and anniversaries, and we forget the lessons of the past. More troubling, we forget what God has done for us. The Jews were no different than us. People forget about God, and it always leads to trouble

At that moment of time, God warned His people of judgment, but He also gave them words of promise. **"The days are coming... at that time I will grow up to David a branch of righteousness; He shall execute judgment and righteousness in the earth. In those days Judah will be saved, and Jerusalem will dwell safely. And this is the name by which he will be called: 'The Lord our Righteousness.'"** In Hebrew, His name is, **"Yahweh Tsidkenu."**

God still promises judgment and righteousness. Even today "The Lord our Righteousness" brings both the judgment and the righteousness we humans badly need. The idea of God coming with judgment is not a pleasant thought. If we are honest about our sins, Judgment Day should be a dreadful thing to think about. It should put the fear of God into us all.

We modern people cannot downplay our sins. Our lives, yours, mine, and the lives of the most prideful people, may appear righteous to the outside world, especially if we compare ourselves to evil doers. We are truly not as bad as terrorists, or murders, or drug lords, or even some politicians. By all outward appearances we may appear to be good people. In fact I am sure there is not a single person here in church today who looks like a sinner.

But remember the saying, *"You can't judge a book by its cover?"* Underneath our innocent smiles and folded hands we are sinful people and worthy of none of the things God has given us. God doesn't see merely our outward lives - He sees our hearts and our thoughts, and they are sinful! And so we must agree with John when he says, **"If we say we have no sin, we deceive ourselves, and the truth is not in us."**

Because we cannot deceive God, we desperately need Jesus - Yahweh Tsidkenu, the Lord our Righteousness – so He can cleanse us from sin. John further tells us in his Epistle, **"But if we confess our sins, God is faithful and just to forgive us our**

sins and to cleanse us from all unrighteousness." (1 John 4:7-8)

Although we rejoice in the day of Christ's first Advent, the time we call Christmas, we'd better be a little skittish about the day of Christ's second Advent, the time we call Judgment. That's why Advent is a good time for repentance, a good way to prepare for Christ's second coming. Advent, then, is truly a penitential time, for it is in repentance that we prepare best for Christ's second arrival. We await His second Advent best by asking His forgiveness for our worst.

Jeremiah waited for this prophecy to be fulfilled in the future, but we today already know this prophesy has been fulfilled. Jeremiah waited, looking for righteousness. We wait, trusting in Christ's righteousness. He looked forward to what he could not see. We look backward with joy to what we know and see - the first Advent of God's Son, our Lord Jesus Christ.

Today in Advent we look forward to what we cannot fully see or realize - Judgment Day. And by faith we trust that Christ's second Advent will a day of joy for all believers. Because we trust in the forgiveness He earned through His first Advent, His first coming, we need not fear any judgment through His second Advent.

The prophets speak to us this Advent, and the first thing they tell us through the prophet Jeremiah is God's promise of righteousness through His Son. **"The days are coming. At that time I will grow up to David a branch of righteousness; He will execute judgment and righteousness in the earth. In those days Judah will be saved, and Jerusalem will dwell safely. And this is the name by which he will be called: 'The Lord our Righteousness.'"**

A few years ago during the season of Advent newspapers carried the story of Al Johnson, a Kansas man who came to faith in Jesus Christ. His story became noteworthy when his newfound faith in Christ moved him to confess to a bank robbery he'd pulled off when he was nineteen years old. Because the statute of limitations on the case had run out, Johnson could not be prosecuted for the offense. Still, he believed his relationship with Christ demanded a change of heart, and so he voluntarily repaid his share of the stolen money. Advent can be a time of change.

4

You and I and believers through the centuries may have sought God's righteousness, but the truth is, God's righteousness has found us. His righteousness comes to us in Jesus Christ and saves us from the destruction of our sins. As we sing in our hymn, *"My hope is built on nothing less than JESUS' blood and righteousness."* (LSB #575)

This Advent, as we are looking for righteousness, we need look no further than to Jesus, to His Word and His Sacrament. Then we can rest assured in the hymn words:

"When He shall come, with trumpet sound,
Oh may I then in Him will be found,
Clothed in His righteousness alone,
Faultless to stand before the throne.
On Christ the solid Rock I stand,
All other ground is sinking sand." Amen.

ADVENT SERIES ONE
"The Prophets Speak"
Week Two

Micah 4:1-7   *"God Will Establish A Nation"*

"In the last days the mountain of the Lord's temple will be established as chief among the mountains; it will be raised above the hills, and peoples will stream to it. Many nations will come and say, "Come, let us go up to the mountain of the Lord, to the house of the God of Jacob. He will teach us his ways, so that we may walk in his paths." The law will go out from Zion, the word of the Lord from Jerusalem. He will judge between many peoples and will settle disputes for strong nations far and wide. They will beat their swords into plowshares and their spears into pruning hooks. Nation will not take up sword against nation, nor will they train for war anymore. Every man will sit under his own vine and under his own fig tree, and no one will make them afraid, for the Lord Almighty [El Shaddai] has spoken. All the nations may walk in the name of their gods; [but] we will walk in the name of the Lord our God for ever and ever. "In that day," declares the Lord, "I will gather the lame; I will assemble the exiles and those I have brought to grief. I will make the lame a remnant, those driven away a strong nation. The Lord will rule over them in Mount Zion from that day and forever."

✠ ✠ ✠

Advent is a time to be thankful, especially since it follows on the heels of Thanksgiving.

A small boy was asked to give thanks at a holiday meal and he proceeded to give thanks for every one and everything around and on the table. He thanked God for his parents, grandparents there at the table and his brother. He gave thanks for the table and chairs, and then he gave thanks for the food – turkey and dressing, potatoes and gravy, pie and even whipped cream. But he stopped and quietly said, "Mommy, if I say I'm thankful for the broccoli, will God know I'm lying?"

What are you thankful for this Advent? Perhaps it's because we are free to worship the Lord God here in America, our nation we know is still a great nation. We are here in this church this evening be part of the "nations" the prophet Micah spoke about. He wrote: **"It shall come to pass in the latter days that the mountain of the house of the Lord shall be established as the highest of the mountains, and it shall be lifted up above the hills; and peoples shall flow to it, and many nations shall come, and say: Come, let us go up to the mountain of the Lord, to the house of the God of Jacob, that He may teach us His ways and that we may walk in His paths."**

Micah, whose name means *"Who is like God?"*, prophesied that people would come from all over to the Mountain of the Lord. If you think of it, we have come from strange and foreign-sounding nations like Iowa, Minnesota, Colorado, Nebraska, Illinois and North Dakota. Micah's prophesy speaks of people coming from all nations, Jewish and non-Jewish, people who hear God's Word and come to faith in God's Son, Jesus of Nazareth. We are invited to go up to the mountain of the Lord, so that He may teach us His ways and help us walk in His paths. People of all nations shall come to the mountain of the Lord, to His House of worship.

One summer I led many worship services in Wittenberg, Germany, during our two weeks there, and Carol and I met Christians from all over the world who'd come to visit that small city so important in the Reformation of the church. At one service, 24 people came representing 10 nations - Lutherans from South Africa, Rwanda, India, Sri Lanka, Tanzania, Switzerland, Indonesia, Sweden, the Netherlands and America! Another service had only 7 people but they represented 3 nations, and another time 42 people came from 8 nations. I even gave a personal church tour to a group of Lutherans from Hawaii. All who came to those services heard the Gospel of Jesus in a tiny chapel called Corpus Christi, built 660 years ago in 1350! You should hear "A Mighty Fortress" sung in that ancient chapel where Martin Luther conducted weddings and baptisms.

God gathers His church from all over the world and brings them to the mountain of the Lord. It is not a physical mountain like the Rockies, or the desert mountains of Arizona. The mountain where God accomplished His greatest achievement was a small hill outside old Jerusalem's walls, a little place called Golgotha, only a mile from the Jerusalem Temple. There Mount Zion was established, God's Kingdom of Grace, His Holy Christian Church on earth.

Today Golgotha (Calvary) is inside the Church of the Holy Sepulcher, a small stone hump left over from centuries of pilgrims chipping off a souvenir, all that is left after Hadrian's soldiers smashed it into pieces. They thought by smashing Golgotha and other Christian sites they could erase Christianity, but instead they confirmed for all ages where Mount Zion was.

Our Advent theme is *"The Prophets Speak,"* and the prophet Micah says, **"It shall come to pass in the latter days that the mountain of the house of the Lord shall be established as the highest of the mountains."** The mountain of the House of the Lord is the highest because it lifts people up, far above the earth, and it shows them the way to heaven.

So here we are today, inside one of Arizona's wayside chapels located on the way to the mountain of the Lord. Here we are taught the Word and ways of God, that we might walk in His path. Psalm 23 says, **"He leads me on the path of righteousness for His name's sake."** Our normal path in life is not a good one. Our sinfulness pushes us off the path of righteousness and into the cactus, onto the spiky yucca plant, and into the smelly greasewood bushes.

The path of righteousness God wants us to walk is the path Christ shows us. If we let Him, He will lead us on that path and also walk with us on the way. By becoming human at Bethlehem, by His sinless life and His innocent suffering and death, Jesus has given us a place in the house of the Lord. In His resurrection on the third day, He built the house we call Mount Zion.

Advent and Christmas are great, but the best is yet to come. Baptized into Christ, you and I are united with Christ. We have been brought into His church where we are taught His ways, and are given help to walk in His path. Sometimes we may travel though the valley of the shadow of death, but we will fear no evil, because He is with us and His rod and His staff they comfort us. We may see our enemies all around us, but they can harm us none. They are judged - the deed is done! One little word - Jesus - can make them fall.

9

This time of year we like to buy or make gifts for others. In Christ we have been given a gift far greater than we could buy or make. Without Jesus, you and I are sinners, speeding to our deaths on the road to destruction. In Germany I drove on the A-4 Autobahn, and once got that VW up to 125 miles per hour! But then I slowed, realizing what would happen if we'd have an accident.

You and I do some silly things in our lives. Some of us even do some really bad things. It's amazing we don't kill ourselves and others by how we live. God is loving, but He is also righteous. He will not excuse those who hate Him or reject Him. He loves those who trust Him and helps us willingly do what He commands. You and I may be lame and crippled by our sinfulness, but God loves us in Christ, and in His mercy He spares those who trust Him.

The Prophet Micah says, **"The law will go out from Zion, the word of the LORD from Jerusalem. He will judge between many peoples and will settle disputes for strong nations far and wide. They will beat their swords into plowshares and their spears into pruning hooks. Nation will not take up sword against nation, nor will they train for war anymore,... for the Lord Almighty has spoken The Lord Almighty! (In Hebrew, "El Shaddai.")**

Will it not be a most wonderful time when God will stop all wars? We never seem to run out of things to fight over in our world. Wars keep happening. Iraq and Afghanistan are never-ending and after 60 years, there's still trouble in Korea. I heard a commentator say something very truthful: *"Only the dead need not fear war any longer."*

That may be true for this earth, but on Mount Zion there will be no more war. Armies, Navies and Air Forces will all be dismantled for good. And I can tell you that on that day, every single soldier, sailor and airman will rejoice! Those who defend us do not glory in their tasks, though they do their duty the best they can. Yet I am certain they will be first in line to have their swords and guns molded into plows and toys, and they will rejoice in the peace that never ends!

The prophet Micah says finally, **"The Lord will reign over them in Mount Zion from this time forth and forevermore."**

Today is that day. We from all over the world are part of the remnant that the world hates. We trust Jesus Christ, not ourselves. We meet to prepare for our trip to Mount Zion.

Although I've never served in the military, I've always admired the bravery and dedication it takes to serve, to lay one's life on the line for the benefit of others, that they might live free. It always is emotional when I see a medal ceremony, when someone is called out to receive a commendation. Few of us may have a medal of valor, but all of us are God's medals. We are what Christ fought for. We, our children and our grandchildren are those whom Jesus died for. We are His medals, His achievements, and we give thanks to be counted among those so honored by God.

Today God needs an army of peacemakers. Today God needs a nation of grace, an assembly of people made holy by the blood of Jesus. Christ reigns over us, and guides and directs us. Our sins are forgiven, and our victory has been won. We are Christians. Because of Christ, we are His holy nation. Praise God for that! Amen.

ADVENT SERIES ONE
"The Prophets Speak"
Week Three

Malachi 3:1-3   *"The Day Of His Coming"*
"See, I will send my messenger, who will prepare the way before me. Then suddenly the Lord you are seeking will come to his temple; the messenger of the covenant, whom you desire, will come," says the LORD Almighty. But who can endure the day of his coming? Who can stand when he appears? For he will be like a refiner's fire or a launderer's soap. He will sit as a refiner and purifier of silver; he will purify the Levites and refine them like gold and silver."

✛ ✛ ✛

In June, 1992, Boston landlord George Carroll did not clean up his broken-down apartment houses, and so he was sentenced to live in them. The Housing Court Judge believed this is the only way the negligent landlord could be persuaded to make necessary repairs. And while Carroll lived in the slums for a week, the people from his slums were to live in his house.

Good story! Too bad the verdict was thrown out by someone who thought it was too harsh. This is like the incarnation – God becoming human. The God of all creation humbled Himself and lived on this earth. He walked where we walk, and was tempted as we are tempted. He became human to buy us back from our sins.

But Christmas isn't here yet – we're still in Advent. Have you ever noticed that most Advent wreaths have three purple or blue candles and one pink candle? Most of us think the pink one is just before Christmas, or else stands for Christmas itself. But actually the pink candle represents the third of the four Advent Sundays. Advent, we learned, is a penitential season. It was set up mostly to be a serious season of reflection on our need for repentance. But whoever set it the use of candles decided Advent shouldn't be all gloomy, and made the third Sunday one of rejoicing. Hence we get a happy pink candle in the midst of purple gloomy candles.

Thinking of repentance in our modern day season before

13

Christmas might lead us to wonder if we need to repent of the excesses or mistakes we bring upon ourselves. We buy so many unnecessary gifts, or get the wrong gifts, or neglect the poor who need our gifts. Government officials tell us our nation's economy depends on this time of year to grow and produce, but somewhere in our heart we wonder how wise it is to pile up the presents and forget this is all so temporary. We've come a long way, baby, from the holy family in the stable. It's an enormous leap from the birth in Bethlehem to Christmas in America.

I've titled this message, *"The Day of His Coming"*, and I want us to think again about the second coming of Christ. As we do, it might make us wish there were more happy pink candles. Judgment can be a gloomy subject. On this third service of Advent we go back to the prophet Malachi, who asks that very question, **"Who can endure the day of His coming?"** As we look at our world with its confusion and struggles, we might wonder what the world is coming to.

We surely know who is coming - Jesus Christ. But when will He come? Will it be during our lifetimes? Some things we wait and wait for, but they never seem to happen. My wife told me week Larry King was retiring. Finally! I think he should have retired long ago, and though I rarely watched even part of his program, I have wondered how that old guy can keep a program going. I know it's good an older person can succeed in a young person's world, but I've thought he should have gone a long time ago. Maybe I'm not the only one – the newspaper said he has been married eight times – wow! I guess he never quite got that straight. Like I said, some things never seem to happen, no matter how long we wait.

This time of year is Messiah time, not just Handel's "Messiah," but Jesus the Messiah. But have you ever heard the circumstances under which George Friedrich Handel wrote his master work? Though a successful composer, historians tell us he had been depressed. At age 41 he'd had a stroke and even though he recovered, no one was buying his compositions. In April of 1741, Handel came home after a long walk and found a manuscript at his door from one of his friends, Charles Jennens, that was filled with Bible references. They told the story of Christ's birth, ministry, crucifixion and resurrection, and all started with prophetic passages from Isaiah. When Handel read

14

"Comfort ye my people," *from Isaiah 40, he later said the clouds of gloom lifted and he began composing a new work. About three weeks later, it was finished. The entire Messiah – nearly 250 pages of choruses and solos – was composed in just three weeks. Amazing!*

We all know that this same Messiah, Jesus, will return again *"to judge the living and the dead"* as we confess in our creeds. This prophesy from Malachi reminds us Christ the Judge will come again. If we think of the sad state of our modern world, we might need a whole crate of pink candles, because judgment will not be a happy time. Or will it? What do we know about the second coming of Christ?

Malachi here talks about what will happen to sinners at that time – those who cheat the poor and take advantage of the helpless. He says God will testify against those do not fear Him, those who have forgotten Him and ignored His commandments. He also prophesied against those who followed other gods, or those who think God winks at sin. The Bible tells us that all people are sinners, and therefore all people will be in deep trouble when Christ comes in Judgment.

Who of us, then, can stand in that day before God without fear? Won't we all be condemned because of our sins? Big sin or small sin – they all condemn us. Shouldn't we all fear that day and tremble at the thought of facing a Just and Holy God? If we just stopped here, and there was no more word from God through the prophet Malachi, none of us could endure the day of His coming. Advent would be all purple and gloom.

But here is where the Gospel, the Good News, becomes so important. The Bible also tells us that whoever believes in Jesus will not perish, but have eternal life. The Bible tells us Jesus came to this earth that first time in order to do what we couldn't do. He lived a perfect life on our behalf. He followed the Commandments that we could not follow perfectly. He gave His life on the cross as a substitute for our lives. He gave His life as a gift for us, and as John 3:16 says, **"Whoever believes in Him will not perish, but have everlasting life."**

Thus, for the believer, the Christian who trusts Jesus Christ, the **"day of His coming"** is a good time, a wonderful time, a bright time of joy. True, Advent is for reflection and repentance, looking back at Christ's first coming, and it is also a time of

15

looking forward to His second coming. We look back at the baby, but look forward to the King. Until Christmas comes, we only glance at the baby in the manger, but our true focus is on the Messiah, who comes to judge the living and the dead.

It's good to have penitential season a couple of times a year, a time to see ourselves as we really are. To jump from Thanksgiving to Christmas, to bypass Advent all together, is to be ill-prepared for the birthday of our Messiah. This prophecy is good to consider. The Jews of Malachi's day understood these words were about when the Messiah would come. They knew the Messiah would purify them of their sins.

They knew what a smelter and purifier would do. A smelter is a furnace that cooks the ore. The smelter heats the raw ore so hot that it melts and separates the good from the bad. In a smelter, the heavier pure metal sinks and the useless slag rises to the top. The guy running the smelter skims off the bad stuff and watches the good stuff become more pure.

Handel's "Messiah" has a chorus rarely sung, called, "And He Shall Purify." It's one of the most difficult chorus in that work. The prophet Malachi says the Messiah is the Purifier. God's sinful people, you and me, and all people of all times, are the ore, full of impurities, but still worth keeping. Only after we are purified can the precious soul we all possess be collected. Only after the purifying forgiveness in Jesus Christ can we be righteous and pleasing to Him.

Maybe some of you have seen the T-shirt that says, "I'm retired and this is as dressed up as I get." Last year once I went to a chorus practice dressed in good clothes. I had a 4 PM Lent service and decided to dress so I could go from chorus practice straight to church. One of the women there looked me up and down and said, "You clean up pretty good." It made me wonder what I usually looked like. That was like the time one of my cousins first saw me in my clergy robes and said, "Bobby, I've never seen you in working clothes before - you look pretty good!"

We all need to be dressed by the Lord, and not in earthly clothes, but holy robes. Isaiah 61:10 says, **"He has clothed me with garments of salvation and arrayed me in a robe of righteousness."** Jesus, our Holy Refiner, can do that for each of us. Praise God that we know this for sure in Advent. Amen.

ADVENT SERIES TWO
"Advent Questions"
Week One

Luke 1:42   *"What Shall We Do About Mary?"*
"In a loud voice Elizabeth exclaimed: 'Blessed are you among women, and blessed is the child you will bear!'"

✠ ✠ ✠

Welcome to our Advent services this year of Twenty Eleven. I have chosen to speak on "Questions of Advent," questions that should help us deal with Christian life in these two thousand plus years after the birth of Jesus, which was the First Advent of Jesus our Savior into the world. We observe Advent to help us be prepared for His Second Advent, when He returns to the earth in Judgment. Tonight's question is, *"What Shall We Do About Mary?"*

When the teenage Mary told Joseph and her family in Nazareth that she was expecting a child, they did not know what to do. They knew what they could have done, but were unsure. Her story of the angel shocked them. They eventually came to terms with her condition, to accept it and make the best of it. But it was not easy. And the Christian Church has wondered ever since, "What Shall We Do About Mary?"

"Hail, Mary, full of grace! The Lord is with thee; (Luke 1:28) Blessed art thou among woman and blessed is the fruit of thy womb, Jesus. (Luke 1:42) Holy Mary, mother of God, pray for us now and at the hour of our death." Those lines ought to get the attention of Lutherans at worship! "Wrong church, Pastor, that's not us!" Of course that's true, but there has always been something fascinating about Mary and the Rosary. These words have often become the object of scorn among non-Catholics, but few of us realize how biblical they are.

It was the angel Gabriel, great messenger of God and protector of His people, who saluted Mary at her annunciation, **"Hail, Mary, full of grace! The Lord is with thee."** (Luke 1:28) And it was cousin Elizabeth who said later, **"Blessed art thou among woman and blessed is the fruit of thy womb."** (Luke 1:42) These verses are the inspired Word of God, words that

17

honored the expectant young mother of the promised Messiah, the mother of the Christ who would save the world.

The last words of the Rosary, however, are unsettling, for they are a prayer that we find unsettling: *"Holy Mary, mother of God, pray for us now and at the hour of our death."* Wait a minute, we say, we pray to God, not to people. No matter how good we think someone has been, God alone is worthy of prayer. How can Mary help anyone while she is in the grave?

Ever since realizing and coming to faith that Jesus of Nazareth was truly the Son of God, Christians have wondered what to do with Mary. True, she was highly honored by God to be the birthmother of the Messiah. But how far do we go in honoring her? What do we know of her, and what is the right way to treat her?

Mary was born in Nazareth, a village of 300-400 people southwest of the Sea of Galilee. Her people were from several clans whose ancestors had returned from Persian exile a few hundred years before. Those released captives had been waiting long and hard for the redemption of Israel, so much that they even named their village Nezer - oth, "branch - town" as some have translated it, the village from which the "Branch of the tree of Jesse" would come according to Isaiah 11:1.

Mary was a descendant of King David through her father's side. Her fiancé Joseph was a distant cousin, probably born in Bethlehem, and also part of David's lineage through his mother's side. Some scholars believe Mary's name comes from "marah," Hebrew for "bitter," very much how she felt when her son died. Mary was in her teens and Joseph probably in his twenties when Gabriel visited them with the news.

Most all we know of Mary is related to Jesus' infancy. After the annunciation, she visited Elizabeth in the Judean hills down south, and then returned home to settle affairs with Joseph and their families. There were undoubtedly problems trying to explain the legitimacy of the coming birth, so when the edict for a census came from Caesar Augustus, she and Joseph set out for Bethlehem as soon as they could.

After the birth and all that happened that first year, we hear nothing of Mary until Jesus is twelve years old. Again the family was back in Jerusalem, and Mary was too busy, probably with her other children, to notice her eldest son was missing. After a few days of looking and then some gentle scolding, we hear little of Mary until her son is grown and they attend a wedding together. Later there were times when she and His siblings tried to caution Him that He'd gone too far with His radical teachings. We know she was present for part of the crucifixion, but the last biblical word about her is in Acts 1:14 where she is identified as part of the small group of early believers. Then Mary disappears from biblical history.

But not from church history! People just can't leave her alone. There's something about Mary that has moved Christians throughout history to honor her beyond her station. They have elevated her from honored mother to venerated saint to near-equality with God. When Emperor Constantine decreed that the Roman Empire officially become Christian in the Fourth Century, hundreds of thousands of pagans were ordered to abandon their belief in multiple gods. But Mary's unique position gave them a excuse to keep looking. Led by Helena, Constantine's mother, Christians began pushing Mary up the ladder of honor. These early half-Christian, half-pagan people prayed to and venerated anyone close to Jesus, including Paul, Peter and also Mary. They figured if you can't have more than one god, you can still pray to those closest to Him.

In AD 431 Mary was labeled "Mother of God," and AD 649 she was granted status of "Perpetual Virgin." Then people began to mold her in the image of her Son. She was declared free of actual sin by the Council of Trent in 1545, as Jesus was, and in 1854 she was decreed to have been conceived by the Holy Spirit, without original sin, as Jesus was. Finally just 60 years ago in 1950, it was decreed she ascended bodily into heaven, again, again just like her Son.

For a brief period during the past few decades Mary achieved the apex of her elevation, being publicly and officially declared "Co-Redempress" with Christ by Pope John Paul II. In other words, some in the Roman church now claim that we are granted heaven as an act of grace by both Jesus and Mary. This places her right up there with God the Father, Son, Mother and Holy Spirit - a "Holy Quartet." No place higher could come to Mary than that! Fortunately few Christians anywhere have taken this last proclamation seriously. But again it shows people don't know what to do with Mary.

Now please understand this is not Catholic-bashing. This is merely about how Christians have made more of Mary than she is. Orthodoxy pushed Mary that high long ago. Officially, the Roman Catholic Church does not worship Mary, but she does have 17 major yearly feasts dedicated to her and millions of people mistakenly pray to her every day.

Some believe that if she does hear their prayers, she's more likely to influence her Son, who would then influence the Father to get what they want, rather like a holy chess game. Aside from this being just plain wrong, it's also too much like politics. Belief in the super-humanity of Mary is the result of rationalization, but it does not make Catholics into pagans. Like other groups in the Church, they are Christians with a lot of unnecessary baggage.

God's Word plainly says Jesus is the only One who intercedes for us with the Father: "For there is one God and one mediator between God and men, the man Christ Jesus." (1 Timothy 2:5) Mary was a humble servant of God, a great person. She'd be embarrassed if she knew what the church has done to her. **"I am the Lord's servant," she said, "May it be to me as you have said."** (Luke 1:38) That's humility.

Prayer to anyone other than God can lead to idolatry. Now understand, Martin Luther always honored Mary as mother of God, but he made it quite clear she was no better or worse than anyone else, yet worthy of honor because of what she did. Luther, who saw the abuses of the church, still considered her an object of human affection because of the role she played in the story of salvation.

You and I need to know what to do about Mary. We should thank God for her, not as a super-mom, but as a vessel who brought the Gospel into human form. She was and should always be highly favored, but not an object of worship. She is right up there with the Apostles and St. Paul, but she's also one of us poor miserable sinners in need of Christ's salvation. No man or woman, no matter how holy, can get along without Christ. Indeed, the more humble and devout we Christians become, the more we should acknowledge their need for Him.

Only the fool thinks he or she is greater than others or equal with God.

Let's give Mary her due. Sometimes Lutherans and other Protestants do not give her the respect she deserves. No other human came so close to God and was still in need of God. No other woman carried the Son of God, Who then carried the cross for her. No mother ever kissed the face of God as closely as she.

No human had such a close look at His infancy, His childhood and His growing years, and no other regular human being in all of history has been so honored by society. Mary of Nazareth has been on the cover of Time Magazine more than any other person. Even the secular media sees something special in Mary. She will always be held up as a most unique person in all of history.

And what would Mary tell us today in the year we live in? Probably that we should listen to her Son. His Father once said, **"This is my Son... Listen to him!"** (Matthew 17:5), and that's what His mother would say, too. Her Son came to forgive us and grant us hope for life in God's presence. He was born of a young virgin who cared for Him like any mother would. He alternately worried her and made her proud, but He also died for her sins, and rose again for her salvation and ours.

Many a mother has saved her son, but no mother has been saved eternally by her Son. Mary takes her place amid the mass of humanity that needs the salvation only her Son can give. She should always be honored, but today her soul she rests with all the saints until the resurrection, awaiting the judgment and life with God forever. May we all rejoice at the gift God has given us in this fine woman, and may we all be ready by faith to meet her Son in eternity. Amen

ADVENT SERIES TWO
"Advent Questions"
Week Two

Luke 1:66   *"What's Going On In Our World?"*
"Everyone who heard this wondered about it, asking, 'What then is this child going to be?' For the Lord's hand was with him.'"

✤ ✤ ✤

Advent means Christmas is coming, and Christmas is a time of year when our thoughts turn to family and friends. Christmas also means programs with children. We saw our four year-old grand daughter's first Christmas program last week and all the cute moments in it reminded me of a nativity program we held in my last church.

Since the new mission was so new, the Sunday School was small, yet well organized. The nativity featured Mary and Joseph kneeling by a manger while a child angel choir sang hymns between readings. The last song was to be sung by all the children, so Mary and Joseph were to walk over towards the other little ones. But Mary still was carrying the doll baby Jesus. Her mother in the front row whispered to her to put Jesus back in the manger. Mary realized her mistake, but instead of carrying the baby doll back to the manger, turned and tossed baby Jesus into the manger, from about 6-8 feet away! And baby Jesus landed right in the manger. Little Mary's clever "solution" brought down the house!

Each time you and I see a nativity, we can be reminded of that fleeting moment when the holy parents first gazed upon the child. The trip was over, the birth pains were in the past, and parenthood had begun. What were they thinking? What were they pondering as they looked at the baby? Do any of you parents remember how you felt when you saw your firstborn and realized all the parental joys and potential heartaches ahead?

Those first hours in the stable were a short and sweet repose from the reality that lay ahead. Every new parent soon sees the major responsibilities of the child brought into this world. I am sure new parents soon wonder, what kind of a

23

world are we giving them? What kind of person will our precious child become? Even the relatives and neighbors can worry. **"What then is this child going to be?"** they asked in this Bible passage, and so also do we wonder.

It's been this way since Eve gave birth to her two sons and one killed the other. It was that way when Jacob saw bitter rivalry arise among his twelve sons, and it was the same when Elizabeth and Zechariah saw their child John being born. The Bible says, **"Everyone who heard this wondered about it, asking, 'What then is this child going to be?' For the Lord's hand was with him.'"**

It is often true that the relatives are more worried about the baby than about the parents. Surely some there thought Zechariah and Elizabeth were too old to care for a newborn. Already they questioned the choice of his name. Though a popular name in Jewish homes, the name John was unknown in theirs. "John" means "God has been gracious," gracious indeed, since God did have great plans for him. He would be the promised prophet, even greater than Elijah, the one who would prepare the way for the Chosen One born a few months later of the Virgin Mary. And there were, of course, rumors about the angels. All this was unusual, unsettling. **'What then is this child going to be?'** was a good question to ask.

Children can be unsettling. As they develop, they often disappoint their parents, and some of this is the parents' fault. We dream of how our kids should be, and they turn out another way. We'd like them to fit a certain mold, but they go ahead and shape their own life. That's how it should be, but still we'd like them to be made of a fabric somewhat like ours.

It's doubtful John turned out anything like his family imagined. Tradition has it he was orphaned at an early age and grew up among the Essenes, a desert community south of Jerusalem responsible for copying and preserving the Scrolls of the Holy Scriptures. Life there was difficult. Essenes lived on little and depended on God for everything. As he grew, John spoke his mind publicly in a way some found to be offensive.

John became a desert prophet proclaiming the day of the Messiah's coming. The baptism he employed came out of Jewish ritual bathing, a baptism of self-renewal and rededication. But John the Baptizer added a key ingredient, "repentance," that holy attitude that would help change lives. His message was simple, *"Change your ways! Don't come to me if you're not willing to change."* (Luke 3:8) For many, John the Baptizer was a great man, but others merely considered him an irritation, an interesting prophet, or the latest fad to see. He was their "prophet du jour," most recent desert celebrity who brought excitement into their otherwise dull existence.

Like charismatic figures today, John had all kinds of followers. Some were wealthy with time on heir hands and others aimless ne'er-do-wells seeking direction. This prophet who as a child was the object of concern by his relatives, never owned more than the clothes on his back, but his reputation for honesty second to no one.

History has considered him right up there with his cousin Jesus. His message prepared them for the greater message of Jesus. The King James Version says it poetically, **"He must increase, but I must decrease."** (John 3:30) John would have to decrease in importance, so that Jesus would increase to the vital role He would play in our salvation. (John 3:30)

Sometimes our kids turn out far better than we expect. My father was twenty years than his youngest brother, Francis. Dad said his mother used to worry about Francis who did poorly in school seemed slower than the others. "What's to become of our Francis?" she often asked my Dad privately. But Francis surprised them all. He married a lovely woman from the North Carolina hills and together they worked successfully in sales and in the upholstery business for nearly fifty years. Some of their work was so good that it made its way into the North Carolina state legislature. As they neared retirement, Francis bought some land from his brother-in-law. They discovered those forty acres of "worthless trees and rocks" held nearly a million cubic yards of pure gravel and a small fortune in precious metals. "Our Francis," the man Grandmother worried about, died a millionaire, the wealthiest of anyone in their family.

John the Baptizer would never be rich, but he would be more remembered than anyone ever thought. He would preach a truth that would shock the common people and shame kings.

He would be greater than his worried relatives could have imagined. He would introduce Jesus as **"the Lamb of God who takes away the sin of the world."** (John 1:29).

I doubt John always knew the meaning of his words, but that's how it is with a prophet. God gives the prophet a complex message, and listeners think he's off his rocker. *"Who does he think he is?"* people ask of the one who speaks God's truth. How easy it is to pass off God's message as meaningless chatter. How hard it is to take seriously God's message that comes amid the tinsel and glitter of Christmas. "Christ the Savior is born," we sing, almost oblivious to the eternal consequences of those simple words.

On a wall of the museum of the Dachau Concentration Camp near Munich, Germany, are many large and moving photographs, and one is of a mother and her little girl standing in a line going to one of the gas chambers. The child, who is walking in front of her mother, does not know where she is going. The mother, who walks behind, does know, but she is helpless to stop what is to come. In her helplessness the mother performs the only act of love left. She places her hands over her child's eyes so that for a few moments the little one will be spared the horror that is to come.

This may well be what Zechariah felt about his son as he said, **"And you, my child, will be called a prophet of the Most High; for you will go on before the Lord to prepare the way for him."** (Luke 1:76-77) As a priest Zechariah knew the difficult life of a Hebrew prophet. He knew their life was usually shortened by their enemies. Though Zechariah was a proud father, he too, must silently have wondered, **"What then is this child going to be?"**

John the Baptizer had a short and inglorious career by today's standards. His garment of camel's hair was the harshest of fabrics, total opposite of today's luxurious camel hair jackets. He ate roasted locusts dipped in honey, high in protein but bitter sweet. His message left no one untouched. John had a few disciples, and in the end, his message cost him his life.

No matter how popular you are, you can't criticize a powerful king without paying the price. This John, wondered about by all, became greatest of prophets, for he prepared the way for the Son of God.

26

That Son of God, and also his cousin Jesus, is our Savior. That baby in the manger is God in the flesh. God's first earthly breath would smell of hay and dung, of sweat and smoke. The eternal love of the Father brought His Son into an unclean world, a world He Himself would need to cleanse by giving up His life.

"What then is this child going to be?" thought Mary and Joseph about Jesus, and later they found out. He who was so loved by his mother and foster father would be hated by the religious people. He who tasted the sweat and smoke of the stable would taste the same on a cross for the sins of an unclean world.

We don't know how our children will turn out. They can alternately fill us with pride and break our hearts. I have a brother who had a few problems when he was young. He drank and caroused far too much and brought tears and grey hairs to his parents. He was on a first name basis with the local cops. But then he went to college and became a high school shop teacher, teaching Industrial Arts. For 35 years he shared his artistic skills with thousands of boys and girls. He was a good teacher and many were grateful for what he taught them. I am thankful he found the Lord again at the end of his life.

He called me one morning and we talked about our boys, his two and my two, both of us wondering how they'd turn out. It's always great to see our children get along better with time. Mary and Joseph, Zechariah and Elizabeth – both sets of parents knew their sons were destined for greatness, but only today can we see the consequences of what they did. Praise God we are recipients of their greatness. Christ the Savior is born! Amen

ADVENT SERIES TWO
"Advent Questions"
Week Three

Luke 2:39-40   *"Will We Ever Get Back to Normal?"*
"When Joseph and Mary had done everything required by the Law of the Lord, they returned to Galilee to their own town of Nazareth. And the child grew and became strong; he was filled with wisdom, and the grace of God was upon him."

✠ ✠ ✠

Christmas and Advent often bring back memories. In my second church they had the custom of having two matched tall decorated Christmas trees in front of the church, and the decorations often changed so that people would wonder what their church's Christmas trees would be like each year.

One year a church member was asked to buy a pair of nice, tall trees in another town. On the way home, one of those trees slid halfway out of his car trunk and was dragged for miles, ruining the lower branches. He and I wondered what to do with the messed up tree. They had no more tall ones, so we had to make do with what we had. Thus, we got inventive! We put pine branches pine in the gaps, but they looked bad. The tree was lop-sided and had to be wired to the walls to keep from falling over. We tried wiring parts of it together but nothing would make it look good. So, we decided to take advantage of the situation and make the trees "symbolic." One tree would represent the true Christian Christmas with red balls, clear lights with white ribbons and lovely star on top. It was beautiful! The other tree would represent the world's Christmas, decorated as garishly as we could make it. We put a big flashing Santa in the middle of it, pinned dollar bills from its branches and hung some small whiskey bottles right in front. We covered it all with tinsel and topped it off with a foot-high dollar sign. Both trees were up front in the altar area for three Sundays, and during Advent several folks told me they were uncomfortable kneeling for communion with all that money, tinsel and whiskey staring them in the face. It was one of the rare times that even some non-church members in town wanted to come over to St. John's just to see that one ugly Christmas tree.

Recently in a store I heard someone say, *"I can't wait for the*

29

holidays to get over so things can get back to normal." I imagine Mary and Joseph wanted things back to normal also, and the Bible text says that finally happened. Some folks also today have been waiting for things to get back to normal in their lives.

But what is "normal" anyway? In our English language, some words radiate feeling. Nice words like: love, wedding, baby, healthy, friend, success – these words are good. But others are not so good: layoff, bankruptcy, accident, failure, cancer – those words are ugly and leave us fearful and feeling empty. How about the word "normal?" How do you react to that? To me, "normal" is a great word. "Your child is normal." "Your test results are normal." "Such feelings are normal."

Normal means you can probably predict what will happen next. Normal means having a good routine, trusting what will happen today or how you'll feel or even how your worship will be conducted in church. Normal means knowing what comes next, and though normal for some people might be boring, it helps keep us sane. Normal is good. In this day and age of so much that is unexpected and unknown, we all need more things we can call "normal."

Often it takes time for things to get back to normal. Life for Mary and Joseph was quite normal until God's angel showed up. They thought they would get married like they'd planned. Then came the angel's message and everything changed. The unanticipated birth of the baby changed everything. The angel's message still changes things for the rest of us today.

From that first angelic message, plans for a normal life were forever altered. Embarrassment of the questionable pregnancy, a hasty wedding, the unexpected week-long trip, the birth in a stable, then shepherds and foreign visitors, a longer trip to Egypt, then finally coming back home to face the relatives! Maybe then life got back to normal for Mary and Joseph, though I doubt it ever was. Nothing gets back to normal when your first child arrives, especially when that child is the Son of God.

Normal is a great word when you're worried or fearful. If you visit the clinic because something seems abnormal, it's music to your ears when the doctor says, "Everything's normal." That's good news! You can relax - you're normal!

30

But for some, normal is boring. It's living in a rut. It's the "same old, same old" and it's no good. It's tedious and no fun. For many, "normal" is a pain. For others, normal is just lot more sin. Their life is filled with sinful deeds they consider normal: misrepresent the facts a little - "Hey, others do it - it's normal!" Under-report the results a little, fudge on the truth a little, cheat a little here, steal a little there. "Don't look at me like that - this is normal."

That may seem normal, but it's also sinful. And compared to God, we're all sinful. As good we may try to be, we'll never be good enough. As hard as we may try, it'll never be enough. Everything we do is tainted by sin. The best marriage has its warts, the best kids do stupid things, and the best job is still hard work. The best church is still filled with sinners, and the best pastor or teacher will disappoint you. To our holy God, the best deeds are still imperfect. Without a Savior, we're stuck in sin. We're in a rut too deep. Without Jesus to lift us out, we'll stay there forever.

The only real solution for our emptiness is the fullness of Christ. The only way to find inner peace is by trusting the Prince of Peace. The only way to eternal life is through Jesus, **"the Way, the Truth and the Life."** The only way to normal is trusting in God -- and for humans, that's abnormal.

People try to find "normal" in the wrong ways. Some will try to get it with knowledge. "Educate them and they'll be fine." But the problem isn't ignorance; it's sin. Some say the problem is poverty or oppression. "Give them more choices, redistribute the wealth, and all will be better." But an empty bank account isn't the problem; it's an empty soul. Others say people have too much guilt and don't think highly enough of themselves. "Help them feel good about themselves, and we've fixed the problem." But our problem isn't lack of self-esteem. It's lack of God-esteem.

The only real solution for our emptiness is the fullness of Christ. He came to fix the unfixable in the world. He came between us and Satan and delivered us to the throne of God which is ours by faith in what He has done. Jesus is the solution, but it cost Him His life.

On May 21, 1946, a daring young scientist was carrying out an

31

experiment to learn more about atomic energy. Louis Slotin had done this experiment many times before to determine the "critical mass," the amount of radioactive uranium necessary for a chain reaction to occur and explode. He would push the two portions of enriched Uranium together slowly, then just as the mass became critical, he would push them apart, all from a safe distance. But one day something slipped and the two portions of U-235 rolled together. Instantly the room was filled with a dazzling bluish haze. Instead of ducking or running, the young man leaped up into the path of the two portions, keeping them from exploding with his bare hands. He had broken the chain reaction and saved the lives of the other people in the building, but he had also doomed himself. Nine days later Louis Slotin died in terrible agony from intense radiation exposure.

1970 years ago the Son of the Living God walked directly into the path of sin's deadly forces. He jumped between mankind and Satan to save all people, and was touched by the deadly power of sin. On the cross Jesus of Nazareth let sin take His life, and He broke the chain reaction. Christ broke the power of sin and set us free. Now we don't have to fear sin's power. It's been broken for all times. Sin separates us from God and mankind, but Jesus separates us from eternal death. In Him, by God's grace, we have eternal life.

Because Christ stepped between us and eternal death, because He sacrificed Himself, things are different now. God has given us new definition of normal. It's no longer normal that we should act according to our sinful nature. We can live by the Spirit, not by the flesh. St. Paul said it plainly: **"Those who belong to Jesus Christ have crucified the sinful nature with its passions and desires. If we live by the Spirit, let us keep in step with the Spirit."** (Galatians 5:24)

For you and me, normal doesn't mean the same as it did before. Normal used to mean sinful. Now it can mean walking in step with the Spirit. When you trust Jesus Christ, NORMAL CHANGES. It moves to a higher level. Normal may always include change, but it will be change when Christ firmly holds our hands in faith. You see, it's not the change, but what we do with change, that will make the coming Christmas special.

In 1636, in the midst of the Thirty Years War, a German Lutheran pastor, Martin Rinkart, saw such hopeless and disaster as can only be imagined. For a few months, the war waged right outside of his village, and as village pastor, he conducted burials, sometimes for 15-20 people a day. Pastor Rinkert saw 500 of his fellow villagers die in that war. And yet, in the heart of that darkness, with the cries of pain and death outside his door, Pastor Rinkert sat down and wrote this table prayer for his children: (German) "Nun danket alle Gott, mit Herzen, Mund und Handen. Der grosse Dinge tut, an uns und allen Enden. Der uns von Mutterleib, und Kindesbeinen an, unzaehlich viel zugut, und noch jetztund getan." (English) "Now thank we all our God with hearts and hands and voices; Who wondrous things has done, in whom this world rejoices. Who from our mother's arms hath blessed us on our way, with countless gifts of love, and still is ours today."

Martin Rinkert was a man who knew that peace with God, and a normal life, come not from outside circumstances, but from the inside, from a heart that is filled with love and faith in Jesus Christ. God willing, you and I, or future generations, will never have to see anything as terrible as a deadly plague.

But as the holidays are completed and "normal" returns, many good and joyful things will happen in the coming new year: Godly things, surprising things, blessed things, normal things, and all by the grace and love of Jesus, our Lord! Joseph and Mary found God's new normal, and so will we. God bless your Advent, Christmas and New Year with a rapid return to normal. Amen.

ADVENT SERIES THREE
"Prophet, Priest and King"
Week One

Matthew 17:5   *"Jesus, our Prophet"*
"A voice from the cloud said, 'This is my beloved Son, with whom I am well pleased. Listen to Him!'"

✠ ✠ ✠

An old pioneer traveled westward across the great plains until he came to an abrupt halt at the edge of the Grand Canyon. In amazement he looked at the magnificent sight: a vast chasm a mile deep, eighteen miles across, and more than a hundred miles long! The old pioneer gasped, "Something musta happened here!" In a similar way, consider our world today at Christmas time: the lights, decorations, trees, parades, festivities, and the religious services. A first-time visitor might also probably say, "Something must have happened here!" Indeed, something did happen. God came to our world on the first Christmas.

But have you ever wondered, why all the fuss? Why special midweek services? Why remember a baby born in an obscure Middle Eastern village and why have a huge festival just to honor His birth? Why? Because big something happened back 2,000 years ago. The Son of God came to earth in the first Advent and that's enough in itself. Jesus of Nazareth is the Son of God. His purpose is to save the human race. That will never happen due to Environmentalism or politics or the economics of shopping or all the good deeds the human race come up with, only Jesus. He is **"the Way, the Truth and the Life and no one will come to God except through Him."**

How did Jesus save the human race? What method did He use? Activism? Economics? Politics? Power? Christians over the centuries have considered from the Holy Scriptures that Jesus saved the human race through fulfilling three distinct roles: He was a Prophet, He was a Priest, and He was a King. Perhaps you can remember those words from Confirmation instruction. Prophet, Priest and King: three words that define the life of our Lord. During these three Wednesdays of Advent we will

35

examine these three roles and how they relate to us today.

Advent means "coming." You and I live between two advents, the first Advent was when He came in His birth at Bethlehem. The second Advent is when He will *come again in glory to judge both the living and the dead,*" as we say in the Creed. Despite the hoopla about Santa Claus, Advent is a time for Christians to prepare to celebrate His first coming. And while Advent is a time to prepare us for His important first coming, during this time we might also get ready for His even more important Advent, His second coming.

The roles of Prophet, Priest and King were foretold by Wise Men in Matthew 2. Did you know that? They surely didn't realize it at the time, but their gifts - Gold, Frankincense, Myrrh - each of corresponded to one of the purposes of His life. Gold is what a King needs to rule and reign, Frankincense is used by a Priest in worship, and Myrrh is used far too often. It's given to the Prophets who spoke God's Word and got killed for it.

Do you know the names of the Wise Men? Tradition does give them specific names, although we doubt these are what they originally were: Casper, Melchior, Balthazar. Today many traditional Roman Catholic homes will have written in chalk over inside doorway this formula: "20 (C+M+B) 09." It's their way of remembering the wise men. And like someone once said, *"WISE MEN STILL SEEK JESUS."*

CHRIST OUR PROPHET

A prophet of God is one who speaks for God, telling God's Word and interpreting God's Will to the people. God the Father designated Jesus as the most important Prophet in Matthew 17:5 when God said of Jesus, **"This is my Son - Listen to Him!"**

In the Gospel of Luke, Jesus calls Himself the Prophet several times. Having a prophet is not unique to Christianity alone. Muslims say Mohammed was a prophet. Mormons say Joseph Smith was a prophet. But you and I know Jesus Christ is THE Prophet, most important of all. John 1:18 says, **"No one has ever seen God; the only Son, who is in the bosom of the Father, He has made Him known."** Jesus' role as Prophet is to give us the Word of God.

In the Gospel of John, Jesus is called the WORD, which in

Greek is "logos." Jesus the Prophet spoke God's Word and today it comes to us through the Gospels. Jesus the Prophet spoke to us and all people of all times through the Apostles and Disciples who had the task of telling God's Word and Will to people as they became new believers. He is the Prophet and we are to **"Listen to Him!"**

Jesus the Prophet told His disciples He would send the Comforter, the Holy Spirit, who would lead them into all truth. Peter told us that holy men of God spoke as they were moved by the Holy Ghost. As Christians we believe that the Bible is the prophetic Word of God, fully and completely inspired by the Holy Spirit. The Bible is God's Word and it is true.

Today, God's Word is still proclaimed, just like it is being done tonight in churches throughout Christianity. The task of being a prophet is given to pastors and all who proclaim God's Word in worship and in teaching. When reading the Bible, this is God speaking and we are to **"Listen to Him!"** The Prophet Jesus brings us God's message of forgiveness and love for sinners. God's Word tells us about sin and grace, which the church also calls Law and Gospel.

The content of the message from God today is the same as it has always been: LAW and GOSPEL. Law is the Ten Commandments, what we should do and not do. The Gospel is what God has done for us by forgiveness in Jesus. Law condemns us, but Gospel forgives us. Law shows us our sin, but Gospel shows us our Savior. Law and Gospel, sin and grace. This has been the message of the God's prophets and pastors, and this message is not always easy to hear and accept.

Prophets have often been unpopular. God calls them through the centuries to tell His Word with faithfulness and it gets them into trouble. A longtime friend of mine who's a Lutheran pastor had big problems one year just for speaking the truth. But his people don't like to hear about sin. *"Grace is fine,"* they said, *"but forget about that sin." That's too negative and it's just your opinion anyway."*

The unpopularity of prophets is where the gift of Myrrh comes in. Myrrh is a burial spice. The prophets often paid the ultimate price for speaking God's Word. Jesus said in Matthew 23:37, **"O Jerusalem, Jerusalem, killing the prophets and**

stoning those who are sent to you." Jesus the Prophet spoke of those who had been rejected in the past, and He also predicted His own death several times. He spoke God's Word and was nailed to the cross for it. John 19:39 tells us the women anointed His body with myrrh and aloes - 70 lbs. of it! It was packed around his body to keep it from spoiling. Jesus is God's true Prophet, so let's **"Listen to Him!"**

Some illustrations can help understand our need to **"Listen to Him!"**

First, we all need the same forgiveness: During a Caribbean cruise all passengers are required to go through a lifeboat drill. It came at the start of the cruise, and when the drill occurs, the passengers are found in various kinds of dress. Some are in furs and tuxes, others in swim suits and blue jeans. Some are rich and some are poor, but each one must wear the same life jacket, same color and style, and they're taught to use it the same way. So also the Gospel offers each of us the same salvation, no matter who we are or how to come to God. We all need it, so we must be ready when the call of God comes.

Second, we all need God's Word of strength: Canada's bull moose battle for dominance. They fight head to head, crashing horns. Antlers can break which means certain defeat. The strongest moose is the one that wins. Yet the battles of autumn are won in the summer, during their time of eating and gaining strength. The one who eats well and becomes strongest in the summer is the one who wins in the autumn. Those who eat poorly are weak and fail. In the same way, you and I need a steady diet of God's Word to strengthen our faith for times of battle against sin and Satan. If we are weak, we, too, will fail. We all need God's Word of strengthen in our life

Finally, we have victory in Christ Jesus. While attending St. Louis Seminary, I did some yard work in LaDue, a wealthy suburb. The muggy climate there help grow lots of poison ivy and in many yards the ivy vines are left to grow old and big and strong and wrap around trees. If not cut down, poison ivy vines grow large and wind their way up tree trunks, choking the tree to death. The solution is simple: cut it off at the ground, and the vine dies. The vine may stay wrapped around the trees, but it's dead and will eventually fall off. Similarly, in our lives sin often starts out small, but if unchecked it can grip us and even choke us off from God. Christ's death and resurrection cuts the power of sin. Like the cut vines, sin may seem to linger, perhaps in guilt, but it can no longer overpower us, because it is dead. Trusting in Jesus Christ gives us victory over sin.

This Advent, listen to the Prophet and His Words. Every morning you rise, trust in Him, "Listen to Him!" Get ready for His coming. Our Prophet has come and He will come again. Next Wednesday we will hear of "Jesus the Priest." Amen.

ADVENT SERIES THREE
"Prophet, Priest and King"
Week Two

Hebrews 4:14   *"Christ Our Priest"*
"Since we have a great high priest who has passed through the heavens, Jesus, the Son of God, let us hold fast to our confession."

✛ ✛ ✛

Welcome to our second Advent service. Advent, as you know, is a time of preparation for Christ's coming, of preparing for two advents, Christ's first coming in the manger, and His second coming in judgment. The world has made a big thing of His birth, but doesn't know what name to call it. But whatever label it chooses, most of the world has certainly embraced it with parties, decorations, concerts, church services, greeting cards, and, of course, the frenzy of shopping. The real meaning of Christmas was supposed to be God's love, but it turned out to be how much money it can generate.

s usual, not everyone is happy this time of year. One large store had really long lines, and when the register tape ran out and the attendant had trouble crediting a customer some coupons, an irate woman in the back of the line grumbled, *"This is ridiculous! Whoever started this Christmas thing ought to be taken out and shot!"* Someone ahead of her said, *"Too late, they already crucified Him!"*

Three Lutheran pastors were tragically killed in the same car accident on Christmas Eve. St. Peter met them at the gate and said, "What special gifts have you brought for the Christ child?" Thinking quickly, Pastor Kelly pulled out a cigarette lighter, saying, "This is the latest in Christmas candles." Peter was impressed and let him in. Pastor Fred pulled out his keys, jingled them and said, "These are the latest in Christmas bells." He got in. Pastor Bob handed him a pair of earrings. "What are these?" Peter asked. "Pastor Bob said, "They're Carol's!" (My wife's name was Carol - Ho, ho, ho!)

The real gifts Jesus received, Gold, Frankincense and Myrrh, foretold the three roles of Jesus: Prophet, Priest and King. Last week we considered His first role, that of being

41

God's Prophet. Jesus our Prophet was God's spokesman who told people the truth of God and was controversial because of it. Most folks loved Him but some hated Him, really hated Him – and it's still that way today. But this is certain: His humble birth in a stable, the angels, visits from shepherds and Magi, those valuable gifts, and the fear it provoked in an old King, all this is history.

The second role of Christ is that of Priest, and to better understand what this means, we need to understand more of the priesthood. A priest is not just someone with a clerical collar wearing fancy robes leading strange rituals. The priest was to be the mediator between God and people, the "go-between" who speaks to God for the people and who speaks to the people on behalf of God. Being both God and man, Jesus did that job very well.

A lot of Christians don't understand why Jesus did what He did, but we use all kinds of phrases, such as, "reconciliation" or "atonement," or even, "He died for our sins." And we don't know quite what they mean. Let's start with "reconciliation."

The Bible tells us that sin separates us, from each other, from nature and from God. Because of sin, mankind needs a way to bridge that separation, a mediator who can help bring us back to God. Sin brought death, the ultimate separation, and if people are to survive, we need to be reunited with God. This is where reconciliation comes in. 2 Corinthians 5:18 says, **"God was reconciling the world to himself in Christ, not counting men's sins against them."** God sent His Son Jesus to become a bridge between Himself and people. That's His primary work as our High Priest.

To achieve reconciliation, someone had to pay a price sufficient for the damage sin had done. Sin not only separates us from God, without reconciliation it can destroy us. Sin is not just mistakes or errors, it brings death. Sin is so powerful that something supernatural is needed to bridge the gap. To make amends for sin requires more than being sorry, or doing good deeds or giving gifts.

God requires reconciliation, and only He can provide. God is offended and God must reconcile. Other religions lay it all on people to make amends, but Christianity believes God has done it for us, starting with the baby Jesus. God sent His Son into the world to bridge the separation, and bring us back together to God. Theologians call this act, "atonement" (at-one-ment). Because of what Jesus does for us on the cross, we are restored, made "at one" with God once again. Jesus our Priest is the divine Mediator, the "go-between" who restores us to God.

Reconciliation involves repayment. For awhile in the Old Testament, God accepted an animal sacrifice in payment for sins. But neither animal sacrifice nor good deeds can remove sin and guilt. A perfect human being had to come forward, one who would give his sinless life in exchange for the sinful people, one who could repair the breach and lead the people back to God.

That man was Jesus, Son of God and son of Mary, who came to do this. His becoming human is called the "incarnation." The incarnate Jesus is God in the flesh, and he became the sacrifice God required. Because Jesus was truly human, He could be the sacrifice for sin. And because He was truly God, He could rise again from the dead and judge the world. All this would take place at a time in history that God chose, a time when the world was ready for a Savior.

The Old Testament priests were the first mediators. For a time they offered sacrifices for sin, and it involved shedding of blood. Sometimes they sent a scapegoat into the wilderness carrying away the people's sins. But the Old Testament priesthood was not enough. It pointed forward to a time when God would send His true High Priest, the Holy One who would provide the perfect sacrifice for all. He would not only be the Perfect Priest, He would also be the Perfect Sacrifice.

The OT priest offered the sacrifice for sins in the temple many times over the centuries. But when the time was right, God sent Jesus the Perfect Priest, and He became the Perfect Sacrifice for sins, once and for all. After Jesus, no more sacrifices were needed. The book of Hebrews explains this. I urge you to read it to understand all this better.

This is the meaning of Jesus our Priest. The gift of Frankincense foretold all this. When Jesus shed His blood on Calvary it ended the need for repeated sacrifice. When the temple curtain was torn in two, the old was over. **"It is**

Finished!" meant salvation was complete, no more sacrifices were needed. The Priest became the Sacrifice.

Through all this we are reconciled to God. 2 Corinthians 5:21 says, **"God made Him who knew no sin to become sin for us, that we might become the righteousness of God."** Jesus our Priest suffered the punishment for our sins. With Him, atonement for sins is complete. That's what Isaiah 53:6 means when it says, **"The Lord laid on Him the iniquity of us all."**

(A story by Paul Harvey) *There was once a modern man, one of us. He was not a Scrooge, but a kind, decent man. He was generous to his family, and upright with his dealings with other men. And he was looking forward to another Christmas season.*

However, he did not believe in what he termed "all that incarnation stuff." "It just does not make sense," he said in his mind, too honest to pretend otherwise. He just could not swallow "that Jesus Story," the one about God coming to earth as man. On Christmas Eve, he told his wife, "I hate to disappoint you, but I just cannot go to church with you tonight." He said he would feel like a hypocrite, that he had much rather stay home, but that he would wait up for them. So he stayed at home and his family went to church.

Shortly after the family drove away, snow began to fall. He went to the window to watch the flurries getting heavier and heavier, he then went back to his fireside chair and began to read the newspaper. Minutes later, he was startled by a thudding sound, then another and another. At first he thought someone must be throwing snowballs against the living room window, but when he went to the door to investigate, he found a flock of birds floundering miserably in the snow. They'd been caught in the storm and in a desperate search for shelter, tried to fly through his picture window.

Well, he could not let the poor creatures lie there and freeze. Then he remembered the barn where his children kept their pony. That would provide a warm shelter if he could direct the birds to it. So he quickly put on a coat and boots, and tramped through the snow to the barn. Once there he opened the doors wide, and turned on a light, but the birds only ignored it. They would not come in. He figured food would entice them in, so he hurried back to the house, fetched bread crumbs, and sprinkled them on the snow making a trail to the yellow lighted doorway of the stable. But to his dismay, the birds ignored the crumbs.

44

They just continued to flop around helplessly in the snow. He tried catching them, he tried shooing them into the barn and waving his arms. Instead, they scattered in every direction, except into the warm lighted barn.

Suddenly, he realized they were afraid of him. "To them I'm a strange and terrifying creature," he thought. "If only I could think of some way to let them know they can trust me so they'd understand that I'm not trying to hurt them, but to help them." But how? Any move he made scared and confused them, they just would not follow. They could not be lead or shooed because they feared him.

"If only I could be a bird myself," he thought. "If only I could be a bird and mingle with them and speak their language, and tell them not to be afraid and show them the way to the warm and safe barn. But, I'd have to be one of them so they could see and hear and understand."

Just then, church bells began to ring. The bells rang so loudly that he heard them that cold night. And listening to the bells pealing their glad tidings of Christmas, and remembering the story of the birth of a baby, he suddenly understood why God became a man. And he sank to his knees right there in the snow.

We all need Jesus. We all need to ask with that jailer at Philippi, **"What must I do to be saved?"** (Acts 16:30-31). We need to trust Paul's words, **"Believe on the Lord Jesus Christ."** Jesus is our great High Priest who became the sacrifice for us. God wants us in heaven with Him. Advent is a time of preparation for His second coming. Christ was born, Christ is risen, Christ will come again! **"Even so, come quickly, Lord Jesus."** Amen!

ADVENT SERIES THREE
"Prophet, Priest and King"
Week Three

Matthew 2:2   *"Jesus, our King"*
**"Where is the one who has been born king of the Jews?
We saw his star in the east and have come to worship him."**

Every society has its heroes. Study the heroes and you'll better understand that society. People and nations honor those who embody its dreams and values. While each nation has its various heroes, there is one character that reflects the world. He is as recognized in Colorado as he is in Columbia, in India as he is in Indiana. His face is known everywhere, even in many underdeveloped societies.

This man was born in 280 AD in modern-day Turkey. He was orphaned at age 9 by a plague, and as an adult he studied Greek philosophy and Christian doctrine and became a priest. He was honored by being chosen a Bishop in the early 4th century, a post he held till his death in 343 AD. He has been canonized a saint, but was often a bit of a troublemaker.

During his early years he was twice jailed, once for religious reasons and once for slugging a fellow bishop. He never married, but was a hopeless romantic. He was best known during his life for his kindness to a poor neighbor who was unable to support his three daughters or provide the customary dowry so they could marry. One night he slipped his hand through an open window and dropped a handful of gold coins on the floor so the eldest daughter could be married. On later nights, he left also gold for her sisters that they also might marry. By now I'm sure you all know who I mean.

When the Wise Men visited Jesus, they brought Him gold. We don't know how much, but it was greatly appreciated by Joseph and helped him provide for his young family. The Magi believed this child was born to be a king. Their asking, **"Where is He born King of the Jews?"** rocked Jerusalem and old King Herod. Herod was so unnerved that he ordered the killing of all the infant boys under age two in Bethlehem, hoping to extinguish a fire that could burn him alive.

It was not until Jesus faced another powerful ruler in a different age that He publicly admitted He was King of the Jews. That ruler was Pontius Pilate. Pilate had been given the dirty work of bringing Jesus to trial. There He told Pilate His kingship was not of the world. And like many kings, this one evoked strong emotions, so much so that the Jews demanded His death.

When Jesus was crucified the soldiers and people made fun of Him. **"Hail, king of the Jews,"** they said as they mocked and struck Him. On His cross Pilate placed the Latin inscription, "INRI," (Yesus, Nazarenus, Rex Yudaiorum), **"Jesus of Nazareth, King of the Jews."** This was nearly equal to **"King of Kings and Lord of Lords,"** the name given Him in Revelation 17:14. But what a king! His scepter a broken stick, His royal robe something from "lost and found," His crown of bloody thorns, and His throne a grizzly cross. And all His so-called "subjects" were nowhere is sight.

How different was that Friday from the Sunday before. Then Jesus rode with a royal procession into Jerusalem while crowds laid their garments before Him and hailed Him king. **"Blessed is He who comes in the name of the Lord,"** they shouted Sunday. **"Crucify Him!"** they shouted on Friday. The whole city turned out for His grand entry on Sunday, but the Friday crowd assailed Him a villain who claimed to be King. How like us who are so easily swayed. So easily we turn our backs on those who have given to us so generously.

Back to our world hero. The legend of the handful of gold coins grew with time. Instead of dropping them through the window, he was said to have dropped them down the chimney. Rather than landing on the floor, the coins landed in stockings hung on the hearth to dry.

In time his wardrobe and even his personality changed. As Bishop he wore priestly robes and a mitered hat. By 1300 AD people said he had a long white beard. By the 1800's he was a fat man carrying a basket of food to share. Soon came black boots, red cape, stocking cap and sack full of toys. By 1930 he had a big smile and a Coca Cola in his hand. And by then the whole world recognized him instantly. He's our international hero, good old Santa Claus.

St. Nicholas of Myra today reflects the desires of people all over the world. Over time he has become the composite of all we wanted, a friend who cares and brings gifts, a wise sage who knows if you're naughty or nice, a friend of children, who never gets grows older. He lets you sit on his lap and share your deepest desires. He's the personification of our memories, the expression of our yearnings and the fulfillment of our childhood desires.

If Santa Claus is considered a hero, then is Jesus of Nazareth one also? Is His face as recognized as Santa's? Certainly what He did is of far greater significance. A hero eventually dies and is buried. Jesus our "hero" died for a purpose, but very soon came back to life.

A hero's life is often expanded and embellished until there is little truth left. But what Jesus did, as recorded by His followers, is as true today as the day it happened. He was king then and is king now. He is not a mere hero of legend. He is, as we thrill to hear in Handel's "Hallelujah Chorus," our **"King of Kings and Lord of Lords."**

Sir Thomas More is considered by many to be a hero. As Lord Chancellor for King Henry VIII, Thomas More was a hero because He stood up for his beliefs. He was a loyal Catholic in a court that had broken away from the papal authority. He opposed King Henry's wishes to divorce his wife in order to marry another. Because of his beliefs, Thomas More died a martyr. For all this call him, "A Man for All Seasons," a man who stands up for what is right rather than what is popular.

In a far greater way Jesus of Nazareth is our "Man for All Seasons." He refused to be made an earthly king. He refused to break God's Law when it had become popular. He defied those who demanded He obey manmade laws. He was condemned to death because He followed God, defying those who believed they knew better than God. Sounds like the kind of person we need today!

Jesus is our "Man for All Seasons," no matter what season of life we are in. Whether we are in the springtime of life with its growth and great change, whether we are in the fruitful summer of life, whether we are in the maturity of life's autumn, or whether we wear the whiteness of winter on our heads, Jesus is our "Man for All Seasons." Jesus is also our God for all seasons. His death was not the death of a martyr, but the death of the Savior. He was **"put to death for our offenses, and raised again for our justification."** (Romans 4:25) Now He is **"King of Kings and Lord of Lords."**

America has never had a king, but Great Britain has had many – queens, too. A king or queen may reign with honor, but he or she rules with power. In England, the last monarch to both reign and rule was Queen Elizabeth I. She was the daughter of Henry VIII by Ann Boleyn. Henry VIII died in 1547, one year after Martin Luther died, and two weak rulers followed Henry, Edward VI and Mary I. In 1558, Elizabeth was crowned Queen reigned and ruled England powerfully for 45 years.

She reigned, that is, she was given all honor and glory due a monarch of that era. But she also ruled. She ruled affairs of state with an iron hand, forming armies, enforcing laws of the British crown rule, even ordering executions. During her reign, science and the arts flourished under her encouragement of Francis Bacon and William Shakespeare. Francis Drake and Walter Raleigh commanded powerful English armies abroad, and in 1588 Lord Howard and the British Navy defeated the Spanish Armada and began domination of the seas. But it was also under Elizabeth's rule that British Parliament developed its power and became the eventual ruler of England. "Good Queen Bess," as she was called, was the last British monarch to both reign and rule. Since then, monarchs have reigned in glory, but Parliament has ruled with law.

The story is told of the King of a small nation who was once visiting the villages of his kingdom, receiving his peoples' cheers and admiration. As the King entered the market square in one village, peasants bowed humbly to his chariot. To the amazement of all, one brash young man stepped up and approached the carriage. "Grant me a favor, Sire," he pleaded. "give me some special blessing only you can give."

The villagers were astounded at the King's response. "Of course," he said. "Come here, get in my carriage and come to the palace. You may marry my daughter, become my son-in-law and live in luxury for the rest of your days." The young man was amazed. It all sounded too good to be true. He was ready to take the step when he stopped to consider the offer. No more Saturday nights at the tavern. No more carousing with his friends. He'd have to take a bath every week! He'd have to learn court manners and have official duties. So the young man lowered his eyes and said, "No Sire, no thank you. It would be too much change. It would take me from the comforts of my home. It would require too much of me." And so the King left him with his greatest blessing declined.

A most remarkable quality of Jesus our King is that He wants to make us even greater than we are. He wants to make us God's children, and give each one of us a high place in His Kingdom. He wishes to adopt us into His family and rule with Him. All we need do is accept His offer in faith. He holds our gift in His hand. It's all ours for the taking. But will we, like the young man, feel it's too much change and reject His offer?

Jesus Christ is our King of kings, and all people are subject to Him, including all the saints. Several years ago I received a card from a friend who tried to find something religious at the grocery store. The card showed a manger scene with various persons kneeling in adoration of the Babe. And there on the side of the group bowing in worship was a chubby little red Santa, kneeling in adoration before the King of Kings. I like that card, St. Nicholas of Myra, good old Santa Claus, worshipping the King of kings and Lord of Lords. Amen

ADVENT SERIES FOUR
"Women of Advent"
Week One

✠ ✠ ✠

ANNA, PROPHETESS OF GOD

A small bird darted into the Temple, past the Court of the Gentiles, past the Women's Court and into one of the inner courts accessible only to Jewish men. Anna, the old prophetess of God, may have blinked as she watched the tiny beating wings swerve into the sunlight and then vanish into the shadows. A privileged little bird had found a corner in the Temple of God, and it reminded Anna of the words of Psalm 84: **"How lovely is your dwelling place, O Lord Almighty! My soul yearns, even faints, for the courts of the Lord; my heart and my flesh cry out for the living God. Even the sparrow has found a home, and the swallow a nest for herself, where she may have her young-- a place near your altar, O Lord Almighty, my King and my God. Blessed are those who dwell in your house; they are ever praising you."**

For most of her 84 years, Anna had been a widow who spent her days praying and fasting in the Temple. A thousand times she must have walked into the Women's Court, passing the warnings inscribed on the walls, telling everyone who could or could not enter the courts, always on penalty of death. As many times she must have heard the men giving thanks to God in prayer they were not born Gentiles or women. Despite how she may have felt about that, Anna accepted this restriction, for her thoughts were not on those who made and enforced the Temple rules. She was thinking about the God who dwelt there.

Suddenly a loud voice interrupted her prayers. Simeon, old friend and fellow temple patron, was holding a baby in his arms and shouting words that thrilled her soul: **"Sovereign Lord, as You have promised, now let Your servant die in peace. For with my own eyes I have seen Your salvation which You have prepared in the sight of all people, a light for revelation to the Gentiles, and for glory to Your people Israel."**

Both Anna and Simeon had lived for little else than to see

Israel's coming Messiah and the salvation He would bring. She must have watched as the old man handed the child back to his mother, saying, **"This child is destined to cause the falling and rising of many in Israel, and to be a sign that will be spoken against, so that the thoughts of many hearts will be revealed."** To His mother Anna heard Simeon softly say, **"And a sword will pierce your own soul too."**

Anna herself then approached the couple, and placing her arms gently around the mother's shoulders, gazed at the sleeping infant. Words of thanksgiving poured forth from the old woman. Her heart felt buoyant and her hope unsinkable. This was the holy Promised One of God! As vividly as Jacob who wrestled with God, or Moses who saw and heard God, Anna experienced the presence of Almighty God, now wrapped in a blanket, and carried by His mother.

Now too, Anna may have felt like that sparrow soaring freely in the Temple. It no longer mattered that she was forbidden entry into the inner courts, for God Himself would soon break down the walls between Jew and Gentile, between male and female, revealing Himself openly to all who hungered for His presence. That day a holy child transformed the Women's Court into the holiest place of all, occupied by the Son of God Himself.

Anna, the prophetess spoken of in Luke 2, was unique. She probably spent upwards of 60 years in the temple, every day. The Bible says she was always there, **"...worshipping day and night, fasting and praying."** (Luke 2:37) Evidence of her devotion was not just in spending that much time there, but in that she recognized the baby as the promised Savior. He was, after all, just 6 weeks old. Anna had chosen to give her life to God, probably cleaning and sweeping, making the Temple tidy after crowds came and went. She was not idle, Indeed she was very much alert when the Son of God came in. Despite any restrictions, she never let up on her hope to see the promised Messiah. Anna and Simeon must have had much to talk about after the holy family left!

Simeon was no stranger to the Temple. Like Anna, he came there often, especially after he could no longer work. Cynics have said those two spoke special words to many couples who entered carrying babies, perhaps most of them. But that makes no sense, for they would have been considered foolish and would not have been allowed to be there so often.

Solomon had built the first Temple, an elaborate white limestone structure inlaid with gold. Zerubabbel tried to build the second Temple, but his work was small potatoes compared to Solomon's majestic edifice. Then came Herod the Great who built the Temple where Anna and Simeon worshipped. This was the most majestic of all. It was on the edge of highest hill of Jerusalem, for every eye to see.

Herod's Temple had four courts, each one more exclusive than the one before it. The outer court was the Court of the Gentiles. This was the only place Gentiles were allowed, and was also the court Jesus cleared out due to improper buying and selling during worship. The Inner Court was divided into two sections: the Women's Court where Anna worshipped, and the Court of Israel, reserved only for men. Men could enter the Women's Court, but only men could enter the Court of Israel. The Court of Priests, called the Holy Place, came next and was reserved only for those of the Levitical priesthood. The Holy of Holies, most sacred of all and separated by the huge curtain, was reserved only for the High Priest who offered sacrifices there for the sins of all the people.

Customs may have restricted access in that great Temple, but no earthly regulations can actually bind someone's worship. You and I today worship wherever we choose, usually in churches, but without restriction to place or gender. Jesus once told the Samaritan woman at the well, **"Believe me, woman, a time is coming when you will worship the Father neither on this mountain nor in Jerusalem. You Samaritans worship what you do not know; we worship what we do know, for salvation is from the Jews. Yet a time is coming and has now come when the true worshipers will worship the Father in spirit and truth, for they are the kind of worshipers the Father seeks."** (John 4:21-23)

Holy Scripture tells us Anna had been married, but doubtless had been childless. She was the daughter of Phanuel, of the tribe of Asher, one of Jacob's sons. "Anna" is the same as "Hannah" and means "gracious." She took her place along side other prominent prophetesses of Holy Scripture, such as Miriam, Deborah, Huldah of the Old Testament and the daughters of Philip in the New Testament. Anna praised God for the child Jesus in the Temple, just as Hannah had praised God for the child Samuel in the Tabernacle 1,500 years before.

Anna may have been allowed to live in one of the dozens of small rooms in Herod's Temple complex, or she may have come there only during the daytime. But whether or not she stayed at the Temple, what matters most is that she was there when the Holy Son of God came in. So she is forever noted in Christian history as one of the primary women of Advent.

You and I need not be bound or restricted in our worship. Liturgies or hymns are but one of many ways to worship God. Churches honor God but do not contain Him. Pastors can teach and preach God's Word, but so may any Christian. The Christian Church is a gift from God to help us serve God and honor God. You and I can serve and honor Him by serving and honoring each other.

There is nothing in our past that need keep us away from God. This is the Gospel: that because of Christ, no horrendous sin, no terrible mistake, no foolish act need keep us from worshiping God and recognizing our Savior. Anna's life revolved completely around prayer and fasting in the Temple. She had no family, no job and perhaps no home. Instead, the Temple was her home, the worshipers were her family, and God was her eternal Father.

Whatever time you and I spend in prayer, reading the Bible, or doing deeds of love, nothing of it is ever wasted. If you long to see your Savior, to experience His presence in life, then let Anna's example encourage you. She and Simeon did not become too old to serve or to worship. She never became too old to give thanks or praise her God.

Anna's legacy is her prayer. She never let up praying to see God's Promised Holy One. She believed in her heart He would come again, and her faith was rewarded. Paul wrote, **"Never be lacking in zeal, but keep your spiritual fervor, serving the Lord."** (Romans 12:10) **"What does the Lord require of us, but to act justly, to love mercy, and to walk humbly before our God."** (Micah 6:8) God grant us such faith, amen.

ADVENT SERIES FOUR
"Women of Advent"
Week Two

✠ ✠ ✠

MARY, WIFE OF JOSEPH

Good evening, friends. I am here to share with you some thoughts from the heart of a man named Joseph, a carpenter of Israel. This message is not about me, but about the woman I married. Mary, O Mary! Where is our son? We have an order to fill before morning. He knows I must do the special work at night- it is a long walk to Sepphoris where we work on the new buildings there. For once I'm glad to be near the Romans, for their new city provides labor for me and Jesus, and wages for our family. It's hard on my old body, but more profitable than making tools or the small jobs of building here in Nazareth.

We are so small here, just a few hundred people. But all the new buildings in Sepphoris is a blessing from God. Thanks be to Jehovah that He has provided work and good health so that we are provided well in all our needs.

When I think back where we've come in the past dozen years or so, it is astounding. We went to Bethlehem with nothing and came away with wealth in gifts from the Persian Magi. Mary and I almost didn't get there in time. Actually, we almost didn't get married. When I heard she was expecting, it just about killed me. We'd known each other for several years and had plans marry, but not in that way.

Mary is from Nazareth and I was born in Bethlehem. We met when my family moved here and Mary was very young. Our mothers were distant cousins, so we visited often and enjoyed each other. She was much younger than I, but I think we liked each other from the start.

As she grew, she became so beautiful it almost took my breathe away. I waited till she was of age before I asked her father for her hand. Our families settled on the bride price, and so I hurried - actually I ran - to her home with the news and the cup of wine. When she drank for my cup, consenting to my proposal, I nearly did handsprings down the street.

57

I then went to prepare a place for her and told her I'd come back soon to take her to be there with me. It would have been an addition to my father's house, but he had already died, as had my mother. So I had begun building our new home with my uncle when the shocking news came. Mary had been visiting her cousin Elizabeth and returned very obviously expecting a child. And it was not mine. Again, she took my breathe away, but for a terrible reason I thought.

She said the child was from God, that an angel had visited her with the news, but I did not believe that. Angels I could believe, but not with news like that. The Law was clear. She had wronged me and had to pay, so I spoke with one of my Levite friends about setting the betrothal aside. The other alternative was stoning but that I could not have allowed. And so I would have gone through with the divorce had not that same angel came to me that very same night, affirming what she had said. The child was from God, literally!

Zechariah had once told me, *"Don't argue with an angel!"* I tried to tell our friends what was going on, but they just snickered and looked the other way. Thus, I arranged for a quiet marriage, and we found a small house of our own. Our reputations took quite a beating those first months until we left for Bethlehem.

I had made the trip several times and Mary had already gone there to visit Elizabeth, so we knew the way well. But this trip for the census was down the Jordan valley and was difficult for Mary and we barely made it in time. I was glad we were alone in that little stable when the baby came, and I was very much amazed how Mary gave birth to her first child all by herself. I was not allowed by Moses' law to help until the baby was born, but then I washed and wrapped Him. What a night it was, the child, the shepherd visitors. Such a gift from God!

The Innkeeper's wife helped Mary and her husband found us a little house the next day. It reminded me of our home in Nazareth that I'd loaned to a friend while we were gone. Then some time later came those wonderful men with their gifts. We would have stayed there a year or more as work was plentiful. But then came the angel's visit once again. *"Go now to Egypt,"* he said, so we did. My, but Galilean women are strong! She seemed never to tire. Weeks through Gaza along the great sea and several months in Egypt. It was good that we found friends there. There is a large settlement of our fellow believers in Alexandria, but it was not home

One day when I came to our dwelling, Mary gave the news that Herod was dead. She told of how he had planned to have people mourn his death, so he had hundreds of prominent citizens locked in the hippodrome with orders they be killed when he died, just so people would have reason to mourn at his death. But thanks be to God one of his officers ignored the order and released them unharmed. Mary often said she still felt sad for the mothers of the infants he'd had killed after we left for Egypt. Such an evil man he was!

But that seems long ago, and now we have four children to think of, including the holy boy. I am only His foster father. Somehow and for some special reason, God gave Him to Mary and to all of us. Mary said last night we must never forget He is the Messiah. but I don't understand all that means. Will He gather an army? Defeat Rome? That's impossible, and I'm not sure that's what the Messiah would do. Oh, there He is now, and His cousin John is with him. Good! I can get both of them to help me carry the table and chairs to Sepphoris.

Boys! Come here. I need you both. Leave your things in the house, for we have work to do. Ouch, there's that pain in my arm again! Sometimes it seems to go from my heart all the way to my fingers, but it goes away quickly.

Mary is such a good mother. Ironically, after the shaky beginning to our marriage, I am now admired for being her husband. She is a model of motherhood. But our family, and especially the oldest boy, is our real joy. He has a mind of His own, but He's a good boy, very obedient. You know, I can't remember even once that He talked back to His mother or me. Now James on the other hand, he's more than made up for that! That boy has a mouth on him. And I wish he'd wash up more often. He gets dirty so quickly!

Come on, boys, let's get these delivered before dark. Mary, we'll be back in two hours, the boys will help me deliver them. Both fine boys, they are, both so different, both so dedicated to God. John has lived among the wilderness people since his parents died. He's bright, but a bit rough around the edges. Sleeping in caves will do that to a person, as well we know. They tell me he spends days discussing the Torah and copying the scriptures. I wonder what he will do for a living. He hasn't learned any trade, but he writes well and speaks to others easily. God will show him the way He has for him.

Here son, take one end of this table, and John, you carry the chairs. Ouch, there's that pain in my arm again! I need a good night's sleep. That's the best medicine for all aches and pains. God be praised we live in peace now. I hope to be around for a long time yet. God willing, Mary and I will play with our children's children. What joy that will be!

Mary said tonight something so true, that joy cannot be purchased. Money can get us things, but not joy. That can only be given by God. When Mary told me her "bad" news back in the early days, I could have despaired, but God give me joy. May God bless you also with joy and peace this night, so that you may all sleep well. Go on ahead, boys, up that street. It will take us time to get there and back, so let's not dawdle! Mother Mary will be waiting for us when we get back.

ADVENT SERIES FOUR
"Women of Advent"
Week Three

✛ ✛ ✛

ELIZABETH, WIFE OF ZECHARIAH

"Blessed are You, O Lord our God, King of the Universe, the God of Abraham, Isaac and Jacob. I praise You for life and health and every good thing. Hear my prayers on behalf of Your people. Deliver us from the hand of our enemies and restore the glory of your Chosen People. May my wife and child bless You like Sarah and Isaac. Give me the strength to be a good father like Jacob, and the faith to be a man of God like Abraham. Hear my prayer, O Lord God of hosts, amen!"

She was very young when I first laid eyes on her, my Elizabeth. Her name means, "God is my Oath," and we took an oath when we were betrothed after our families agreed on terms for marriage. Elizabeth was an exemplary child, and she carried her godly nature into adulthood. Her friends called her **"upright in the sight of God,"** so well did she observe our laws and regulations. She was remarkable woman in every way.

Our marriage was like that of most Israelites. We had little, but we shared with all who came to our home. As a Levite priest, I was compensated meagerly, but we always had enough. She helped me with my work and was like an angel to the poor and sick. Our sorrow in marriage was in not having a child. To be barren was the greatest burden a woman of Israel could have. But that all changed one day.

We'd been married nearly 40 years. I had been chosen by lots to burn incense before the Most Holy Place, a rare privilege. But during my week of service I was nearly frightened to death by the appearance of an angel as I sprinkled incense. I knew it was an angel, though I can't tell you how. It said, **"Your prayers have been heard. Your wife Elizabeth will bear you a son, and you are to name him John. He will be a joy and delight to you, and many will rejoice because of his birth; He will be great in the sight of God."** (Luke 1:13-14) I told the angel I could not believe this, and so I was made speechless as proof.

Elizabeth could not understand my reaction. When I left

61

the Holy Place I could not speak and so she thought the experience had terrified me. But once you have seen a heavenly being, what is there to say? If I had not been skeptical such a thing could happen at our age, I would not have paid the price.

Imagine us having a child! It was like Sarah and Abraham all over again, or Rebekah and Isaac, or Rachel and Jacob. God was once more growing a tree in the desert, making a fire with two dry sticks. Elizabeth soon devised a way for me to scratch messages on a stone slate, using a soft white stone. And she quickly came to know how to speak with me so I could answer in short written words.

But despite my inability to talk, I felt a vigor in my soul that had long since left me. God, the creator and giver of life, blesses us as He chooses, and there is no greater blessing than looking into the eyes of a newborn child.

The days that followed the angelic visit were memorable. Elizabeth's golden brown eyes sparkled. Like currants in pastry, they winked at the world from cheeks that had baked too long in the sun. Snowy strands of hair straggled from beneath her woolen shawl, and her small hands became busy with things only God could have given us. In no time at all, she told me of the new life stirring within her. The first time I felt movement within, it was a shock to me. But then I knew it was real, and not a dream.

We were content in our quiet home, for I could do little of my duties without my voice. Soon she began to sing, as she had during our first years. She sang the ancient Psalms of David and Moses. She sang our tribal cradle songs, and she sang new songs. Her sweet music filled our home with joy.

Each morning she awoke and opened her eyes as though waking to a fantastic dream. Sometimes at night she shook with giggles and laughter, and I knew she was thinking of how God had rearranged her life, planting new life inside her old body. And her body seemed to be growing younger each day!

In her sixth month we had a visitor, or rather, I should say Elizabeth had a visitor. Her cousin Mary came all the way down from Nazareth, and when she called out her greeting, Elizabeth fairly jumped out of her chair as our child leaped within her. She then stepped carefully down the stairs to welcome Mary as she spoke in a loud voice even our neighbors could hear, "Blessed are you among women, and blessed is the child you will bear! But why am I so favored that the mother of my Lord should come to me. As soon as the sound of your greeting reached me, the baby in my womb leaped for joy. How blessed is she who has believed what the Lords has said to her will happen." (Luke 1:42-45)

After greeting each other so memorably, I left for the temple so they could speak of things I would little understand. Mary stayed nearly three months, helping make Elizabeth ready for her birth. I was home each night, but rarely spent more than a few hours there during the day. Mary's visit so blessed my wife. It was the perfect preparation for our new arrival.

We learned much during Mary's stay. We learned that the same angel, Gabriel, who spoke to me, also had visited her. The magnificent song of praise Mary sang for Elizabeth seemed not just for her, but for the whole world. Their bond of friendship grew those months, and yet something told me all would not be perfect in the years to come. This world held dark, sinful shadows for both children, and yet as always, we trusted God to get us through.

When it came time for Elizabeth to give birth, neighbors and relatives came to our home, and news that it was a boy brought joy and laughter to all in the village. On the eighth day Elizabeth called a Rabbi came to our home for the circumcision, and we nearly had a serious problem. Because I could not talk, my family took it upon themselves to name the babe after me, but I waved them off and objected. It was then that Elizabeth said firmly to all, **"He is to be called John!"** Some grumbled, *"No one in our family has that name!"* Others said, *"A father should name his son."* So they came to me and I wrote on the slate, **"His name is John."**

As soon as I wrote the words, my tongue was loosed and I praised God loudly for all to hear. And over all the singing and praises, I could hear my beloved Elizabeth, praising God and giving Him great glory. Everyone wondered what kind of child John would be, for they knew the Lord's hand was with him. And I wondered the same. What kind of gift had God given Elizabeth and me?

That was a few months ago, and now everyone has gone home. Our days are filled now with quiet baby cries, rising often in the night. Though this is her first child, Elizabeth has an uncanny way of knowing just what to do. I try to suggest something and sometimes I am right. Most often she rolls her eyes at me, especially when I suggest what I want to do with the baby and how I shall teach it. She recently told me to act my age, and so I reminded her she certainly is not doing that. Neither of us want to, for we know this time will end soon enough.

Word has now come that Mary has given birth. Praise be to the God of our Fathers, Abraham, Isaac and Jacob, who has not forgotten His people. Elizabeth believes Mary's son will be a blessing to all mankind, not just our families. I believe John will, also. Meanwhile, I wish to speak with Joseph. I would like to know if Mary rolls her eyes when he says things, like my Elizabeth does. God be with you all!

ADVENT SERIES FIVE
"Getting Ready"
Week One

Mark 13:34-37   *"Getting Ready for Christ's Return"*
"It's like a man going away: He leaves his house and puts his servants in charge, each with his assigned task, and tells the one at the door to keep watch. Therefore keep watch because you do not know when the owner of the house will come back--whether in the evening, or at midnight, or when the rooster crows, or at dawn. f he comes suddenly, do not let him find you sleeping. What I say to you, I say to everyone: 'Watch!'"

✠ ✠ ✠

Good morning and Happy Thanksgiving a few days late! I'm happy to say our trip to visit our son and his wife in Florida was a success, complete with giving us a little Florida tan. I always appreciate getting together with friends and family on Thanksgiving, but the only drawback this year is that we have no leftover turkey in the frig. While some of you may think that's a blessing, I do miss making all those great sandwiches. But I'm sure God will provide.

Today is Advent, the beginning of the new Church Year. The Church Year is divided into two halves: the Lord's Half which deals with the life of Jesus, and the Church's Half Year, which emphasizes the teachings of Jesus. Today's the first Sunday in Advent, beginning a new Church Year. Advent is a season of waiting and getting ready, so I've chosen the theme, "Getting Ready" for our services during the coming weeks, "Getting ready ... for Christ's Return" "Getting Ready or a Blessed Event, and "Getting Ready for Christmas. May God bless us as today we consider briefly the business of "Getting Ready for Christ's Return."

Advent comes from two Latin words meaning "to come to." At this time of year we remember Christ's two advents, (1) when He first came at Christmas and (2) when He will come again in Judgment. We're living between the two. We remember well His first advent when He came to the world as the child

65

born in Bethlehem. But Scriptures tell us the babe didn't stay a baby. He grew to manhood, completed the work of salvation, and then returned to heaven until His second advent, on Judgment Day.

Most people can be confused about the significance of Christmas and Easter. The most important festival of the Church is not the one recalling His birth, His first advent. It's Easter, the festival recalling His resurrection. Everyone has a birth, but only Christ had a re-birth in the Resurrection. It's good to get ready for Jesus' birthday party, but trusting in His birth won't get us to heaven. But believing He rose from the dead will! Christmas may be a joyful season, but it doesn't hold a candle to meaning of Easter.

Today we're between those two advents, and as the days pass, we'll mostly be thinking how to celebrate His first one. But it's imperative that we're ready for His second advent also. We must always be ready for His return in glory.

Our Lord was a practical person. During His ministry He accomplished His greatest and most difficult task, saving the world. But His second greatest task may have been almost as difficult, teaching His disciples and preparing them to carry on after He returned to heaven. But He did His work well, and when the disciples were prepared, they would teach all the people who would follow. So His teaching methods were extremely important.

One of His most practical methods of teaching was through stories, and today's short parable is a good example. He was talking about being ready: **"It's like a man going away: He leaves his house and puts his servants in charge, each with his assigned task, and tells the one at the door to keep watch. Therefore keep watch because you do not know when the owner of the house will come back--whether in the evening, or at midnight, or when the rooster crows, or at dawn. If he comes suddenly, do not let him find you sleeping. What I say to you, I say to everyone: 'Watch!'"**

When you and I leave home, we lock our doors and perhaps turn on the alarm. My son and his wife have an alarm and have done this out of habit so much that it can shock their guests. The day after Thanksgiving when my daughter-in-law

66

left to do some early shopping, I opened the door and mistakenly tripped their alarm. She had reset it when she left the house! Are those things ever loud inside a small house! And our former track star son can still move fast when he's motivated!

Jesus says waiting for His return is like watching over the Master's home while He is gone. You don't know when He will return, so he posts servants to watch for His coming. They must stay awake. A sleeping servant can't guard anything. And we can't either. He's put us in charge of watching over His house, and we can't afford to fall asleep.

But sometimes we do. It's easy to fall asleep when times are good. Our prosperity has lulled a whole lot of us American Christians into dreamland. We're so caught up in our search for enjoyment and fulfillment that we're in danger of losing our first love, to do God's will and share our faith. When the times are this good, there's almost no way God can keep us on our toes. I have tried and tried and found no workable solution for this. God will have to shock us, to get us awake, because we won't stay awake in such good times as these.

Jesus says we must stay awake because even He doesn't know when He'll be coming back. During His time on earth before the Resurrection, which we call His "State of Humiliation," His chose to limit His divine wisdom. Wouldn't you love to know exactly when He's coming? Wouldn't that be a wonderful bit of knowledge? Actually, it wouldn't be as helpful as you think. A roadmap to the future can be more a hindrance to faith than a help. Certain signs have been given us, but not for the purpose of making a detailed sequence of predictable events. Faith is absolutely necessary, and anything that short circuits our faith is bad for us.

We're nearing the end of 1999, the possible beginning of a new millennium. I'm among those who don't believe it starts until 2001, but that's just semantics. And it surely doesn't stop those who firmly believe something catastrophic will happen sometime the early days of year 2000. They're hoarding food, generators and gold, thinking it's all going to collapse. That doesn't seem to be an attitude of Christian faith, but of an alarmist with little faith.

67

What's involved with being ready for His coming? It's simple: know your faith and be ready to defend it. 1 Peter 3:15 tells us, **"Always be prepared to give an answer to everyone who asks you to give the reason for the hope that you have. But do this with gentleness and respect."**

A philosophy professor there was a deeply committed atheist whose goal in teaching was to prove that God didn't exist. (That seems to be the goal of a whole host of elite educators these days.) Most students feared arguing with him because of his impeccable logic. For twenty years he had taught the class and few had the courage to stand up to him. Some tried arguing, but to no avail.

The last day of each semester, he would say to the class, "If there is anyone here who still believes in God, stand up!" In twenty years, students had stopped standing up because of what he would do next. He'd shout, "'Anyone who believes in God is a fool! If God existed, he could stop this piece of chalk from hitting the ground and breaking." And every year he would drop the chalk to the floor and it would shatter. The students would remain silent, and many were convinced that God could not exist. A number of Christians attended the class, but in twenty years few had stood up for their faith.

Then one year a Christian freshman enrolled in the class. He'd heard the stories, but this was a required course, so for the entire semester he prayed that when the time came he would have courage to stand up as a witness. He didn't want to deny his faith, but he was scared. When the last day came the professor said again, "If there is anyone here who still believes in God, stand up now!" And the young man quietly stood. The professor and the students were shocked. Twenty years of conceit, twenty years of harassment and twenty years of storm trooper tactics were threatened! The professor shouted, "YOU FOOL! If nothing I have said has convinced you God doesn't exist, then you're truly just a fool! If God existed, he could keep this piece of chalk from breaking when it hit the ground!"

But as the professor dropped the chalk, he was so rattled that it slipped out of his fingers, bounced off his pant leg and shoe, and rolled onto the floor, unbroken. The professor was speechless as he stared at the unbroken chalk. He looked at the young man a moment and abruptly left the lecture hall. The young man then spent a few minutes sharing his faith in Jesus. And all the students stayed and listened to his witness.

Knowing your faith means the need for Bible study, and if there's one thing I plan to emphasize in the coming year, it's Bible study. We all need it. There's no one here who has learned enough. Study it in groups or alone, at work or at home, by reading or by listening to it on tape. Every Christian home with a computer should have a Bible search program or a Bible study on it that gets used.

You've heard me talk about Small Group Ministry here in this church, and those all center on Bible study. People share and care for each other, but all they do centers on God's Word. And we have Sunday morning Bible study, 9 AM right here each Sunday. And we have midweek Bible study as well. We have midweek Advent services this Thursday at 7:15 and that service, too will center around God's Word. Know your faith and be ready to defend it.

That's what really matters, to know God and His Word, that He loves us and that He cares enough about us to give the life of His only Son for us. As our Lord tells us, **"Therefore keep watch because you do not know when the owner of the house will come back... If he comes suddenly, do not let him find you sleeping."** Be ready for His return. Don't fall asleep on your watch! Amen

ADVENT SERIES FIVE
"Getting Ready"
Week Two

Luke 1:13   *"Getting Ready for a New Arrival"*

"The angel said to him, 'Do not be afraid, Zechariah; your prayer has been heard. Your wife Elizabeth will bear you a son and you are to give him the name John.'"

✛ ✛ ✛

Our Advent theme this year is "Getting Ready" and today we are "Getting Ready for a New Arrival." Zechariah the priest and Elizabeth his wife wanted a child. She had been unable to have children, but they prayed and kept on praying. In their old age they had by then probably lost hope, given up on God that their prayers would be heard. But in His own wonderful way, God answered their prayer.

And what a child! John was full of the Holy Spirit, a source of joy to his aging parents. But He was also John the Baptizer, the prophet, a wild man. God was willing and able to give them a child, but His answer to their prayer was much more than they expected. Zechariah at first didn't even believe it would happen, so the angel Gabriel rendered him speechless as a sign. The lesson here is clear: God answers prayer, and He is willing and able to do what He decides.

Zechariah had drawn his turn to burn incense in the temple, a job that took him away from home for about six months. It must have been a long six months during which he couldn't talk with other priests or family or friends. It was a long time for him to think quietly about God's promise through the angel. When he got back home, his wife conceived their promised child. But only when the child was born could old Zechariah speak again.

Never doubt it! God is able to answer our prayers. He CAN and He WANTS to! In Matthew, Jesus said, **"If you who are sinful know how to give good gifts to your children, how much more will your sinless Heavenly Father give you good gifts?"** God is willing and God is able to answer our prayers with good things. We must get ready for His answers.

71

My father was a willing and able father, but not always at the same time. When I was a senior in High School I wanted to buy a car, a brand new blue 1963 Corvair convertible, with a stick shift on the floor. And only $2300! I would go to the dealer and stare at it for hours. One Saturday I spent so much time looking at it, Dad got tired of waiting and left me in town. I had to walk part of the 10 miles home. I asked him to loan me the money to buy my dream car, but he said no. He was able, but he was not willing, a good thing as I look back on it now.

Another time Dad was willing but not able. I had just moved and found a nice small home at an unbelievably low interest rate and only $283 a month! But I needed a $10,000 down payment, so I asked Dad for a loan for just 30 days so I could buy it before someone else did. Dad wanted to help, but he had no funds to loan at that time. He was willing but just not able. It turned out all right because I found another source for the down payment. But He always felt bad. *"You've never asked me for a dime and now when you do, I can't help,"* he said. Fortunately he'd forgotten about that blue Corvair!

Our heavenly Father is both willing and able to grant our requests, even in the face of big odds. He is able because He can do all things. He is willing because He loves us. And in His love He often surprises us, as He surprised Zechariah and Elizabeth.

I met Joe and Martha on the 4th of July, 1971. I remember the date because it was the day their son Clyde drowned. He was not just their only son, he was a wonderful boy, a nice boy, a compliant, obedient boy, a real joy to know. His death devastated them. They weren't members of my church, but their priest was gone that day so I helped as best I could. Later I visited them on their farm near Lincoln Valley, ND, one of those little towns that no longer exist.

About a year later Martha asked me an amazing question, "Should Joe and I have another child?" They were both in their forties, so I told them to pray about it. About six months later she called to tell me she was expecting and how pleased they were. Aaron was born a few months before my son Chuck, and what a boy he was, a fiery red head who came out bawling and squirming and demanding. He was totally the opposite of Clyde, full of the dickens, energetic and almost wild. They were ready for a new arrival, but not quite a child God gave them - a wild, wiggly red head!

Zechariah and Elizabeth had it nearly the same. They prayed for a child and God gave them John. He was no ordinary man, but full of energy and the Holy Spirit, a fiery prophet who spoke God's Word with power and sometimes even with pain. When we pray, we must get ready for a new arrival, God's answer for us. God is willing and God is able to answer us. He heard Zechariah and Elizabeth, and through their son John we were introduced to Jesus, the Messiah, the Savior of all. John prepared His way and we all are blessed through him.

Jesus was born nearly two millennia ago, even secular history books tell us this. What they won't tell us, however, is why. As Christians we know He was born to bring salvation to a world lost and without hope. We know why He came, but we can't rest on that information.

Each one of us here this morning is responsible to the Lord for our own faith and relationship to God. We cannot rely on what our parents or grandparents have believed. God has no grand children. He only has children. Each person of each generation must come to Him in faith in order to be saved. If your parents and my parents are believers, that's wonderful! But even more wonderful is that you are a believer, and I am a believer. There is no other way to eternal life with God except through Jesus. The baby grew up! He's no longer in the manger, so how shall we respond to Him? Will He be our Lord, or will He only be Lord of our parents?

God is willing and able to answer our prayers. If you ask Him for something, get ready for a new arrival, His answer! He'll always follow His own timetable, but He's a Father Who loves us and He will answer our prayers, even when the odds seem against us.

When I came to Colorado 1985, I was a single widower but I had no plans to stay that way. I dated a few women and one of them asked me, "What are you looking for, Bob?" My answer was simple: a Christian single woman my age and similar values who had never been married and was willing to raise my sons as her own. She laughed and said, "Good luck!" But God heard my prayer and answered it in exactly the way I wanted when I met and married Carol. So God had the last laugh because He is willing and able.

I'd like to give you something special to pray about this morning, something that affects our whole church. Last week the owner of our chapel called and said they are planning to sell. They are first offering it to us to buy, but its price tag is high, about $2 million. While I love this place, I am not sure this is the best location, or that we can afford the price.

That means we must begin praying right now for the Lord to show us His will. I am asking each of you to remember our church in your prayers, that God would point us in the right direction. The worst case would be we'd need to find a new place to hold Sunday worship services, and begin paying higher rent. But this won't happen right away, since selling a mortuary will probably take time. But let's begin praying now that God would let us stay here or, if not, show us a new place.

Last January I and a dozen or more others prayed for the Lord to give us a place to hold our services, and He gave us this chapel, such a beautiful place. Now we must all pray for Him to help us keep it or else show us what to do next. Our Church Council meets this week and will discuss this, so share your thoughts with the Elders or one of our officers.

But don't lose heart! God hears our prayers and He will answer them. He is willing and He is able. When you pray, get ready for a new arrival, His answer to our prayer. Consider the prayers that brought about the existence of Epiphany Lutheran Church. Remember Joe and Martha, and remember Zechariah and Elizabeth. God hears us when we pray. And what wonderful blessings He gives because He is willing and able to answer our prayers.

Pray and get ready, get ready for a new arrival, whether it's a child, a job, that special person in life, or a new place of worship. I ask that you keep this news close to your heart. We'd rather not make it public until we're ready. But we must pray and get ready for a new arrival. God is willing and He is able. Let's pray right now: *Oh Lord, our faithful Savior, we thank You for giving Your life for our salvation. We thank You for earthly life and for eternal life. Today we come with this special request, to show us what to do, and where to go next. We ask if it is Your will, to bring us the right place for our permanent church site. Make it affordable, in the right location and make it obvious, amen!*

ADVENT SERIES FIVE
"Getting Ready"
Week Three

Romans 13:11-12   *"Getting Ready for Next Year"*
"And do this, understanding the present time. The hour has come for you to wake up from your slumber, because our salvation is nearer now than when we first believed. The night is nearly over; the day is almost here. So let us put aside the deeds of darkness and put on the armor of light."

We stand just 19 days away from a significant time change in human history that has been only observed once before, the change to a new millennium, Year 2000, or Y2K as it's commonly called. Although many, including myself, say the new millennium won't begin until 2001, most people believe it will happen in 19 days that we might as well go along with them. And never mind that the birth of Jesus happened in 5 BC, so the real Y2K happened already four years ago.

To me an interesting aspect of the coming year change is that we all can say we lived in two centuries and even two millennia. My father and mother were both born at the turn of the 20th century and lived in two centuries. Something about that fascinated our family. Perhaps those in our families born after Year 2000 will think us special, products of two centuries, like I thought of my parents.

What makes this time change significant is not so much the date as the technology surrounding it. One invention, the computer, governs our daily lives more than any other. We have given so much of our lives over to computers that we're unsure right now if they'll help us or hurt us in the change from "99" to "00." People have imagined their financial portfolios disappearing, reverting back to 1900, when none of us here were yet born. And if the computers don't "think" we're born yet, then they may treat our money as if it doesn't exist and simply erase it.

To insure this won't happen, billions of dollars have been spent, and extraordinary measures have been taken, but still

75

many people don't trust electronics. They have taken measures into their own hands, buying generators because they think electricity will fail, storing food and water because utilities will fail, converting their assets into gold and silver because Wall Street will fail, and buying weapons to protect themselves from the coming chaos. So many generators have been ordered that catalogs now refuse to accept them back. You bought it, you got it, and don't try to return it. That already shows skepticism that Y2K will really be a problem.

Some have said Y2K will be the biggest non-event in human history, greeted with a big yawn, and that our fears will prove unfounded. Personally, I agree with that, and yet if enough people believe something will happen, they could make it happen. If enough people fear financial collapse and remove their money from circulation, they could cause a major financial upheaval. If enough people panic, their panic could spread. But again, I doubt that will happen.

What about us Christians? How should we live and act in the coming days? How did Christians handle the change from 999 to 1000? As Y1K, approached, Christians feared the end of the world. When midnight mass was celebrated at the Vatican on Dec. 31, 999, most there believed the Apocalypse would scorch the earth that night. But nothing happened, just as I believe nothing will happen Dec. 31, 1999, beyond perhaps some scorched brains from too much partying.

In Year 1000, Viking longboats raided cultures from Russia to the Americas, and the religion of Islam extended its influence through Asia, Africa and the Middle East. The Song dynasty ruled China with an iron fist, and warring Indian tribes jostled for supremacy. Starvation, illiteracy, poor transportation, war, disease and slavery were all part of everyday life. The global population was 300 million and life expectancy was in the low thirties. You were an old man if you lived to age 55. People probably thought things couldn't get much worse than they were.

Yet the new millennium brought unimaginable advances in every phase of life. Today we have 20 times that population and people live into their 70's and more. Rapid advances in science and technology, genetics and communications startle even the

76

most scientific of minds. We're moving faster, but with a more shallow existence. We have more but enjoy it less. Some want to move us towards a religion-free society and yet people are starving for meaning in life. What does it all mean?

What does God want from us, His people today? St. Paul has a good word in Romans 13: **"The hour has come for you to wake up from your slumber, because our salvation is nearer now than when we first believed. The night is nearly over; the day is almost here. So let us put aside the deeds of darkness and put on the armor of light."**

We Christians sleep too much. There's a whole world dying around us in unbelief and we're asleep in our comfortable life bed. Sometimes our bed is financial security, and sometimes it's busyness. Sometimes it's the bed of fun and pleasure, but whatever it's called, we're asleep in it. We may think we're awake, but when it comes to witnessing to a world lost in sin, most of us act like we're sleeping. St. Paul says it's time to wake up! **"The hour has come for you to wake up from your slumber, because our salvation is nearer now than when we first believed."**

You can't get ready for something if you're asleep. How does God want us to get ready for Year 2000? Simple, in the same way He wants us to get ready for any day of any year: by Faith, by Prayer, and by Service. Luther said that if he knew the world would end tomorrow, he'd still plant a tree today. In other words, live today as if it were your last. Do things that show your faith and trust in God. Do the things that need to be done for the welfare of others.

In Paul's day, people thought the world would end soon, so some early Christians just quit working. That's why Paul wrote in 2 Thessalonians 3:10, **"If a man will not work, he shall not eat."** He meant slackers who used the times as an excuse should be held accountable. No matter what day it is, we must keep working. You and I must keep doing the things God has called us to do, and in faith trust God will provide for all our needs.

Some Christians today are really showing their lack of faith. A Christian couple I heard about has stocked up on food essentials, bought guns and ammunition and converted all their assets into gold nailed into the floorboards of their house. So certain are they of social chaos that they have take such extreme measures. Not surprisingly, their house has already been robbed by people who knew of their plans. God has not called us to be stupid, but to be faithful. No matter what will happen in Year 2000, God will still be God, and we will still need to trust Him, and rely on His divine providence.

Our Lord Jesus calls us to trust Him, no matter what day it is. He loves us and has given His life for us. He rose again to give us hope and a future. He hears and answers our prayers every day, no matter who we are. He wants us to trust Him every day for everything.

So how can we get ready for Year 2000? Faith, Prayer and Service. These will prepare us more for Y2K than all the manuals, food, generators, gold or guns ever will. Everything in our life begins and ends with faith in God. If we trust Him for eternal life, why shouldn't we trust Him for our daily life? If we do our work today, serving Him in our jobs, homes and communities, why will we not do the same on January 1, 2000 or on January 1, 2001?

Everything in the Christian life begins and ends with faith, but prayer is a central part of our faith. If there's one thing Christians need do to more, it's pray. And not just pray for God to give us things. God is not a divine vending machine. We owe Him more than to treat Him like one. Because of Jesus we owe Him our very lives, and should praise and adore Him for that fact. If our prayers to God show we treat Him as only a Divine Answer Man, we have missed the point of faith.

Our prayers can contain four elements: Adorations, Confessions, Thanksgivings and Supplications. The first letters of these spell ACTS. Prayer is the central act of our faith and worship. If we're not praying, something is wrong with our faith. You and I can't have a relationship with our kids or parents if we never talk to them. So also we can't have a relationship with God if we never talk to Him. Prayer is talking to God. Let's not talk in our sleep.

Paul tells this morning, **"The hour has come for you to wake up from your slumber, because our salvation is nearer now than when we first believed."** We all need to wake up.

Recently I've found my days and nights a little mixed up. Maybe it's because I have a home office and can walk downstairs and work at any hour of the day. But I sometimes find myself napping during the day because I've been working too late. Paul says wake up! Get your life in order! Salvation is nearer now than ever. It will be nearer still on January 1, 2000. Let's not be sleeping when He comes!

So, my friends, don't get alarmed about the future, because it's all in His hands. Year 2000 may bring some surprises, but nothing God and you can't handle together. There's nothing in all creation that can separate us from the love of God that is ours in Christ Jesus. Remember those words of St. Paul (Romans 8:35-39) Nothing can separate us from God's love, it's His guarantee. Amen!

ADVENT SERIES SIX
"What To Do In Advent?"
Week One

Matthew 24:42   *"In Advent, Keep Watch!"*
"Therefore keep watch, because you do not know on what day your Lord will come."

✚ ✚ ✚

It's good to be back! Carol and I had such a wonderful trip. The Caribbean weather was perfect, the food was delicious and the cruise restful. We visited the two Bahamian islands and shared the "Sovereign of the Seas" with 2200 other cruisers and a staff of 800. We were kept busy with many choices of events, and when I could think of nothing else to do, I sat and watched the people. And what an assortment of people go on a cruise! All shapes and sizes, nationalities and ages, in all manner of dress, at all hours of the day. People are so different - no two are alike, and they all seem to wear whatever they felt like. Sometimes I saw more of some people than I cared to, but others were a pleasure to watch! And I brought back the one thing that proves we really were there, an island shirt! Now Carol can find me in a crowd of thousands. Colors like this just shout your presence. *"Look at me, I'm here!"*

But it was a hard landing to come back to the Colorado snow and chill, and also to the beginning of Advent. Today is the first Sunday of the new Church Year, so happy new year! The Church Year is divided into two halves: the Lord's Half Year which deals with the life of Jesus, and the Church's Half Year which emphasizes the teachings of Jesus. Today we begin anew once again to tell the story of our Savior Jesus.

Advent is a season of watching and waiting, something we Americans have never done very well. Advent comes from Latin words meaning "to approach" or "to come to." This time of year we remember our Lord's two advents, when He came the first Christmas, and when He will come again in glory and judgment. Today we're living between the two. We remember well His first advent, the babe born in Bethlehem's stable. But Scriptures tell us the baby didn't stay little. He grew to

81

manhood, completed the work of salvation for all people, and then returned to heaven until the day of His second advent, on Judgment Day.

Many people today are confused about the significance of Christmas. Contrary to what we read in the ads, it's not the most important festival of the Church. That's Easter, the festival celebrating His resurrection. Early Christians right away began celebrating His resurrection, first by selecting Sunday as their day of worship and later by an annual Resurrection Day festival. But it wasn't until the Fourth Century that the church selected December 25 to remember His nativity. At the same time they chose January 6 as Epiphany Day, the festival of lights to commemorate the Wise Men's visit to the holy family.

You see, everyone has a birth, but only Jesus had a resurrection re-birth. It's good to give Him a birthday party, but merely believing He was born gets us nowhere. Believing He is God's Son and that He rose from the dead for the sins of the world, that's what counts! Christmas is a joyful season, but it doesn't hold a candle to the eternal significance of Easter.

As we live between the two advents, and as the coming days pass, we'll be thinking about His coming into the world. Our Sunday services will center on certain words - Watch, Prepare, Rejoice and Behold. I pray all our worship services will help us be ready for His second coming by faith, ready for a day known only to the Father.

But waiting is so hard for us! Waiting drains us. You and I can't hold our anticipation level high for long. As a child asks on a long road trip, *"Are we there yet?"* so we often ask, *"How long, O Lord?"* Watching and waiting can wear a person out. Yet our Lord tells us, **"Watch, because you do not know on what day your Lord will come."**

Every week when we worship on the first day, Sunday, we recall His Resurrection. Once a year we have a big celebration with all the festivities of Easter. Add to that our annual remembrance of His birth at Christmas, and every year we have the chance to be rejuvenated by holy praise and joy. Without those great reminders of God's presence in history, life would be dull and drab. Imagine a winter without Christmas or a spring without Easter! What great blessings God gives us in

82

these two special seasons of holy joy.

Do you know how our weekdays got their names? They were first named by the Romans in honor of their gods. Our present English names for days of the week come from the Saxons who conquered England and named the days of the week after their gods. So we have Sunday = Sun's day, Monday = Moon's day, Wednesday = Woden's day (important god to them), Thursday = Thor's day (another big one), Friday = Friya's day (wife of Woden), Saturday = Saturn's day. That leaves only Tuesday. Legend says that day was named after the daughter of Woden and Frigga. Her name was "Toots" from which we get Tuesday. (And if you believe that, I have some swamp land to sell you in Florida.) Tuesday was named after Tiwa, a Saxon harvest god. But I like the legend better.

We all know it's really hard to wait, wait for a call from the doctor, wait for test results, wait for that new job opening, or wait for your day in court. Parents spend a great deal of time waiting for their child to walk and talk, and then they wait for them to sit down and be quiet. Sometimes you wait for that certain phone call, the one promised that never comes. Ever noticed how often people are in meetings when you call? I can't imagine the number of times I've called a local government agency and been told that person is in a meeting. I really think there are only two kinds of government workers, those in meetings and those taking messages for those in meetings.

Today's Bible verse comes from a time when Jesus was talking with His disciples. They were taking a city tour of Jerusalem, and those Galilean country boys were impressed with the grandeur of the buildings, sort of like a Midwesterner's first impression of New York City. I never saw the World Trade Center in person, but I visited Times Square years ago and nearly fell over trying to look all the way up to the top of the skyscrapers.

It was like that with the Disciples. They were bowled over with the height and size and beauty of those impressive buildings. The pinnacle of the Temple was thirty stories high! The size of the stones in the temple foundation was simply staggering. One of them still in place today measures 32 feet long, ten feet high and eight feet thick and weighs over 200 tons!

But as they marveled, Jesus brought them back to reality.

He said all they saw would be torn down, not one stone would be left standing. I doubt they believed it would happen, but forty years later, Jesus' words came true, as they always do. After the Roman soldiers invaded Jerusalem, they spent nearly a full year tearing apart all the buildings and burning the city. The Jews thought it could never happen, but God's Word always comes true.

But He wouldn't tell them when it would happen, just to be prepared when it did. He said, **"Therefore keep watch, because you do not know on what day your Lord will come."** Over the centuries false prophets have tried to foretell when the world would end, but it never has. I'm told there was a little-known book a few years back entitled, 88 Reasons Why the World Will End in 1988. It sold well enough that the publishers planned a reprinting in 1989! I wonder how well the second edition sold.

But waiting for Christ's return doesn't mean watching the clock. Nowhere is Holy Scripture does God tell us to sit around and wait, but to serve Him with all our heart while we wait.

In the 1987 NCAA basketball Regional Finals, LSU was leading Indiana by eight points with a few minutes left in the game. Despite their superiority, LSU began playing a different ball game. It became apparent LSU was watching the clock rather than playing the game. As a result of their shift in focus, Indiana closed the gap, won the game by a point, and eventually went on to win the NCAA championship. God does not want us wasting time watching the clock. He wants us to be involved in service to Hi and our fellow people..

Right now we're all waiting for something, for a phone call, a letter, an Email, a job, a good relationship or even maybe for this sermon to end so you can go home and watch the Broncos. But just remember, you and I don't have to wait for eternity. Heaven starts the moment we believe. In John 6:47 Jesus said, **"He who believes HAS eternal life,"** not *"will have eternal life"* or *"hopes to have eternal life,"* but *HAS* eternal life. The benefits of heaven are ours right now, because of Jesus and His love for us. Heaven is His to give, and He gives it to all who trust Him.

All of us will one day come to the end of the road, the time when life has run out. Will we be ready for the Lord because we've been faithful in our wait? Or will we have grown tired of watching or gotten side-tracked by the excitement of human passion or the cares of our everyday life? Don't become a clock watcher, serve the Lord with gladness! Don't get pulled away by the temptations of life, stay faithful to Jesus! He's promised won't be tempted beyond our ability to bear it. He's also said, **"He who endures unto the end shall be saved"** (Matthew 24:13). May we all be among those who hear Jesus tell us, **"Well done, faithful servant. Enter into the kingdom prepared for you."** Amen

ADVENT SERIES SIX
"What To Do In Advent?"
Week Two

Matthew 3:1-3   *"In Advent, Prepare!"*
"In those days John the Baptist came, preaching in the Desert of Judea and saying, "Repent, for the kingdom of heaven is near." This is he who was spoken of through the prophet Isaiah: A voice of one calling in the desert, Prepare the way for the Lord, make straight paths for him.'"

✦   ✦   ✦

Welcome to our Church, where people talk about God, sing about God, pray to God and aren't afraid of God. Here you can say "Merry Christmas" without threat of lawsuit, and you can parade anywhere you like, silently or singing hymns. You can carry a Bible without being fired and talk about absolute truth without being ridiculed.

We believe there is only one way to heaven, through faith in Jesus Christ, for we are conservative Lutheran Christians, and we praise God for what He has done for us. We believe in freedom of worship, and we do it openly for all to see. And if all this means we're out of step with the rest of society, so be it! Welcome to all in the precious name of Jesus Christ!

Every year in the weeks before Christmas, the church seems totally out of step with the rest of society. While most people, including those in the church, are putting up trees, decorating homes, buying gifts, and going to parties, the church talks about - are you ready for this? - the end of the world and the Second Coming! It's almost humorous. Secular society is spending like there is no tomorrow, and the church is warning us that just might be true.

Many church bodies have abandoned Advent all together, preferring to spend all of December thinking only about Christmas. And yet one billion and a half people, about 2/3 of the world's Christians, do observe Advent. During the four weeks before Christmas, they hear Bible lessons that deal with end of the world, repentance and getting ready for Christ's second coming.

Does this mean the church is out of touch? Maybe the rest of the world is, and we're the ones who are being realistic. It wouldn't be the first time the majority of the world is in denial of reality. Yes, it would be nice to sing Christmas carols the whole month of December. But others say hearing about the second coming is a welcome relief from a two-month Christmas, that huge commercial rush between Halloween and New Years.

John the Baptist wouldn't know what to do with our world today. He didn't even like the modernization of his own world, so he went to live in the desert, not for its beauty or mystique, but just to be with God. He went there to find a faith relationship more pure and less distracting. John was a prophet who needed to be alone with God and with the few people who followed along to hear what he had to tell them. He was a prophet, and a prophet's life is lonely.

John was the forerunner to Jesus, the King of kings. He came to get the world ready for the Lord of lords. He prepared the way for the Messiah by baptizing people and getting them to change their ways. We know some things about John's ministry, that his parents died when he was young, that he renounced the world and had disciples and denounced hypocrisy. He got his world ready for the Christ, this we know. What we don't know is what it means for us today to be prepared for the coming of the Lord.

Maybe you've heard that some stores are prohibiting Salvation Army bell-ringers this year. like some of you, I don't go to those stores anymore. Did you hear about the Salvation Army woman back east who was informed by a policeman that a local ordinance prevented her from ringing her bells to ask for contributions? "No bells - too noisy!" they told her. But a stupid law never stops a smart person. The next day business was better than ever as she waved two signs in the air. One said "Ding," the other said "Dong." Her contributions doubled!

So what the ding-dong we can do to get ready for Christ's coming today? Some of us are already in the desert, and it has too much snow on it anyway!

We can't all become prophets. Nobody will work today for locusts and honey. So I offer three words - a new "Three R's" that we can use to prepare the way today: REPENT - RENEW - RESPECT. Let's look at each one.

1) REPENT: We're more scared of this word than we need to be. Repent means to stop doing wrong, ask God for forgiveness, and start doing right. All of us have things we need to repent of, but sometimes we aren't ready to give them up. Years ago old-time Christians took Advent very seriously. A pastor friend of mine recalled an uncle, an old Norwegian bachelor farmer, who upon hearing that it was Advent, said, *"Holy cow, now I gots to change sumting!"*

Repent may mean changing a bad habit, but it can also be changing a whole life. That same pastor related to me that in his early years before he became a pastor, he spent days in a motel, in fasting and tears and prayer because he knew his life was out of control. Repentance means to stop doing wrong, ask God for forgiveness and start doing right. REPENT - John the Baptist would say that's a good way to prepare the way today.

2) RENEW: We modern Americans live a disjointed life. We're disconnected from our heritage and often our families. We need to renew relationships. We need to re-connect with our roots, who we are, where we've come from, what brought us here. We're not here by accident. God brought us to this place, at this time, and He wants us to use our abilities, time and resources to further His kingdom.

In Advent, renew means learning again the stories and songs of Christ's birth. Renewal means praying more regularly, reading the Bible more often, and worshipping God more faithfully. When you walk inside this church, leave the cares of the world behind you, just for one hour. Here you are loved and forgiven. Here you are a precious human being, not just a number or a body in the work place. Here you are renewed by God Himself. RENEW is a great word for Advent.

3) RESPECT: Advent is a time to respect others and respect ourselves. We need to eat and drink less, to love and forgive more. We live among vastly different people. No longer are we a little settlement of Norwegians or Germans. No longer is everyone we know a Christian and no longer are all Christians alike. We don't have to agree with those who are different, but we need to respect them, as God does. RESPECT - RENEW - REPENT: Three "R's" to prepare the way today.

Someone has said it's time the Church took back Christmas.

But I think we already do. Each year the world tries to hold it hostage, with its gadgets and toys and debts. The world tries to drive us to the poor house. It makes outlandish demands and expectations on us, but they never really work.

The birth of the Christ child is just too powerful and loving, too real for Hollywood, too smart for the intellectuals, too expensive for Wall Street and too honest even for the politicians. Despite the atheists and the ALCU, we still observe Christmas every year. Despite the glitz and the glamor, Madison Avenue can never throw out the baby with the bath water. The beauty of a "Merry Christmas" makes the glitter of "Happy Holidays" look pale and sickly. The quiet cries of a baby in a distant Bethlehem manger always overpower the shrill noises of this world we live in.

A man and his wife received a new DVD for Christmas from their son and spent all afternoon trying to hook it up to the TV. The directions were complicated and their son was too far away to come over. "Call Tech Support," he said, and gave them the number. After ten minutes on hold, a tech person tried for half an hour to help them. Finally, the father said, "I don't need better directions, I need my son to come along with this gift!"

The Son of God is our gift. He came to live with us and die for us. Come to Him in faith, and you will truly be prepared today. As we sing in the Advent hymn:

O come, our Dayspring from on high,
And cheer us by Your drawing nigh.
Disperse the gloomy clouds of night
And death's dark shadow put to flight.
Rejoice! Rejoice! Emmanuel shall come to you, O Israel.
Amen

ADVENT SERIES SIX
"What To Do In Advent?"
Week Three

Philippians 4:4-6   *"In Advent Rejoice!"*
"Rejoice in the Lord always. I will say it again: Rejoice! Let your gentleness be evident to all. The Lord is near. Do not be anxious about anything, but in everything, by prayer and petition, with thanksgiving, present your requests to God."

✛ ✛ ✛

It's the third Sunday of Advent and time for a change of mood! The early fathers called this Sunday "Gaudate," because they knew Lutherans needed some rejoicing. While Advent is primarily a time for repentance, the ancients wisely broke the sobriety of the season with joy and a little mirth. Sadness turns to laughter, seriousness to levity, and purple to pink. St. Paul once said, *"Rejoice in the Lord always. I will say it again: Rejoice!"* Amazing words from a man who seems so often stern and unbending!

It's always a challenge to stand before a crowd of Christians during Advent and move them somewhere, to action or to higher faith or out the door, to serve God, of course. I hope some of you today aren't moved to spend the whole sermon taking notes. This isn't going to be that good. Most of us pastors are self-effacing, we try not to praise ourselves, but rather praise God. Some are self-effacing, others are self-erasing. After we're done speaking, no one can recall a thing we've said. We're like good campers; when we leave, you didn't even know we were there.

But the measure of a sermon is not whether it's memorable, but whether it nourishes. We prepare thousands of meals, and after we eat them we rarely remember them. Yet they all nourish us. Whatever we say this time of year, let's make sure it nourishes. And let's, *"Rejoice in the Lord always. I will say it again: Rejoice!"*

For most of our members, Advent and Christmas are times of mixed emotions. The busyness can be exhausting. *All this reminds me of the woman who was out Christmas shopping with her*

91

children. After enduring parking lot traffic and hours of looking at row after row of toys and everything else imaginable, and after hours of hearing her children beg for everything they saw, she finally made it to the store elevator. She was feeling what most of us feel during the holiday season time of the year. You know what I mean - the pressure to go to every party, taste all the rich food and get a perfect gift for everyone on her list, to get the cards out, go to the school events and maybe squeeze in church once or twice, and finally, to figure out a way to pay for it all. Finally the elevator doors opened and the car was packed. She pushed her way in, dragging in her kids and all her bags. When the doors closed she said in a cranky voice, "Whoever started this whole Christmas thing should be strung up and shot." From the back of the car a quiet, calm voice responded, "Don't worry, we already crucified Him."

For many, anxiety mounts about going home. It's all some kind of sacred routine set up years before, by forces unknown. It goes like this: you spend Thanksgiving at the home of his parents, so for Christmas you must go to hers. This can go on year after year, with an occasional switch here or there. So when the year finally comes that Mom and Dad are coming to your house, it's almost like a Lutheran Bar Mitzvah. *"Today I am a man!"* Or for the daughter-in-law, *"Today I am a cook!"*

Many mothers are like Queen Bees. They hover over the kitchen, in charge of baking and cooking. Forty pound turkeys are baked with twenty pounds of potatoes in 3 pounds of butter. Queen Mothers bake hundreds of Christmas cookies and expect a compliment on each. And daughters-in-law can't do this well. They are lovely people, nice for the boys, but simply not qualified to prepare holiday food like Queen Mothers!

So when these trophy daughters-in-law finally are called on to do Christmas at their home, how can they say no? Just make sure the pie crust is made with lard, and cranberry relish is freshly ground. Pity those poor people, those retired workers on fixed incomes who have Thanksgiving at Country Buffet. How can they possibly enjoy the five kinds of meat, salads and vegetables fit for royalty and the freshly baked cinnamon rolls they'll get there? And what can make up for the true Lutheran fellowship of the Rite of Washing Dishes? I always enjoy the traditional family meal. We come home from church, and gather at the house with the biggest color TV. We watch a little football, drink a little beer, and then about an hour before dinner, someone goes to the phone and orders Kung Pao Turkey or Holiday Pizza. Or maybe we'll have our specialty: chopped ham and pineapple, layered over spiced tomato sauce, covered with a finely grated cheese and baked atop special round flat bread. That's a real Minnesota holiday dinner! *"Rejoice in the Lord always. I will say it again: Rejoice!"*

But it's not always good news. Sometimes we're just so surprised at what happens around the holidays. *A few weeks before Christmas, a man called his son. "Son, your Mom and I are getting a divorce. We've gone far enough with this marriage and have decided to start proceedings after the holidays." "But Dad," he said, "you can't do this! 30 years of marriage and now a divorce? At Christmas? I can't believe it!" The boy hung up and immediately called his sister. "Did you near what Mom and Dad are doing?" he asked. "Yes," she said, "and I'm furious! What about all that faithfulness and commitment they showed us? I'm going there for Christmas and I'm going to do everything I can to stop this from happening." "I'm coming too," he said, "and bringing my family." The son called his father and told him he and his were coming and bringing their families. As the father hung up, his wife walked in the door, "What was that all about, honey" she said. "Good news, dear!" he smiled. "The kids will finally all be home for Christmas and they're paying their own way!"* *"Rejoice in the Lord always. I will say it again: Rejoice!"*

Christmas is a wonderful time for children. Remember those days? Whatever they got under the tree was easily be broken that day, but the batteries were guaranteed, for 24 hours if you could find them. As for their clothes, it was "trip and tear" time. And the closer you lived to church, the later you got there, because kids always know how to spring an emergency at the last moment. No matter what you feed or don't feed them beforehand, at least one child in the Christmas program learned the surprise value of projectile vomiting. *"Rejoice in the Lord always. I say it again: Rejoice!"*

(Any current church conflict can replace the next section)

On this Sunday named "Gaudate'" consider where Paul writes these words. In prison. hardly a place to rejoice! Many of

93

our fellow Americans are not rejoicing today, and it's not the economy or the flu or the war. The wet blanket on the party is disunity. We're a nation divided and sometimes even a church divided. Well-meaning intentions have given way to heartless actions. Hatefulness has replaced love, even in the church.

A few years ago some pastors I was with agreed there's probably no solution for peace in the Middle East, or in the Missouri Synod. If we believe what the Bible tells us about the Last Days, "Satan's Little Season" is only going to get worse, until Christ finally comes in His Second Advent. It doesn't mean we run out and buy guns, or more cell phones, or that we reserve a hotel "war" room for the next Convention. But it does mean we recognize the signs of the times and be ready for the Prince of Peace with faith. We rejoice somewhat now. It's just muted until the Final Great Rejoicing with God in heaven. *But how long, O Lord?*

At times it seems the church has lost its way. Anonymous criticism can not replace fraternal conversation, and the Gospel of God's love must not give way to nit-picking. And I have a solution: Let's remove synod control from all the preachers, sem profs, Board members and self-proclaimed theologians, and to turn the whole church over to the laity. They would certainly not make any bigger a mess of it than we have. But of course that would mean our trusting them to understand the Bible without us. Could we stand that?

The Good News, my brothers, is that despite our ecclesiastical lunacy, God still loves this church and its people. His mercy and righteousness will prevail, even in the LCMS. We just need to trust what Isaiah said: **"Be strong, do not fear; your God will come, he will come with vengeance; with divine retribution He will come to save you."** (Isaiah 35:4)

This message today may lead you to wonder. If today is to be a Sunday of rejoicing, why end it with negativity? That decision is up to us. It is very easy to turn our joy of life into a rant over injustice. We can choose to take the happiest time of the year and find something wrong with it. Or we can be glad God puts a season of peace and joy in the midst of darkness and sin. The reason for this season is what we make it. If we wish God's joy in our lives, then we must share it with others.

94

May our Lord this Christmas fill us all with true joy, a little levity, and a lot of wonder of the child's birth. He who could have skipped this world for better things chose to enter human life. He who could have forced everyone to believe gave us a brain to make choices. Thus, may we, by the Spirit's power, choose to reflect the love of Jesus, and rejoice eternally with the hosts of heaven. *Grant us this, dear Father in heaven, amen.*

(These Lent sermon series were written for a specific congregation and time)

Sermons For Lent

LENT SERIES ONE
"Certainty for Uncertain Times"
Week One

Luke 22:1-23   *"Making Wise and Godly Decisions"*

✠ ✠ ✠

His name is Joe, an ordinary guy at a crossroads. He told me, "I've got a tough decision to make, Pastor, but I just don't know what to do. I've prayed but get no clear sense of direction. I think I know what I want to do, but what does God want me to do? My friends and family give me conflicting advice, but one way or other, I need to make a decision. I just hope it's the right one."

At some time or other in life, all of us have been where Joe is. Should I take that new job or not? Should I move to a new town? Should I find a new career? Should I get married, have children, retire early or take a chance with that investment? Should I go to a counselor, send my children to a different school, hire an attorney, or just call in sick and crawl under the covers?

Decision making is a fact of life for everyone. Decisions arise from circumstances and they result in consequences which can be pretty scary at times. Romans 15:4 says, **"Everything that was written in the past was written to teach us, so that through endurance and the   encouragement of the Scriptures, we might have hope."** We all want to make the right decisions because we know they will bring consequences that will affect us later on.

We begin the season of Lent once again. In tonight's Passion History from St. Luke, many decisions were needed. The chief priests and teachers of the law had to decide what to do with Jesus. The Disciples had to decide where to prepare for the Passover meal. Those were two very different kinds of decisions, for one would affect only a meal, but the other would affect an individual's life. One decision would influence their

97

appetite, but the other would influence the entire course of world history.

Tonight, as we recall the beginning of Christ's suffering and death for us, we meet on a day called Ash Wednesday. Ashes are a biblical sign of repentance, and repentance is that change of heart necessary to straighten out a crooked life. Thousands of people met together yesterday in the revelry of the Mardi Gras, a day they call *"Fat Tuesday."* I guess they've been partying and living the excessive life so they'll have something to repent about during Lent. Repentance is changing something. Some of us may have to make decisions whose consequences we'll carry with us for the rest of our lives.

It's like the tragic young man I read about whose decision to drink and drive nearly killed him. He miraculously escaped death when his car slammed head-on into a bridge abutment, but when he stepped out of his car, he was electrocuted by a downed electrical line. His air bags saved him from the accident, but not from the electricity. Every decision we make is prompted by circumstances, and every decision we make brings with it consequences we must live with – or we must die with.

The theme for midweek Lent services this year is, **"Certainty for Uncertain Times."** I'd like us to consider three Key Concepts tonight: (1) Decisions come from circumstances, (2) Decisions bring consequences, and (3) Learning to make good decisions is a lifelong process.

The Disciples thought they were preparing only for a simple Passover meal. I'm sure they'd done it before. Find the place, buy the food, prepare the table and have the supper. Simple, no-brainer decisions they wouldn't have given a second thought. Yet tonight's meal would be different. It would be the last Passover for them with Jesus, but it would be the first Lord's Supper that millions of Christ's followers would repeat until judgment. Their decision was prompted by circumstances, and it brought consequences they could never have imagined.

The chief priests and teachers of the law also had a decision to make. They wanted to rid themselves and their religion of a trouble-maker. Rabbi Yeshua ha Nosari, Jesus of Nazareth, was a nuisance, a thorn in their foot, a bug to be squashed, so they sought a way to kill him. But what they were doing wasn't new.

Practitioners of a twisted religion of works righteousness had been killing God's prophets for generations. Jesus once sadly lamented for them, saying, **"Surely no prophet can die outside Jerusalem! O Jerusalem, Jerusalem, you who kill the prophets and stone those sent to you."** (Luke 13:33-34)

One thing that Lent always brings home is how wonderful it is that Jesus made the right decisions. True, being God He was not going to make wrong ones, but He didn't have to do all this – He decided to. This, despite that one of the disciples doubted Him, others argued yelled and argued, and another wanted to remove Jesus permanently. Yet Jesus loved every one of them, including Judas, and He loves every one of us too, no matter what our past.

As with the Disciples, the decision of the chief priests and teachers of the law was prompted by circumstances, and it brought consequences they could never have imagined. They thought they were the masters of their destiny, but they were only a small part in a plan God had set into action long before. The Son of God had to come into a corrupted world. God had to take on human form, had to become a person, so that He would rescue a fallen world from its own destruction.

The decisions to sin by Adam and Eve, by Jacob and Esau, by Sodomites and Gomorrahians and every living person, moved God to set into action a plan that would save them. God become a life preserver for drowning people. When the chief priests and teachers of the law had a problem, they made decisions with eternal consequences. This illustrates two of the three Key Concepts in decision making: (1) Decisions come from circumstances, (2) Decisions bring consequences.

A third Key Concept is learning to make good decisions is a lifelong process. Someone has said there are five things about making a good decision: (1) Analyze, (2) Get Advice, (3) Pray, (4) Decide, and (5) Evaluate. That sounds like a business plan. And in the business of making decisions, I guess it is.

In 1982 I took a call to a church in Southern California, and realized it was a huge mistake. I tried to find a way to undo what I'd done. I'd left North Dakota and driven a large truck there with all our possessions, but left it loaded in a parking lot as we were waiting to get into a place to live. As I saw the congestion and smog, traffic and foreign languages and tasted the polluted air, I wanted to go back. But how could I? I had accepted the call and was sure I had mad a wrong decision in coming there. But my wife and boys rallied to my side and helped me make some decisions. In the end I used those Five Principles of Decision-Making without realizing it.

(1) First, I analyzed the circumstances the best I could. I had no other place to go, but the thought of staying was repulsive. Then, (2) I asked for advice. Phone calls to friends, talking with local pastors and asking members for direction helped. (3) Then I prayed - desperately - and asked others to pray, but I really wanted only one outcome – to leave. But the Lord didn't give what I wanted. Instead He gave me what I needed. (4) Finally I made the decision to stay. A wise pastor there told me, "Either unload that truck or drive it back!" Hard words to hear but necessary, so we unloaded it. (5) Evaluating the outcome took time. My ministry there was short and painfully bumpy, but it was fruitful. The church grew, and I grew. And my family didn't fall apart like I'd feared.

All this because I wanted to preach the Gospel. The fact that Jesus died and rose again for my sins keeps us going in the worst of times. Every day we need to trust God and His love for us. It helps if we pray with faith and worship Him regularly. Jesus Christ is the Savior of the world, the Savior of every man, woman and child. Believe He is Your Lord, trust Him to forgive you, to accept you and to change your life. Trust in Jesus because He's the only one really worth trusting in life.

You and I can't escape making decisions, but we can make them in a way that will help us and those around us. The Disciples got their problem solved very easily – they had Jesus make it for them. The Jewish Church leaders also got their problem solved by someone else when Judas walked in the room. Sometimes solutions and decisions come easily, but most of the time the big ones are not easy. I can say from experience that as a parent these days you can't advise a son or daughter about getting married. And perhaps it's better not even to advise our spouses in some things.

In the coming months and years of this world we've been given, we all, especially our young, will need to take great care in the decisions we make. In this century, there will be more amazing strides made than we can imagine, strides of technology and science that will force us to make decisions that will reach far beyond ourselves. This is true in nations and politics, in companies and congregations, in homes and in personal lives. May we all ask ourselves what Jesus would do, and then do it. God grant us grace let Him guide us. Amen

LENT SERIES ONE
"Certainty for Uncertain Times"
Week Two

Luke 22:24-26   *"Testing Your Character"*

✛ ✛ ✛

St. Paul once wrote, **"We also rejoice in our sufferings, because we know that suffering produces perseverance; perseverance produces character; and character produces hope."** (Romans 5:3-4) Paul didn't write this by accident, but by experience. Like many other early Christians, he found that character can be a result of perseverance, that quality of keeping going no matter what. Perseverance, unfortunately, often comes as the result of much suffering.

A test of our character is rarely known ahead of time, but the nature of our character will show itself clearly when the test happens. Testing our character is more a pop quiz than a prepared exam. It comes unexpectedly in the form of an accident, or illness, or a nasty turn of events. How we react determines what kind of character we have.

Brooke Westcott, a Bible scholar once said, *"Great occasions do not make heroes or cowards; they simply unveil them to eyes of the world."* Today, in these days of uncertainty, our character will be tested often.

Our character is the sum of the qualities that make us different from all others. We can use "character" to mean self assurance, as in when we "have it all together." And so we say, *"She has real character."* Character can also mean an extreme individualist, like when we say *"Now he's a real character!"* Our true character is made up of personal qualities, plus experiences and what we've learned from them. Like the wall plaque that says, *"Good judgment comes from experience; and experience comes from bad judgment."* We could add, *"Character grows in being tested by bad experiences."*

Character can develop when we go through a crisis and respond to it in such as way as to become a better person. But this wasn't the case when the disciples argued over who was the greatest. Tonight's Gospel shows us grown men wanting to

103

be at the top, first in the pecking order. James, John and the other boys wanted to be *"King of the Mountain."*

Later these men may have become Christ-like, but not tonight. They were loudmouths and louts, each wanting to be Christ's favorite. He brought them down to earth, saying greatness comes from service, not privilege. Favored places in the Kingdom do not come to those who seek them. They are gifts of God's grace, given but not deserved. Whoever wants to be first must be the servant. Service, not privilege, develops a person's character. They saw this in their Rabbi, their beloved master, when He knelt down and washed their feet, work of the lowest servant.

Peter must have been trying to mediate this, but Jesus tells him, **"Simon, Simon, Satan has asked to sift you as wheat. But I have prayed for you, that your faith may not fail. And when you have turned back, strengthen your brothers."** Not long after that Peter's character would be tested, and he would fail that test miserably. Like Jesus' Parable said, **"But many who are first will be last, and many who are last will be first."** (Matthew 19:30) People can quickly see a person's character in whether or not they are willing servants.

The Winter Olympics have begun and those are always exciting games, especially short track speed skating! In 2002 an unknown teenager was going for the gold. In the medal race, Apolo Anton Ohno was second, but fell on the last turn, yet somehow scrambled across to get the silver. The leader was out. So who won the gold? The Canadian skater who had trailed all the others, not just once, but in all the prior heats. That skater came in first because those in front of him fell down! He won the gold after trailing the whole race. The last truly was first and the first were last.

My eldest son was a talented track runner and his race was the high hurdles. Watching him cruise to victory in the Colorado State Championships was a thrill I'll never forget, and as he smiled up at us from the track it brought back the memory of his being disqualified in the state meet two years before due to a false start. He never let that disqualification get him down, but moved him to work harder, not only winning state but later setting records and being ranked nationally in college. Losing can grow character faster than winning. A humble loser passes the test by picking himself up after defeat. The humble winner may grow by showing grace in victory, but character is usually built by how we deal with loss.

We don't always learn from our testing. Don won the Lottery years ago. He took the lump sum of $2 million and lived it up, bought new cars and spent freely. In a year or two it was all gone, money, marriage and even his health. Last I heard Don was poor, sick and broken, yet still buying lottery tickets, trying to win the jackpot one more time! He won big, but he lost bigger because he didn't learn.

The disciples lost the big one that first Holy Week. They argued for position, fell asleep during prayer, and then ran like rabbits when the soldiers came for Jesus. Peter tried to make up for his boasting, but he failed as badly as anyone. The only one who stuck by Jesus was John, the youngest. The older guys all hid. Only young John was there at the cross with Mary.

We people don't know how we will react when our character is tested. Even Jesus was tested as He saw His coming suffering. **"Father,"** He said in the Garden, **"if you are willing, take this cup from me; yet not my will, but yours be done."** (Luke 22:42) Think of it - Jesus wanted out! He was hoping the Father might find another way, to change plans at the last moment. He knew the suffering ahead of Him, and, just like any of us, He wondered if there was an easier road.

The Good News is that Jesus stayed the course and because of it, you and I are forgiven. Because He persevered we are set free from the penalty of our sins. We are redeemed because of His endurance and sacrifice. Heaven does not come because we're great, but because He's great. Christ's reluctance was human, but His determination and trust were divine. As sinners, we may share in His suffering, but as saints we surely will share in His glory.

Judas failed his character test. Perhaps he was disappointed in Jesus. He believed in an earthly king, one who would push the soldiers out of Israel. Then Jesus started talking about a spiritual Kingdom, and about forgiving your enemies and doing good to those who hate you. Somewhere in there Judas gave up on Jesus. His weak character could not accept God's way - he wanted his own way. Betraying Jesus for a handful of silver was not what he planned after following Jesus.

He faced a difficult decision, and instead of shining in faith, his lamp went out. The traitor went dimly into the night, and in the end snuffed his own light out.

The outcome of a hard test can be strengthened faith. By God's grace we can grow from what happens to us. When St. Paul wrote, **"suffering produces perseverance, perseverance produces character; and character produces hope,"** (Romans 5:3-4) he didn't mean it always happens that way, but that it can. Suffering can also produce bitterness, and bitterness can bring resentment. But that's the way of defeat. The outcome of facing a test can be a deepened trust in God. It can mean a stronger faith if we go His way and let Him lead us. Once again, the Good News is that Christ stayed the course, and because He did, we are Children of God by faith.

For two centuries, the farmers in southern Alabama had been accustomed to planting the same crop every year - cotton. They'd plow as much land as they could and plant it all to cotton. Cotton was their life, their meal ticket. Then one year the dreaded boll weevil devastated the whole crop. The next year those farmers mortgaged their homes and planted cotton again, but again the weevils destroyed their crops. The third year happened the same. But this time a few who survived tried something new. Instead of cotton they planted peanuts, and their peanuts brought in a fine harvest. Weevils left them alone and the price was good. Peanuts proved so hardy and profitable, that everyone started raising them. Those farmers paid off their debts and lived prosperously. Today in several town centers in southern Alabama you will find monuments, not to stately Civil War heroes, not to "good old days," but to the boll weevil. If it hadn't been for an ugly insect, they'd never have found prosperity. Even in disaster God can richly bless us.

Dear friends, as we see in our Lord Jesus, every moment of suffering is an opportunity for growth. In a perfect world there would be no economic downturn, no depression, no earthquakes that kills a quarter million such happened in Haiti this past month. Faith in Christ does not guarantee a good life. But He guarantees an eternity of joy to all who call on His name. Jesus isn't looking for perfect people, just forgiven sinners who come to Him in faith. Thanks be to God He gives us this certainty in uncertain times. Amen.

"Certainty for Uncertain Times"
Week Three

John 13:34-35   *"Healthy, Helping Relationships"*

✛ ✛ ✛

A family was sitting around the dinner table one evening waiting for Dad to get home. Finally, he came in late because it had been a rough day. Dad came in, sat down at the table and offered thanks for life and especially this food. As soon as he finished his prayer, he began to complain and grumble about how awful things were going at work. The boss was a jerk and the other workers were lazy. The world was going to pot, and on and on he went.

Then Mom brought in the food. Since he was so late, food that was supposed to be cold was warm and what was supposed to be hot was cold. The casserole was overcooked and the bread was hard. And of course Dad pointed out what was wrong with everything. When the complaints finally stopped because Dad was eating, little daughter asked a question. "Daddy, do you think God heard you when you prayed?" "Well, yes, sweetheart. Of course He did." Then she asked, "Do you think He heard what you said after that?" "Why, yes, sweetheart. God hears everything." Then she asked, "Which one do you think He liked?"

If there's one thing for certain, it's that we live in an uncertain world. We may think we know what's coming next, but we are continually surprised. So many people long for love, but are fearful of commitment. There may be wealth in our bank accounts, but there is poverty in our souls. We seek good news but hear only bad news. And nowhere is this uncertainty more evident than in the shakiness of basic human relationships.

People want a close relationship, but there are risks. For many it is safer to keep people off at a distance or to live together without commitment. Young men and women want intimacy but can find it in destructive ways. It's not that we don't value good relationships, we do. Indeed, we invest much time and effort in them. But our world often works against us, isolating us from each other.

We're encouraged to communicate, but not in person.

Can't find a friend? Get Facebook? Looking for that special someone? Go to eHarmony. No time to visit? Use Email, or Twitter. Electronics will take you anywhere on the planet except face-to-face. We have cell phones or message machines because we're rarely home. We have to schedule a week ahead of time to visit or have a cup of coffee, and pity the poor person who drops in on us without calling us first. No longer do we welcome people to our homes unannounced.

What would we do without our Day-Timers? Or our watches? Or our computers? Perhaps some of you are thinking, *"That's not me. I don't go in for those things."* But we all must admit times have changed significantly in human relationships, and mostly not for the better. What can we do? What does God want us to do in 2010? What can God do for us, and what can we do for each other to make our lives more fulfilling?

Yet history shows all this is not unusual. If there was ever a time of shaky relationships among Jesus' disciples, it was the night before He died. His disciples argued like kids and fell asleep on watch. One of them betrayed Him, His closest friend denied Him with curses, and all the rest ran away. Talk about dysfunctional! Even though Jesus knew something like this would eventually happen, it must have been a jolt to see these people He'd loved and nurtured for so long, fall apart and fail so miserably.

People are sinful and nothing shows it more than our excuses. Excuses are different from reasons. Reasons have reality and truth behind them while excuses are meant to justify bad behavior. A mother may cover for her son's faults, and do this so often that he becomes irresponsible. Yet she excuses it by saying it's because she loves him so much. Or a father pays his daughter's bills so often that she never learns responsibility. *"I am just trying to help!"* he says. *"We thought we were doing the right thing."*

You can almost hear Peter saying the same. *"They'd have arrested me. How could I have admitted I knew Him? I was just trying to help by being there."* Or Judas saying, *"I had to stop Him before He got us all killed."* Or the others saying as they ran away, *"I have responsibilities!"* Excuses are not very helpful in life, especially when they hide the truth. You and I need to see them for what they are, our poor attempts to sidestep our sinful actions and attitudes.

What makes for good relationships in today's busy world? How can we make families or friendships or churches better? Let's talk about three short principles. Life teaches us we should, 1) Aid those in need, 2) Help without hurting, and 3) Learn when to say "no."

1) <u>Aid those in need</u>: Faith shows itself in works of love. In Matthew 25, Jesus talks about the judgment, and ends His story saying, **"I was hungry and you fed me, I was thirsty and you gave me drink, sick, imprisoned and naked and you helped me.:** He didn't say, **"You had the right theology,"** He said, **"You helped me."** Christ wants us to aid those in need, not just form a committee to discuss their problems. Did you know there is no monument on the face of the earth dedicated to the memory of a committee? We must seek to aid those in need, not just discuss their problems.

To do that, we must look outside ourselves and give back as we've been given to. Those who keep their blessings all for themselves will never have fulfilling relationships, but only passing acquaintances. People can see self-centeredness a mile away. Use your gifts to aid those in need. It's the first principle healthy, helping relationships.

2) <u>Help without hurting</u>: You can almost hear Judas say as he throws down the coins, *"Nobody understands me - I was just trying to help!"* I'm sure he felt he had just cause to hand Jesus over before soldiers came and killed everyone. The chief priest and other Jewish leaders surely would have agreed with him that it was the right thing to do before things got out of hand. But appealing to the greater good can also be an excuse, if it hides selfish motives. We must take care not to hurt with our good intentions. Not everything we think will help, actually does. It's easy to hurt others if we don't teach responsibility. Good intentions badly placed have left a trail of bruises. God wants us to help without hurting

3) <u>Learn when to say "No:"</u> There is a book called, *When I Say No I Feel Guilty.* People bought it in droves because they shared a similar fear that if they spoke honestly, others might not like them. Many requests should be answered "Yes," but

saying "no" is not necessarily shirking our duty. Sometimes we need to say it, to our children or our friends. A good relationship requires an honest "yes" or "no." The hard part is knowing when to say what at the right time.

Our Lord wishes us to help people in need, and that we help them without hurting. If we do, we won't just feel better, we'll know it is the right thing to do. While we're at it, here are "Ten Rules for Getting Rid of the Blues." It's very simple: Go do something good for someone, and then repeat it nine more times. Nothing helps a bad mood like helping others.

In the midst of these bad relationships in the lesson, we see Jesus doing it right. He stopped to help others. He helped, and the only thing He may have hurt were some feelings. And He knew when to say "no." Jesus gave without thought of return. The divine "ray of hope" in that hard world of Judea was this gentle man, son of Mary, Son of God, giving the thirsty man a drink of water, healing the sick, forgiving His enemies, and giving His life to forgive us our sins.

It's this same Jesus who comes to us in Lent with love and gentle firmness. Jesus offers us the best relationship of all, to be our Savior and Brother. No other religion shows the heart of God like this, that God wants us His children. Praise God that He loves us so much.

Remember that father who criticized the supper and complained about work? Across town there was another Dad who also came home late after a hard day. On that very same night he also was late from work and sat down, not to dinner, but to breakfast! Instead of a dinner casserole, he got ham and eggs, and they weren't very good. Mom handed him a plate of hard eggs, dry ham and burnt toast. The children were a little worried what he'd say. But Dad buttered the cold toast, smiled at Mom, munched the hard eggs and asked the kids how their day was at school. He smiled and ate every bite as he listened.

When they got up from the table that evening, the kids heard Mom apologize to Dad for the supper. He kissed her and said: "Honey, I love burnt toast, and you can make me ham and eggs anytime." Later that night one of the children asked him if he really liked his toast burned. He hugged her and said, "Your Momma works hard. A little burnt toast never hurt anyone!"

There are times wemust overlook what our loved ones do,

110

and there are times when we shouldn't. Jesus forgives our faults so we can forgive others. He died for our sins because He loves us. Jesus loves us just the way we are, although He may not leave us that way for long. Jesus loves us enough to make us better people. More about that next week. Amen!

LENT SERIES ONE
"Certainty for Uncertain Times"
Week Four

Luke 22:66-23:12   *"Depending on God's Planning"*

✛ ✛ ✛

We live in uncertain times. We can't take a vacation or visit a public building any longer without feeling this uncertainty. There's something about a passing through a metal detector in a high school, an airport or a courtroom that makes us uneasy. Perhaps it's all a sign of the coming End Times. The New Testament speaks often of the close of the age, with its heightened distrust, dishonesty, and disrespect.

Even churches, or I should say, especially churches, are not immune from this uncertainty. Did you know dozens of churches in Colorado now have plainclothes armed guards and ushers carrying weapons during their services? I've even heard of some pastors licensed and carrying a weapon. Of course, the infighting in many congregations and denominations gives a sad witness to those outside the church. Jesus knew this would happen, and so He said in Matthew 24:12, **"Because of the increase of wickedness, the love of most will grow cold."** There seems to be a chilly wind blowing all around these days as the End Times comes steadily closer.

In Luke 22, our Lord's time had finally come, and the culmination of His life's work was at hand. Jesus was born into the world for one main purpose, to fulfill the plan of salvation God had set in place. He came to fix this damaged world Adam and Eve had started. All our Lord's teaching, all His miracles, good deeds, and all He did pointed to His own end. That started with His trial in Jerusalem.

After being arrested in the Garden, Jesus was taken to the house of Caiaphas the High Priest. Today you can see the foundation that house and sit in the actual courtyard and walk the actual steps our Lord walked. It was there in the courtyard, right next to the modern church called Petra Gallicantu, which means "Peter of the Cock Crowing." There a frightened Peter sat by the fire with the others, and there a cowardly Peter

113

denied he knew his Rabbi.

I wonder whether Jesus slept at all that night. One tradition says He was kept in the dungeon beneath the house of Joseph Caiaphas in upper Jerusalem. I've been inside that dungeon. Even as a visitor, you don't want to stay long. Dug from solid rock there are no windows, you can see places where prisoners were chained to the wall or hung up by their wrists. The tiny rooms have floors that slope into a drainage trough for obvious reasons. It still smells bad in there. Little air ventilation except two small holes near the ceiling. Sooty torch stains are on the walls. It says a lot about a religion when the High Priest has a prison in his own basement. So much for religious tolerance, so much for love and mercy, all those things that are easy to talk about but hard to practice. Jesus once said those guys could **"strain out the gnat, but swallow a camel whole."** (Matthew 23:24) Some in the Church still do that today.

I wonder why God's people can often be so cruel. There's a series of books about Cadfael, a mythical twelfth century monk who solves crimes, a kind of Dark Ages Sherlock Holmes. The series takes place in Shrewsbury, England, during the English Civil War and the reign of King Stephen. These are novels about life among the monks in this Benedictine abbey, mostly good men but also pompous watch dogs. They piously demand others follow rigid rules at every step of life. Rather than showing mercy, the medieval Pharisees delight in finding fault with others. It is fiction, yet it does point one truth: when the self-righteous spring into action, love and mercy fly out the window, and so does common sense. Fault-finders love to point fingers. Thank goodness we're not like them!

It's sad that Pharisees have gotten such a bad name. They were supposed to teach people but instead became critics. They were experts at telling others how to live but didn't practice what they taught. Jesus opposed them often during His ministry, but never so boldly as when He stood before them in chains on that Good Friday morning. They were delighted to see Him! Now He was on their turf. They had planned this moment for months. They now could be rid of this "loose cannon," this thorn in their foot, this "Rabbi of the rabble."

As Jesus prepared to face them, I wonder if He had a plan. Probably not. Remember how He told His disciples not to worry what to say when they face an adversary? **"But when they arrest you,"** He said, **"do not worry about what to say or how to say it. At that time you will be given what to say, for it will not be you speaking, but the Spirit of your Father speaking through you."** (Matthew 10:19-20) I'm sure He took His own advice, just praying to His Father as he went into court. We can learn something from that.

I went traffic court once as result of being in a accident and had carefully rehearsed what I wanted to say. I was certain I was not in the wrong and that my traffic ticket was unfair. I had my charts and photos and speech all rehearsed. When I arrived at the appointed time, however, plans changed. The judge said my evidence was inadmissible! My carefully written defense could not be considered. Of course, I lost the case in front of a judge, and not long later it was discovered he was a corrupt judge. He was disbarred a year later for too much personal dallying with his court reporter during work time. But that day I paid a double fine for arguing my own case. I represented myself and really did have a fool for a client.

It was much different with Jesus. They would allow no evidence except what was against Him. The Chief Priests, Scribes and Pharisees had Him right where they wanted Him, and no one was going to deprive them of the opportunity to remove Him from society. When evil has set its sights on a target, evil will do everything it can to get its way.

We know these events, so what can we learn from them? How about three more Key Concepts? Tonight let's look at these three, 1) Begin each day with the Lord, 2) Prepare for the unexpected, and, 3) Look to God for results.

1) Beginning each day with the Lord is not as hard as it sounds. All we need do is sit and read His Word a few minutes, and if you can, try to do that! But if you can't, at least utter a prayer for guidance as you drive, or think of God and His will during your day. What would God want you to do? What would He want you to avoid? Jesus probably started each day with prayer. What would He do if He were in your shoes? Our prayers don't have to be long, but remember James who said, **"The prayer of a righteous person bring results!"** (James 5:16) Begin each day with the Lord, and see good things happen.

2) Preparing for the unexpected should be part of life by

now. I usually know what I'd like to do each day, but I also expected some of the unexpected. It was that way in a former large church I pastored, but not quite the same since retiring. But retired or not, I still make a list of activities to do each day, and I've learned to expect the unexpected. A suggestion or interruption can alter your whole day. Getting sick can change your plans. A phone call can turn your world upside down. And no matter when it happens, forgetting an appointment can disrupt everything! Yet, if we learn to expect the unexpected, we won't necessarily get derailed. We will survive!

3) The best to do every day, however, is to Look to God for results. While Jesus knew the outcome in advance, He didn't always know all the details. There was plenty of room for anticipation and even some very human fear. It's human to fear the unknown. It's also human to try to avoid pain. Like us, Jesus did not relish pain or disappointment. And like us, He had His Father to turn to, One who has all of life in His hands and in His plans.

It was the Father's plan to lay the sins of the world on the shoulders of His Son. It was the Son's plan to follow the Father to the smallest detail and bring us salvation. It was the Holy Spirit's plan to convince us Jesus is our Savior. And He will still help us with that every day. Through Word and Sacrament the Holy Spirit helps us trust Jesus and do good. Give thanks that Holy Three had a plan and followed it, and saved us from eternal death. They did for us what we could not, and so we are children of the Heavenly Father by faith in Jesus.

At the end of last week week's message I said, *"God loves us just the way we are, but may not keep us that way for long."* God does love us sinners, no matter how bad we are, even while we are still sinners. He doesn't wait for us to get good enough – He loves us just the way we are, but He will change us, if we let Him. His plan was to forgive us and help us become better people.

The German poet Goethe one said, *"If you treat a person as he is, he will remain that way; if you treat the person as he can become, he will tend to become that person."* God loves us, even the sinful person we may be, but He helps us become better. The Holy Spirit gives us strength to trust Jesus, do good, to live better, and to be less selfish. The Spirit helps us trust God more and ourselves less. Yes, God does love us the way we are, but He may not keep us that way for long.

Smith Barney used to tell us in their ads, *"We make money the old-fashioned way - we earn it."* Good advice about investing, but not with God. Heaven is not earned, it's a gift from God's grace. Lent is not about us, it's about Jesus. Lent is all about His suffering and death. But remember, Lent ends with His resurrection. We live on the Easter side of Good Friday! **"He is not here, He is risen!"** Thanks to God for the hope we have in Jesus. Amen.

John 14:27   *"Peace In An Uncertain Future"*

✠   ✠   ✠

The longer we live in these uncertain times, the more it is evident: Uncertainty is one of the few things that is certain. I was puzzled the other day when I read a bumper sticker: *"When you think all is lost, the future still remains."* I'm not sure if the writer was an optimist or a pessimist, but either way, the future remains and is filled with uncertainty.

No matter how hard we try to approach it with confidence, we can't control the future and it always surprises us. I believe the coming days are going to throw us some curves. We'll not be able to prepare for everything. But while we don't know what the future holds, we do know Who holds the future, and that's good enough.

The Cold War may be over, but the fighting continues. We're bogged down in the war against terrorists. The Palestinian-Israeli conflict is goes on. Drug lords seem to be winning. Earthquakes keep burying bodies, politicians keep pointing fingers, and people keep finding new ways to sin.

William Cowper lived during the 1700's in England. A Christian poet and hymn writer, he suffered terrible fits of despair and twice even attempted suicide. This, despite his dedication to Jesus Christ and the Christian church. People tried helping him, and one friend even moved into his home to help him, but still his melancholy persisted. Once during a dark night in his soul, he set out from his home in London with the intention of jumping into the Thames River to drown himself. Instead, he got hopelessly lost in the London fog and wandered around blindly for hours. Eventually, lost and confused, he bumped into a house and decided to go inside just to get out of the fog. The home he walked into? It was his own. God had guided him all over through the fog and then brought him back to those who loved him. Spiritually moved by this experience, Cowper sat down and penned the words of the beloved hymn, "God Moves in A Mysterious Way". Two verses of that hymn are these:

119

God moves in a mysterious way His wonders to perform;
He plants His footsteps in the sea, And rides upon the storm.

You fearful saints, fresh courage take; The clouds you so much dread
Are big with mercy and will break in blessings on your head.

I once spoke of Cowper's experience in a Sunday sermon, and later that day received a phone call: *"Pastor, you have no idea what your message meant to me. I was laid off from my job in December and I was starting to despair. I was thinking that God is not in my life at all. Everywhere I turn, I get rejected. I was beginning to think I am a worthless person, yet I know God is in control. I just hope and pray that He will show Himself before I hit the brick wall. Thank you for your message to me today."*

We need peace in our lives, at least some of the time. It's not always the actual problem that bothers us most, it's the uncertainty of solving it. I wonder how the disciples felt while Jesus was on trial, where they were and what they were doing. While He was fighting for His life, were they were together or separately hiding? While He was making His defense, were they making excuses? While He was facing execution, were they were crouched in a corner filled with fear? Yet we can't blame them, because we'd probably have been right there with them. Uncertainty frightens us and weakens us. Uncertainty makes us wimps instead of warriors, the hidden instead of the heroes.

How can we make peace with a future that holds so much uncertainty? You may find this question humorous since our futures today are much more certain than in Jesus' time. We today live longer, richer, better and more peaceful lives. Yet there's something about the present that still brings uncertainty. Maybe it's because we feel we're being watched so closely. Maybe we are! Like the bumper sticker says, *"They ARE out there and they ARE out to get you."*

It's easy to be paranoid, because our lives are becoming less and less private. Satellites can see our houses from miles into space, and computers keep track of where we go and what we buy and what our habits are. Files record even our most innocent activities. Eighty year-old nuns are frisked at airports and school kids are taught morals we can't agree with. "Speech police" patrol our campuses, and we'd all better remember to check our pockets if we go into a public or government building. The day may even be coming when we'll have to walk through metal detectors to shop at Wal-Mart!

So how do we make peace with that kind of uncertain future? Here are three more suggestions: 1) Live Confidently, 2) Do the Right Thing, and, 3) Wait Patiently.

1) Live Confidently: You and I are tempted to believe all our irrational fears, fearful that someone will molest our kids, rob our home, or take us to court. But as God's people, fear must not control us. 1 John 4:18 reminds us, **"There is no fear in love, but perfect love casts out fear."** Live confidently, because God lives with us. He holds us in the palm of His hand. Follow His will and live confidently. That new and better job will come, our children will not become atheists or delinquents, and we can trust most people. Live confidently, because God is near, near in the shadows of the fog, ready to pull you back from the river of death. That's why St. Paul said, **"He who did not spare his own Son, but gave him up for us all--will he not also graciously give us all things?"** (Romans 8:32) Live Confidently!

2) Do the Right Thing: When the road gets rough, when the wheels have come off, when we think life is nothing but sucking lemons, it's tempting to think no one cares, not even God. And we're tempted to quit caring too. But we can't stop doing what's right. Ask God for help and do the right thing. No matter what troubles you face, you're still a child of God, a father or mother, husband or wife, child, student or worker. Do the right thing! Whether you feel left out or hemmed in, do what's needed. It may seem like a dead end, but look at what good can come from it. Now that you're out of work, you have time to read. You have a chance to get to know your kids better. Now that you're struggling, maybe you can show others how to face adversity with grace. We're not all good examples under tribulation; but some are. With the help and guidance of the Holy Spirit, do the right thing. Do the right thing! And finally,

3) Wait Patiently: Some things can't be hurried, no matter how much we'd like to push them. *A man decided to plant a garden. Growing things would make him feel better. So he rented a tiller, dug up a patch and planted the seeds. After awhile most of the seeds sprouted, but one part of a row did not sprout. All the rest of the*

garden was doing great, but half a row of radishes wouldn't grow. The man investigated and found that little fingers had been digging up seeds to see if they were growing yet. Then the soil was carefully patted down and as if it had never been moved. Someone was not patient to let the seeds grow, and by trying to hurry the process had killed the little sprouts. He later found out it was his little boy!

I once tried planting a garden in the desert. Gardening can help a person practice patience, but in the desert it takes a lot of patience and even more water. Jesus knew what patience was. He was patient with His disciples when they quarreled, and with His accusers as they bumbled their way through the Good Friday trials. He was patient with the needy and sick who tugged at His robes, as well as with hypocritical church leaders as they split hairs and acted self-righteously. And Jesus is patient with us today as we worry and fret about an uncertain future. Wait patiently! God will give us the right results.

As Jesus carried His cross to Calvary, the women wailed loudly, and so He said, **"Don't weep for me; rather weep for yourselves and your children's children."** We will all have times of weeping, but we should save our weeping for something worthwhile. He knew trouble was coming for them, so He told them to keep watch. Be ready for whatever happens, ready by faith, ready by prayer, ready by following Jesus instead of the world. We need to trust God's way, not the world's way. Satan and the world want us to be scared and untrusting. Remember, God walks with us on the way. Don't weep for what doesn't matter. God will take care of you.

Peter once wrote, **"Cast all your cares on Him, because He cares for you."** (1 Peter 5:7) He said those words long after he denied Jesus. He was weeping for himself then. He was a miserable man wondering if he ever could do anything right. He eventually came to realize that only God could help him do anything right. If there was ever a night that Peter would remember, it was then. After he made it through that dark night, God made him a better a person.

Whatever we may think, whatever may worry us, let's not forget the facts: Jesus is God's Son and He holds the key to our futures. *He knows what's best and He will not let us down.* People may disappoint us, but God won't.

The Father accepts us as His adopted children through Holy Baptism. No one can tear us away from God's love, and no one can force us to abandon Jesus without our consent. If you're struggling with something big in life right now, consider those three: 1) Live Confidently, 2) Do the Right Thing, and 3) Wait Patiently for the results. God's blessings will come. God will give us peace again. We are not alone. Someone always has it far worse than we do. May the God of peace bring you His certainty in all your endeavors. Amen

LENT SERIES ONE
"Certainty for Uncertain Times"
Week Six

Psalm 51:10-12   *"God's Perfect Provision"*

✛ ✛ ✛

We've been talking the past weeks about "Certainty for Uncertain Times." I want to talk tonight about the Three R's, but not the ones from school we usually think of. Instead of "Readin', 'Ritin' and 'Rithmatic", I want us to think about Redemption, Rewards and Renewal. They are the Three R's of Jesus for us in Lent.

Redemption is the heart of the cross. Redemption is why Christ came. It's why He taught His Disciples through parables and miracles, and why He willingly submitted to misguided authorities. **Redemption** is why He let them arrest Him, torture Him and try Him for crimes He did not commit. **Redemption** is why God permitted His only Son to die a brutal death. God knew that sin would destroy people, so God had to redeem us, to buy us back from the pit we'd all dug for ourselves. And thanks be to the highest heaven that redemption is what God did for us.

"Father, forgive them, for they don't know what they're doing," He said. All people need the forgiveness He prayed for. It's always amazing that we so often think we have everything under control. We might be awash in an ocean of trouble that will drown us at any moment, but, yes, we have everything under control! Everyone else sees us drowning, but we think we're swimming just fine, thank you very much! Because of sin we don't know what we are doing, and we need someone who does. **Redemption** is the heart of the cross. It's why Christ came and gave His all for us.

God sometimes surprises us in our redemption. Last week Carol and I were on a short trip with another couple. Instead of driving it in one day, we decided to take two days, staying overnight along the way. Fellow traveller Dan booked us into a motel ahead of time and said he'd pay for both rooms since we were driving our car. Dan checked us in, and later that night, he spoke with the hotel desk clerk again in the

125

computer room and discovered she was from Minnesota, a little town called Windom. When he told her I was also from Windom, she asked my name and nearly fainted. t was my cousin Jodi behind the counter, and we'd not seen each other in 25 years. She was living in there with her sister Bev, so we three cousins had a mini-reunion and spent the evening reminiscing. And we did it just in time, since Jodi was moving to another city in a few days. There are lots of "ifs" in this story -- if we'd have made the whole trip in one day, if Dan had chosen another motel, if he hadn't gone to the computer room, if we'd have come a few days later, if Jodi had that day off... But the Lord brought us together after all those years. He really is a God of surprises.

Redemption comes from God, and so do **Rewards**. A person doesn't last long when nailed to a cross. One of the two thieves still thought going along with the crowd was best, that it might ease His predicament, but the other one knew better. Each three had only hours to live and in that moment of reckoning, one joined the crowd, while the other joined Jesus. One thief was blinded by self, and the other was bonded to God. **"Remember me, Lord,"** he said, and within hours he was with the Lord in paradise. **Rewards** come from the hand of God, when we do not merit them and least expect them. **Rewards** are a joy because they God's gifts.

Nancy sat alone in the front pew of the small chapel. The young woman was at the funeral of her dearest friend, her mother, who'd finally lost her long battle with cancer. The hurt of loss was so intense, and Nancy found it hard to breathe at times.

Mother clapped loudest at her school plays and held a box of tissues while listening to her first heartbreak. Mother comforted her at her father's death, encouraged her in college, and always prayed for her. When Mother's cancer was diagnosed, it fell to the 27 year-old Nancy to take care of Mom. But she considered it an honor. "What now, Lord?" she thought as she sat there. Her life looked empty. Her brother had his wife, her sister held her son next to her husband, but Nancy felt all alone. Her grief was as great, but no one sat with her.

A door opened and closed in the back of the chapel. Footsteps hurried along the carpeted floor. A young man looked around briefly and then walked to the front row and sat next to her. He folded his hands and placed them on his lap. His eyes were brimming with tears.

"Sorry I'm late," he said. After several eulogies, he leaned over

and said, *"Why do they keep calling her Mary, when her name is Margaret?" "Because," said Nancy, "that was her name - Margaret." She wondered why this strange and annoying guy sat with family. Who was he, anyway? "But she's Mary, Mary Peters," he insisted, as several people glanced over at them. "You're confused," she said." "Isn't this the Lutheran church?" he asked. "No, this is the Methodist Church. The Lutherans are across the street." "O Lord, I'm at the wrong funeral," he said and blushed.*

The realization of the his mistake made Nancy giggle. She cupped her hands over her face, hoping it would be interpreted as sobs, but her giggles gave her away. Sharp looks from other family made the situation hilarious. Nancy peeked at the bewildered man next to her. He was both crying and laughing but he stayed, deciding it was too late for an embarrassed exit. Nancy imagined her Mother laughing, too. When the pastor finally said "Amen," they both darted out a side door. "I do believe we'll be the talk of the town," he smiled. He said his name was Rick and since he had missed his aunt's funeral, could he stay for a cup of coffee?

(This is a true story) That afternoon began the lifelong journey of a woman left alone and a man who attended the wrong funeral. Yet both were in the place God intended them to be. A year after they met, they were married at a church where Rick was the assistant pastor. This time they both arrived at the same church, and on time. In their time of sorrow, God gave them laughter. In place of loneliness, He gave them love. Rick and Nancy recently celebrated their 35th wedding anniversary. Whenever anyone asks them how they met, Rick says with a smile, "Her mother Margaret and my Aunt Mary introduced us. Ours was a match made in heaven."

Redemption comes from God's grace, as do His **Rewards**, and usually when we least expect them. **Renewal** flows from God's presence. We all need to be renewed. Forgiveness is **Renewal** of the best kind. Getting up in the morning is renewal. Being reconciled is **Renewal**.

"Father," said Jesus as He was dying, **"Into Your hands I commit my spirit."** A few minutes later He died, and in so doing, returned home. He was with the Father again. He had left Heaven's presence 30+ years before, exchanging glory for a life of limitations and struggle among sinful people. And now He was coming home. Not as a Prodigal Son, begging for forgiveness, but as the Good Son who kept doing His Father's work to completion. **Redemption** comes from God's grace, **Rewards** come from God generosity, and **Renewal** flows from God's presence. We all need to be renewed, and forgiveness is the best kind of renewal.

In Texas, on the McLennan County line, there was once a bar called Charlie O's. In fact, there had been a whole string of bars there, but locals prayed them out of existence. They also prayed for the salvation of the people who went into them. God answered their prayers. One was sold, another burnt down, and the owner of Charlie O's became a believer. He wanted to sell his bar, but no one would buy it. Finally Charlie decided God wanted it and that he should give the building away. Maybe the Latham Springs Baptist would take it. They were meeting in just a leaky tin shack.

Charlie went to the pastor's house one rainy day and the pastor's wife answered the door. He asked if he could give the church a "building," but didn't explain further. She said they would probably accept, but that he needed to talk to her husband who was at his office. He found Pastor Jerry and asked if he would be willing to accept the former bar. It was in poor shape but a good location, so Pastor Jerry agreed. With the help of the Waco Baptist Association, the site has a church sitting on it. Instead of Charlie O's, it's now called the New Life Fellowship.

God always provides, and His provision is perfect. The death of Jesus Christ on Calvary is God's greatest provision. It's His certainty of forgiveness for a uncertain world. It's the story of divine **Redemption, Reward** and **Renewal**. The Son of God gave His life for our **Redemption**, to buy us back from a world of sin. His life to us was a **Reward** we didn't deserve. And now Christ gives us **Renewal** a chance to change our life to walk in His ways. Each of us who believes in Jesus has **Redemption**. By grace, we have God's **Reward** of eternal life in heaven. Because of Jesus, we are saved. Knowing this can lead us to a changed life, a life of **Renewal**.

Renewal was what the Centurion at the cross received. Perhaps he was the Centurion whose servant Jesus healed, the one who said, **"Lord I am not worthy to have you come to my house – just speak the word and my servant will be healed."** (Matthew 8:8) Perhaps he was the Centurion who built the

128

synagogue in Capernaum and sought to learn more about Jesus. At the crucifixion He would have known Jesus' power and how He could have come down from the cross. That Centurion said, **"Surely he was the Son of God."** **Renewal** may have come to Joseph of Arimathea who Gave away his valuable tomb to bury the body of Jesus. And in doing so, gave away his own right to be buried there in the future. You see, if someone outside your family was buried your tomb, you forfeited all future family burials of there. Joseph exchanged his family tomb for a changed life.

Redemption, Reward and **Renewal**, all are ways that show God provides for us perfectly. There are many other certainties, but these show themselves in Luke's Gospel. May God grant us all the joy of trusting His grace, grace to give us such *"Certainty in Uncertain Times."* Amen

LENT SERIES TWO
"Were You There?"
Week One

✠ ✠ ✠

"WERE YOU THERE WHEN HE WAS BETRAYED?"

Grace, mercy and peace be unto you from God our Father and from our Lord and Savior, Jesus Christ. Amen.

We again have come to the season of Lent and our theme this year is "Were You There?" Each year in Lent we study the events of cross, examining what happened in Jesus' day, and then applying what we learn to what's going on today. Sunday services during Lent are usually about certain stories in the life of Jesus, while our midweek services usually focus on a particular subject. Whatever the service during Lent, we always look to Jesus, **"The author and finisher of our faith,"** as Hebrews 12:2 tells us and what His life means for us each day. Today, Ash Wednesday 2012, we begin anew with a new focus.

This year our subject is "Were You There?" This theme, "Were You There," will place us into the lives of Christ, His disciples and the people around Him. We will focus on disciples named Judas and Peter, and on the Roman soldiers, and on Pontius Pilate and others. But instead of just looking at their stories and saying, "Look what they did wrong," we will try to walk next to them. We want to understand them a little more, their lives, and maybe even their sins, because they are much more like us than we might think.

I must be honest with you. I got the idea for this theme from another Pastor. He is also a member of the Lutheran Church-Missouri Synod, but he's from another state, Iowa. I like the theme he has come up with, so I am sharing some similar thoughts with you, although I have re-shaped them with thoughts that are my own or from the Bible. These are not sermon copies, but borrowed concepts. Some pastors call this, "ecclesiastical recycling," and in this case I hope you will find such recycling to be helpful.

Tonight's theme is, "WHERE YOU THERE WHEN HE WAS BETRAYED?" Predictably, we will focus a lot on Judas.

131

Judas is a man we all know. He's the person probably most hated within the Passion Story. He betrayed our Lord Jesus of Nazareth, which is a despicable act in itself, yet made worse because he was a close friend. Judas was right there in the close circle of friends, the Twelve who were called to follow Jesus. How then could he turn on Christ? Indeed, how could Jesus have even called Judas to follow Him, knowing what he'd eventually do? I don't think we'll ever fully understand this, but we do know that Christ knew what Judas would do from the start. And yet He called him as a disciple.

Yet before we start to point the fingers at this rather pathetic man, we need to ask where we are in this story. Where are we in the betrayal of Jesus Christ? We know what betrayal is. We may have been betrayed in our life, and perhaps we've even betrayed someone else. Betrayal is hurtful thing.

Back in Junior High I thought I was in love. She was the perfect girl. Her name was Judy and even as an 8th grader, I was thinking that she was going to be the one for me. It didn't matter that she was a year older, or that she went to the Catholic Church – she was "The One," a really cute girl and she had agreed to let me sit next to her at a Friday night football game. I told my friends what I thought about her, but I didn't tell her. Actually I never got a chance. Know why? A friend of mine, someone I thought was my friend, liked Judy, also. And before I could sit by her, before I even got to the game, he sat next to her. And he held her hand – the whole game! He betrayed me and that was the end of our friendship. That was also the end of Judy for me, too. So you can see, I do know a little about betrayal. I'm sure you have your stories of betrayal as well.

So here we are tonight, talking about the betrayal of Jesus of Nazareth, the greatest teacher the world has ever known, the one who changed the history of the world. Remember, we believe Jesus of Nazareth really is the Savior of the world. He is "The One." When we read again about Judas betraying Jesus, it ought to anger us. "Why would he do that? Why would he betray his friend, and even take money to do it?" After two years with Jesus, how could he? And after two thousand years, it still doesn't make sense, does it?

We look at Judas. We see what he did and we ask why did

he betray Jesus? He saw the miracles. He heard the amazing stories and parables. He saw the dead raised and the lame walk. He spent days and weeks with his Rabbi, up close and personal, and still he betrayed Jesus for a month's wages. And if you're like me, you've probably thought, "I'd never do that." A child betrays someone, but who betrays a great teacher? Would you betray the great evangelist Dr. Billy Graham or Dr. Paul Maier, Lutheran author and theologian? Would you even betray some politician you didn't agree with? (Well, let's not go there!) But a friend? Would any of us, you or I, take money to have an innocent person arrested?

First, who was Judas? In the Twelve he was the treasurer, the money guy, the one in charge of the purse. He bought food when they needed it and kept the gifts people gave them. There was always someone wanting to help out Jesus financially, and those funds were turned over to Judas. The all trusted Judas. He had impressed them, but they never realized until later what he was capable of doing.

Judas witnessed miracles. He saw things that must have shocked and amazed him, and yet he gave Jesus up to the Pharisees. For some reason he could stand there and say, "Yeah, I'll give you Jesus." And then not turn down money for doing it. What led him to do that? Well, for starters there was greed. Greed is the sin of always wanting more, one of the Seven Deadly Sins. Greed whispers in our ear, "You deserve more, and thirty silver coins is just a start." The Gospels tell us Judas was always wanting something more.

Judas was in the house when that woman came with the bottle of perfume and poured it on Jesus' feet. He was the one who said, "Don't waste that expensive perfume! We could have sold it and given the money to the poor or the hungry or people in need." I'm sure what Judas made sense at the time, but John's Gospel adds something. John 12:6 tells us, **"[Judas] said this, not because he cared about the poor, but because he was a thief, and having charge of the moneybag he used to help himself to what was put into it."** Greed was in his heart and it led to theft. Greed tells us, "You deserve more," and Theft says, "Take it!"

Thirty pieces of silver must have seemed like a lot. The

Pharisees probably understood Judas and though they could have given him more, knew that much would turn his head. The second sin of Judas comes out when we see how he interacted with the other disciples. Judas seems to want power, authority among the disciples. Being with Jesus and being Treasurer wasn't enough. He wanted more authority than he already had. That's why he spoke up rather boldly whenever money matters came up.

Maybe that's behind why he decided to betray Jesus. His quest for power made him think Jesus was weak and more dangerous than helpful. Judas wanted Jesus to do certain things and Jesus disappointed him. Maybe there was envy too, because envy makes a man feel he deserves more power. Money or greed can turn a person's head, but envy can push him over the edge. Greed will enslave you, but envy and jealousy can turn you into a murderer. Wanting power can lead you away from God faster than money or pleasure. It was the historian John Acton who correctly said, "Power corrupts, and absolute power corrupts absolutely."

There were so many other sins shown on the night Jesus was betrayed, the lying and abandonment and blaming others. When Jesus was with His disciples in the upper room sharing a Passover meal, He turned to His disciples and said, **"One of you is going to betray me."** The Bible says they all said, "Not me. It's somebody else. There's no way it'll be me." Judas could right then have admitted to Jesus that it was him but that he wanted to change his mind. But Judas didn't do that. Instead, he left. When the going gets tough, the greedy and power-hungry cut and run. "He got Himself into this, He can get Himself out."

Walking away when you're needed, wanting to have it your own way all the time, or just wanting more and more, do you find yourself in any of those sins? I know I do. I've walked when I should have stayed. I've pushed myself into a position of power when I couldn't handle it, and I've wanted more when I had enough. Right now I want a convertible. I've wanted one for years, but I'm not sure I want to be lumped in with Judas. Or does it?

Romans 8:7 tells us, **"The sinful mind is hostile to God. It does not submit to God's law nor can it."** God often tells us in

His Word, "Here are the things I want you to do, the commandments I want you to follow," but we say, "You can't ask me to do that." Or, "God I know a better way." Or we say" Organized Religion is wrong - I got my fill of church when I was a kid. All the church wants is money," things like that.

But in our hearts we know Paul is right when he says (Romans 3:23), **"All have sinned and fallen short of the glory of God."** We have all known greed, we've all wanted power, we've all lied and run away. Yes, we have all betrayed Jesus at some time or other. Looking at Judas, can all see ourselves in the mirror.

So we all need the forgiveness Christ earned for us on the cross. And this Lent we can all have it! God has not just called us to repentance, He has forgiven us. Lent is not just a time of reflection on the past, it is knowing in the present that we are forgiven. During Lent, we hear more than just new versions of the same old story, we need to hear the story with our names in it. We know the life of Jesus doesn't end at the cross, but at the open grave. We can know and trust that all who believe in Jesus will receive the crown of eternal life.

All this is why we come to church during the season of Lent, and reflect upon His life and our life, and know that God has forgiven us and will continue to forgive us when we trust His only Son, and accept the payment for sins He earned for us on the cross.

"WHERE YOU THERE WHEN HE WAS BETRAYED?" Today you and I can't only point the finger at Judas, because we, too, were right there nearby him and the others in the Garden of Gethsemane when he betrayed the Lord Jesus. Thanks be to God for Christ's forgiveness that is ours. Amen!

LENT SERIES TWO
"Were You There?"
Week Two

✛ ✛ ✛

"WERE YOU THERE WHEN HE WAS DENIED?"

Today is the second Wednesday of Lent. It is also Leap Day, February 29th, the day placed on our calendars to correct it. Our earth revolves around the sun every 365¼ days. To compensate for that extra quarter day, every four years one extra day is added to the calendar. We use the Gregorian calendar adopted by Pope Gregory 13th in 1582. This calendar is used over most of the world today, although a few countries use other calendars. Some ancient calendars can cause concern, such as the Mayan calendar slated to end on December 21 of this year and supposedly cause all kinds of troubles. All calendars have variations which require corrections if they are to be accurate. No matter how carefully we humans make our calendars, the earth's irregular revolutions around the sun require correction.

Humanity requires correction also. No matter how carefully we may try to live our lives, we have variations that require correction. No matter how perfectly we attempt to set up systems of behavior or organize our ideas, we cannot do it perfectly. Only God possesses perfection. Only He can establish perfect laws. People are imperfect. We are sinful. Thus, we all need correction in life.

Peter learned this. He thought he could keep a simple promise. Peter promised Jesus he would be loyal and that no matter what happened, he would not leave him. No matter what happened to Jesus, Peter would not run. Things might get deadly, but he, Peter, would still stand and protect Jesus. He would even die for Him. That's what Peter promised. And of course we know what he did.

Peter did run away. He came back but ended up denying he even knew Jesus. That had to be a painful time for Jesus who was on trial and one of His best friends was right around the corner saying, **"I don't know that man."** And he didn't just say it, he almost shouted it. The Bible says Peter even cursed and

137

swore, calling down heaven as his witness, he did not know that man. What a shameful friend he was when needed.

I've been reading a book about two school boys, ages 13 and 14. That's a hard time of life because you're not adult, although sometimes people expect you to be. You're not a kid anymore, but you still think like one. In the book Malcom and Billy are friends and are continually being harassed by two big, rich kids who seem to run the school. Even the teacher is afraid of the big rich kids. One day Billy comes to school smelling of alcohol and the kids start teasing him. The teacher accuses Billy of being drunk and everyone laughs at him. Malcom is Billy's friend and they do stuff together all the time. But today kids start kidding Malcom about Billy. "You're his friend? What a loser – why waste your time with him?" And finally, under pressure from all the other kids, Malcom starts laughing at Billy too. Instead of sticking up for him, he laughs at him. Because he feels he must be like the others, Malcom denies his friendship. Instead of helping Billy, Malcom denies him.

Some people say a person's life passes before his eyes when they fear for their life. I wonder if that happened to Peter in that courtyard. I wonder if he thought about when he was called from his fishnets to follow Jesus. Or when he went to get his brother Andrew, and together with John and James, all from a little village north of Galilee called Bethsaida, the four of them followed Jesus. Those fellows were fishermen and worked hard to catch enough fish to sell so they could feed themselves and their families. Then one day a man called Yeshua ha Nosari, Jesus of Nazareth, said He'd help them catch people. And they all became really close, living together, eating together, walking and talking together, like good friends. They laughed and learned and saw Him do miracles. Those three years with Him must have been a great time.

Peter was the kind of guy who spoke first and then thought later. Once he scolded Jesus about speaking of his death, and Jesus stopped him cold. In front of the others He called Peter Satan's helper if he kept talking like that. Peter was impulsive, quick to take over. If somebody needed help, Peter was right there. He bragged at defending Jesus, once even drawing his sword. But he could also run away when the going got tough.

138

Peter always wanted to do the right thing, but he also was big at doing the wrong thing, like when he ran away from Jesus in the Garden when the soldiers came and Jesus needed him.

I didg something like that. When I was about 10, a boy named Richard came to visit his grandparents in the summer. One day I gave Richard a ride on my old horse, Mae. We rode Mae bareback and we one day we rode her double. But we rode too fast and Mae turned so fast that Richard fell off against the corner of the barn. He yelled and held his shoulder and I knew he was hurt. You know what I did? I turned Mae and rode her straight home. I'd seen Richard's grandma coming out of the house, and instead of waiting to face her, I ran away. And I never forgot that. Later we went to high school together, but we were never friends again. And when he died in Viet Nam, I felt bad that I'd never apologized to him.

Peter was always on the edge of trouble when he was with Jesus. Once Jesus said the devil was going to test Peter, but that He would pray for him so he wouldn't fail Him. Peter, of course, said that would never happen. **"Oh no! Even if I have to go to prison with You or die for You, I will never run away!"** he said. (Mark 14:31) We know how that turned out.

You and I make promises to God, too. We make promises when we stand before Him and our family and friends on our Wedding Day and we don't keep them. We make promises to love our spouse and to always be faithful. We make promises when we bring our little babies up in Holy Baptism, that we'll bring them to church all the time and be good examples and teach them the Bible. We Christians make all kinds of promises to God. And like Peter, we don't always keep them.

On our Confirmation Day we promise never to fall away from the Christian Faith no matter what. And then we get older and smarter, maybe in college or when we're in the military or get married. Then we stop going to church awhile. Maybe even a long time. Most of us, like Peter, make promises and then forget them. Or we get angry and blame God when hardships start coming.

Sometimes we don't realize what we're promising. We even might put our hand on the Bible and say we're going to tell the whole truth and nothing but the truth, so help us God.

Then we lie like a rug. Sometimes we even lie to those who love us. Just like Peter we don't always tell the truth or keep our promises. He broke his promise to the Son of the Living God, and we have, too.

But one thing is sure, God keeps His promises. He tells us in 2 Corinthians 1:20, **"No matter how many promises God has made, they are all 'Yes' in Christ."** God's promises are all kept. They are all made true in Jesus Christ. And what does God promise us? He promises us forgiveness. When we repent and say we're sorry, God promises to forgive our sins as far as the east is from the west. Jesus was already on the cross when He said, **"Father, forgive them, because they know not what they do."** God also promises us a life in heaven after this life on earth. When our days come to an end here, we have a beautiful place to go, a place God has prepared for us. It's all ours, not because of what we've done, but because Jesus earned that place for us by His death on the cross of Calvary.

Heaven is a happy thought when we're children, but the older we sinners get, the more wonderful and peaceful that thought becomes. When we say goodbye to grandparents or parents or brothers and sisters or spouses or even our children, and bury them in the ground, the thought of a heavenly reunion becomes vivid and real and important. When we trust in Jesus, God promises us heaven. He also promises He will be with us in life, no matter where and no matter what. **"Never will I leave you, never will I forsake you,"** He says (Hebrews 13:5). God promises never to abandon us, even if we abandon Him. He promises to help us and comfort us and provide for us all through life.

Promises. We make then and we break them. But God keeps His. The Good News today is that our salvation does not depend on us keeping our promises, but on God keeping His. God loves us, no matter what. He considers us worth dying for and He has paid the price for our sinfulness. All that's left for us is to trust Him. And He even gives us help doing that! Faith in Jesus comes from the Holy Spirit, and faith in Jesus is all it takes. WERE YOU THERE WHEN HE WAS DENIED?

Years ago while visiting Jerusalem, Carol and I walked down the actual stone steps and stood in the courtyard of

Joseph Caiaphas, the High Priest who put Jesus on trial. On those very stones Peter denied knowing Jesus. Do you remember what happened then? The Bible says a rooster crowed. Peter denied Jesus and a chicken squawked, how appropriate! I'm sure every time afterward that Peter heard a rooster crow, he remembered his broken promise. Later on, after the crucifixion, Jesus told Peter personally that He forgave him. Three times he asked, **"Peter, do you love me?"** (John 21:17). I'm sure that was a touching moment. Bring forgiven always is.

WERE YOU THERE WHEN HE WAS DENIED? Some days I feel like I'm right beside Peter, in the courtyard, denying like a drunkard and lying like a rug. Tonight let's all remember that no matter who we are or where we are, and no matter what we have done, God forgives us. He doesn't like it when we deny Him, but it's not the end of the world. Listen for that rooster, my friends, or whatever reminds you of your sin. Listen and then remember: if Jesus can forgive Peter, then He can forgive you, too. And to that, all God's people should say, "Amen!"

:

142

LENT SERIES TWO
"Were You There?"
Week Three

✠ ✠ ✠

"WERE YOU THERE WHEN HE WAS ACCUSED?"

So far in our midweek Lent services, we've asked two questions: "Where you there when He was betrayed?" and "Were you there when He was denied?" Tonight we ask a third question: "WERE YOU THERE WHEN HE WAS ACCUSED?" The first two questions involved two disciples, Judas and Peter. Tonight's question involves the religious leaders back then who wanted to get Jesus out of their way for good.

Some background here will help. After Jesus was betrayed and arrested in the Garden of Gethsemane, He was taken to the palace of the High Priest at the time whose name was Joseph Caiaphas. There He was given a short trial before some members of the Sanhedrin.

Every Jewish city in Israel was to have a Sanhedrin of at least 23 judges, but the Jerusalem Sanhedrin was made up of 71 judges, and acted as Supreme Court in the land. Its task was to judge cases brought before it that involved enforcing religious laws. These laws covered all the people's religious and political life.

The Sanhedrin could also make new laws, so it was both court and congress. Anyone brought to trial before the Sanhedrin was usually presumed guilty or he wouldn't have been there. Nevertheless, the judges needed to have witnesses to a crime if someone was to be found guilty. The Sanhedrin had great power and could even pronounce the death sentence. Trouble was, under Roman control at that time, they couldn't carry it out. Only a Roman judge or court could put a person to death.

The trial against Jesus didn't start off well. There were barely enough members to convene the court. Nicodemus wasn't there. He was the man who came to Jesus at night asking spiritual questions and Jesus told him **"You must be born again"** (John 3). Maybe the others knew Nicodemus was

143

sympathetic to Jesus and so they didn't notify him of their meeting. Joseph of Arimathea wasn't there either. He supported Jesus and would later donate his grave for Jesus' burial. He probably wasn't notified either. Politics means winning at all costs.

But the people there that night knew exactly what they wanted, and it was to get rid of Jesus. Caiaphas the High Priest was President of the Senate and he had it all planned out. They had arrested Jesus, this time to get Him accused and convicted. Finally they'd take the convicted man Jesus to a Roman court to get Him sentenced to death. Caiaphas was a true politician who worked behind the scenes to get his plan accomplished. So things were well under way. Jesus was identified by Judas and arrested by temple guards. Now they needed someone to give a believable testimony that would draw a conviction. Justice was not the issue here, only conviction. Whether or not the evidence and witnesses were true was not the point – just conviction.

There were also a few Scribes present, acting as court reporters or perhaps legal advisors. Pharisees would be there to act as lawyers for the prosecution. There would be no lawyer for the defense. Jesus was on His own for that. There may have been a few others, some extra witnesses, and some curious people, of course. Perhaps there was also a liaison with Pilate so they could take their decision to him for the sentence.

But there was a legal problem. They were not quite sure what to charge Him with, and so they lacked the right kind of witnesses. How do you find a man guilty when you're not sure what he's done wrong? You know he must be found guilty, so you stretch the truth or you fabricate some story. You're desperate, so you obfuscate (I like that word). You trump up a charge that will look good enough to crucify Him. Life imprisonment was no option, and hey didn't do that back then anyway. If you were convicted, your life lasted only as long as it took to hang you on a cross or cut off your head. Anything less was for sissies. They wanted the job done quickly, ruthlessly and publicly as an example to all.

Dave was volunteer director of a children's choir, for twenty years Dave gave countless hours to help young people develop their musical talent, make friends and feel better about themselves. But all that ended when Dave was accused by two young girls of misconduct. What they swore in court he did ended his career, not only as choir director, but as a school teacher. But Dave was completely innocent. It seems he had found the girls smoking marijuana and told their parents. The girls retaliated by saying Dave wrongly touched them. Dave was sentenced to jail and branded a sex offender. A few weeks after his conviction, the girls admitted they made it all up. They said they were angry and wanted to retaliate for telling their parents they smoked dope. Though he was released, it took Dave a year and huge legal fees to get the sex offender charges removed. But Dave's reputation, his career and even the youth choir were all destroyed. False accusations can destroy people.

So what had Jesus of Nazareth done wrong? What could they accuse Him of? Here's where the Pharisees came in. They had to fabricate something. They got one fellow to accuse Him of healing sick people on the Sabbath, but that wasn't a capital crime. Another man said He called the Pharisees hypocrites, but others agreed with him on that. Someone accused Him of saying, **"He said he'd tear down the temple and rebuild it in three days."** But what did that mean? Making a threat against a building wasn't a capital offense.

So the High Priest of this "Monkey Court" had a problem, there were no credible witnesses. He also had another problem, Jesus wouldn't talk. Court rules required the accused to give some kind of response, but Jesus just stood there silent. Caiaphas was furious over that. **"Aren't you going to answer? What is this these men are saying against you?"** That was a really dumb question if you think of it. It wasn't Jesus' job to define his accusation. He was there to defend himself, not explain their charges. Jesus' defense right then was brilliant - just stay silent. The whole court was looking pretty stupid right then, and so He said nothing.

The trial happened in the wee hours of the morning and people were exhausted. Some had been up all night. Others had been dragged out of bed too early. The witnesses made no sense, and Caiaphas the judge was furious because his plan was breaking down. He knew he could convict Jesus of blasphemy, but that was not a capital crime to the Romans. Treason! That's the accusation he needed. He needed to convict Jesus of treason, so he secretly asked his associates to trick Jesus to say something against Rome. But that didn't work either.

Let's look at Caiaphas for a moment. Caiaphas was top dog, the High Priest of all the high priests. Josephus the historian wrote that Caiaphas ruled the Jerusalem Sanhedrin for nearly 20 years. Yet he wasn't the real power there. The real top dog was a wealthy old man named Annas, who also happened to be Caiaphas' father-in-law. He had been Jerusalem High Priest earlier but was deposed by the Governor for carrying out illegal executions. But whatever plans Caiaphas made, insiders knew that Annas had a hand in them.

But it was Caiaphas who said that **"One man should die rather than the whole nation."** He blurted that out during a secret meeting recorded in John chapter 11. That happened right after Jesus raised Lazarus from the dead, and the religious leaders were getting nervous because so many people were following Jesus. They were afraid the Romans could come in and take away their religious influence. John 11: 50 tells us, **"Caiaphas said, 'You know nothing at all. Nor do you understand that it is better for you that one man should die for the people, not that the whole nation should perish.' He did not say this of his own accord, but being high priest that year he prophesied Jesus would die for the nation."**

So, we know who some of the people are when Jesus was accused, but there were more there, some not even alive yet. His trial has been studied throughout history by all who have ever wanted to demean Jesus, to accuse Him of something. Ever since Jesus healed the sick, people have accused Him of faking it. He's been accused of not being the Son of God, of not being resurrected, and of not even being a good teacher. The enemies of Jesus have always accused Him of something falsely. Question is, are we among them?

Even some so-called Christians have joined the chorus of accusers. Instead of seeing Christianity as being behind development of universities and hospitals, of music and art, or feeding the orphans and widows and homeless, and even government laws, they have blamed Christians for world's problems. Instead of believing Jesus is the only way to heaven, they say He's just one of the ways to get there. I hear there's a well-known Christian pastor trying to bridge a gap by teaching that God and Allah are the same god, just with a different name. He hopes to connect Christians and Moslems. I wonder what Elijah would have said if he'd heard that God and Baal were the same. I don't think I'd have liked what he'd have said.

Caiaphas and his cronies couldn't find any evidence until he asked, **"Tell us if you are the Christ, the Son of God."** Jesus said to him, **"You have said so..."** Then the high priest tore his robes and said, **"He has uttered blasphemy. What further witnesses do we need? You have now heard his blasphemy. What is your judgment?"** They answered, **"He deserves death."**(Matthew 26). Caiaphas finally got his way.

In 1990 archaeologists unearthed an ossuary, a hardened clay covered bone box with the inscription that said, "Joseph, son of Caiaphas." It held the actual bones of Caiaphas, the man who falsely accused Jesus. They found the bones of Caiaphas, but they'll never find the bones of Jesus of Nazareth, because He is no longer dead. He is alive!

Were you there when He was accused? That's a hard question. We don't want to accuse Jesus. He's our Savior. He's brought us blessings. We see an innocent man hanging on the cross, a good man falsely accused. The cross shows Jesus was innocent, but we are the guilty ones. Caiaphas and the Sanhedrin knew He was innocent. Pilate's wife knew He was innocent. We know He was innocent. But our sins put Him there.

Our Lord Jesus prayed, **"Father, forgive them, for they know not what they do."** There's something beautiful and hideous in the cross. Its beauty is in the forgiveness it brings us, but it is hideous how it took place, His false accusations, beatings, the suffering, and finally His death. All for us. He did it all for each of us.

Every Lent that we come into this place, look upon the cross and imagine the pain and the suffering it caused Him, but we also know the beauty of the victory it gives us. Were we there? Absolutely - you and I and all mankind. It's hard to admit, but it's true. Thanks be to God that He loves us and does not hold it against us. Amen.

LENT SERIES TWO
"Were You There?"
Week Four

✛ ✛ ✛

"WERE YOU THERE WHEN HE WAS CONDEMNED?"

Were you there when Jesus was betrayed? Or denied? Or accused? Now tonight we ask, were you there when He was condemned? You may be noticing that our Lent Series this year contains a lot of history and culture. This is to help us understand how Jesus ended up on the cross, not only because of the sins of mankind which was His first purpose, but also to learn the culture which put Him there.

Sunday sermons during Lent often speak of Christ's teachings. I consider it the task of these midweek Lent messages to explain more fully how and why His suffering and death happened as it did. I want to show you that details do matter to God. Our God is not God only of the broad brush strokes of history, He is also the God of details.

The Passion Story of Christ's suffering and death now takes Him to Pilate for condemnation. The Jews could only accuse Him; Pilate only could condemn Him. This drama includes Pilate's wife Claudia who tells him to leave Jesus alone because she'd had bad dreams about Him. Pilate probably dismissed what she said, but both Catholic and Orthodox Christians made her a saint for it, St. Claudia.

But as the morning progressed, details became tangled and troublesome. Pilate knew the Passover would not go smoothly, because it never did. But not in his wildest dreams did he think the day's events would lead to two thousand years of Christians repeating in their creed over and over, millions of times saying Jesus, *"Suffered under Pontius Pilate."*

Pontius Pilate is an interesting man in this drama. He is called Governor but had the power of a Prefect. The Pontius family members were equestrian noblemen connected to Sejanus, a favorite soldier of Emperor Tiberias Caesar. Pilate was responsible for the financial and political governing of Judea, which was no easy job. He spent ten years there and was

149

often involved in troublesome events. As a leader, he was inflexible and merciless, yet effective. The Jews hated him for his harshness and lack of consideration for their culture.

Historians say Pilate averted a riot by removing some images of Tiberius which had been set up in Jerusalem, and it led to some bloodshed. This is the incident mentioned in Luke 13 where Jesus speaks of Galileans whose blood Pilate mingled with the sacrifices. As a governing politician, Pilate was anxious that no negative reports should be sent to Rome concerning his rule in Judea.

Besides governor, Pilate was also soldier and politician, the highest Roman authority in Judea. He usually stayed at Herod's palace in Caesarea on the Mediterranean with his garrison of half a legion, or 3,000 soldiers. During the Passover, Pilate and his family came to Jerusalem with a Cohort of 800 soldiers. When there, Pilate presided over court cases among the Jews. John 18:28 to 19:16 gives us interesting details of what took place next. I tried summarizing all that happened, but the biblical account itself says it best:

"Then they led Jesus from the house of Caiaphas to the governor's headquarters. It was early morning. They themselves did not enter the governor's headquarters, so that they would not be defiled, but could eat the Passover. So Pilate went outside to them and said, "What accusation do you bring against this man?" They answered him, "If this man were not doing evil, we would not have delivered him over to you." Pilate said to them, "Take him yourselves and judge him by your own law." The Jews said to him, "It is not lawful for us to put anyone to death." This was to fulfill the word that Jesus had spoken to show by what kind of death he was going to die. So Pilate entered his headquarters again and called Jesus and said to him, "Are you the King of the Jews?" Jesus answered, "Do you say this of your own accord, or did others say it to you about me?" Pilate answered, "Am I a Jew? Your own nation and the chief priests have delivered you over to me. What have you done?" Jesus answered, "My kingdom is not of this world. If my kingdom were of this world, my servants would have been fighting, that I might not be delivered over to the Jews. But my kingdom is not from the world." Then Pilate said to him, "So you are a king?" Jesus answered, "You say that I am a king. For this purpose I was born and for this purpose I have come into the world— to bear witness to the truth. Everyone who is of the truth listens to my
150

voice." Pilate said to him, "What is truth?" After he had said this, he went back outside to the Jews and told them, "I find no guilt in him. But you have a custom that I should release one man for you at the Passover. So do you want me to release to you the King of the Jews?" They cried out again, "Not this man, but Barabbas!" Now Barabbas was a robber. Then Pilate took Jesus and flogged him. And the soldiers twisted together a crown of thorns and put it on his head and arrayed him in a purple robe. They came up to him, saying, "Hail, King of the Jews!" and struck him with their hands. Pilate went out again and said to them, "See, I am bringing him out to you that you may know that I find no guilt in him." So Jesus came out, wearing the crown of thorns and the purple robe. Pilate said to them, "Behold the man!" When the chief priests and the officers saw him, they cried out, "Crucify him, crucify him!" Pilate said to them, "Take him yourselves and crucify him, for I find no guilt in him." The Jews answered him, "We have a law, and according to that law he ought to die because he has made himself the Son of God." When Pilate heard this statement, he was even more afraid. He entered his headquarters again and said to Jesus, "Where are you from?" But Jesus gave him no answer. So Pilate said to him, "You will not speak to me? Do you not know that I have authority to release you and authority to crucify you?" Jesus answered him, "You would have no authority over me at all unless it had been given you from above. Therefore he who delivered me over to you has the greater sin." From then on Pilate sought to release him, but the Jews cried out, "If you release this man, you are not Caesar's friend. Everyone who makes himself a king opposes Caesar." So when Pilate heard these words, he brought Jesus out and sat down on the judgment seat at a place called The Stone Pavement, and in Aramaic, Gabbatha. Now it was the day of Preparation of the Passover. It was about the sixth hour. He said to the Jews, "Behold your King!" They cried out, "Away with him, away with him, crucify him!" Pilate said to them, "Shall I crucify your King?" The chief priests answered, "We have no king but Caesar." So he delivered him over to them to be crucified."

This is really a continuation of the injustice started by High Priest Caiaphas. Pilate stands before the crowd of accusers, using Jesus as his visual aid. "What's the charge?" he asks those who brought Him. But he doesn't work too hard at this seemingly minor trial. Pilate didn't want to condemn an innocent man, but even more so he didn't want to get himself into trouble with the locals. He tried passing Jesus off to the current King Herod, but Jesus ignored him, too, so Herod tossed Jesus back to Pilate. Finally, Pilate gave in to their demands and allowed them to take Jesus to be crucified. He could have released Him, but instead opted to condemn an innocent man to a terrible death. Of course, he washed his hands of the whole thing, very literally.

There's something surreal about this. The Rabbi, Yeshua ha Nosari, Jesus of Nazareth, was guilty of merely trying to bring people closer to God which alienated the religious leaders. His case is so weak it falls apart. He breaks no laws and yet is condemned. There is no proof, yet He's handed over for crucifixion. What? That's injustice. We know the anger and frustration that come from being treated unjustly.

Maybe we didn't get the promotion we deserved, or maybe we didn't win the award we thought was ours, like the membership in the National Honor Society I didn't get in High School. That was 50 years ago and it still irks me that certain others got it but I didn't. Or maybe someone is not brought to justice. Last week I met a man whose wife was kidnapped and murdered 30 years ago, and it still hurts him to mention it because the case was never solved.

Or maybe a spouse divorces you and takes every penny, or someone guilty gets off scot-free. Or soldiers in Afghanistan are killed because a Koran got burned. (By the way, did you know the Army burns all religious materials if they are no longer needed, including Bibles?) Or the rich get richer and the poor let others feed them instead of working. Or maybe your child rebels in spite of the good way you raised him.

Injustice. It's everywhere. We've all said, "It's just not right. It's not fair. How can they get away with that?" But what do you do when injustice just washes over you like a flood?

I once had some things going in my life that involved unjust treatment. I asked a trusted friend what to do, and he said I should pray for the other guy. "I'd like to pray that a truck runs over him," I remember saying, but I knew that wasn't right. My friend told me to pray that the other person might change a bad attitude, and he also said I should pray to change my own attitude. No matter how unfairly life may be to us, or how evil others might be to us, we probably also need an attitude adjustment. Others might need our forgiveness, but maybe we need God's forgiveness, too.

In Jesus trial, injustice was everywhere. Wicked people did wicked things to a dear man. They released an evil man, then crucified a good man. But this injustice, this innocent suffering and death was all a part of God's plan. It was all necessary to fulfill God's righteousness. 1 Peter 2:24 says, **"He Himself bore our sins in His body on the tree, so that we might die to sin and live for righteousness; by His wounds, you have been healed."** Did you get that? He bore our sins. That's injustice. He suffered in our place. Now that's just not right.

When Jesus was condemned, He took our place. When He was whipped, it should have been our backs. He was the victim of the injustice, but we are the beneficiaries. Somebody else usually benefits when there's injustice, right? It's usually true – someone else gets the job, somebody else wins the award, someone else has perfect kids, or the loving and faithful spouse, or enough money or the good health. It's always somebody else.

But when is it going to be us, we may wonder? Actually, in Jesus, it is us. He's the Somebody Else who was condemned, and we are set free. He is that other guy who gets the beating, looks the fool, or pays the price, and we are the ones who look good. **"God did not send His Son into the world to condemn the world, but to save the world."** (John 3:17) God did not want us to perish, that's the bottom line. God made His choice for injustice and chose it for His Son. But we get the prize.

Acts 4:12 tells us, **"Salvation is found in no one else, for there is no other name under heaven given to men by which we must be saved."** There's no other name, religion, philosophy, no other culture, path or plan that will save us. Only the name of God's precious Son Jesus can do that. Were you there when He was condemned? I was, and I was standing right next to you. Praise God that in Jesus Christ there is justice for us all. It's ours in Jesus Christ. Amen.

LENT SERIES TWO
"Were You There?"
Week Five

✠ ✠ ✠

"WERE YOU THERE WHEN HE WAS CROWNED WITH THORNS?"

If there's one thing we should learn from this Lent series, it's that everyone seemed to get their turn with Jesus. Judas did, the religious leaders and High Priest did, Pilate and now even the soldiers did. Tonight it is the soldiers' turn to abuse Him shamefully, to beat Him up, torture Him and to enjoy it. If you recall that movie a few years ago, "Passion of the Christ," it graphically showed the brutality involved.

This treatment is made all the worse because Jesus was innocent. He was a kind and loving teacher, not some evil convict. He loved little children and took time for sick people and gently corrected his friends. This kind Rabbi taught mercy, but was given back brutality. He offered new life to people, but was crucified for it. The Roman cross was the worst kind of death imaginable, worse even than the famed "hang, draw and quarter" technique of medieval England. Jesus' love for people was rewarded with cruelty by people.

Let me read one Bible record about what the soldiers did, **"Then the governor's soldiers took Jesus into the Praetorium and gathered the whole company of soldiers around Him. They stripped Him and put on a scarlet robe, and then twisted together a crown of thorns and set it on His head. They put a staff in his right hand. Then they knelt in front of Him and mocked Him. 'Hail, king of the Jews,' they said. They spit on Him and took the staff and struck Him on the head again and again."** (Matthew 27:27-30)

These soldiers were not out of control. They may have been treating Him like an animal, but it was expected. A prisoner in the hands of soldiers got abused, and badly. But it's God's Son they're beating, it makes us furious just thinking about it.

I think we should, though, to take a moment to see what it was like from the soldiers' perspective. Who were these guys, these soldiers? What was their life like, and why were they so brutal? I recently bought an interesting book called, *Daily Life in the Time of Jesus*, by Miriam Vamosh and I want to quote a portion of it, a way for us to enter the world of a Roman soldier and see what life was like.

"Enlistment in the Roman army most often took place between the ages of 18 to 23. Among the most important requirements of a recruit was height. At six Roman feet tall, he towered over the local population. Once selected, a full month course of basic training would begin but not before the soldier was tattooed and given a seal bearing his name, which he would wear around his neck for the duration of his service. Though service was long, some 25 years, and most soldiers were forbidden to marry, its benefits were great. A regular salary was awarded and expenses defrayed. Although wealth was an advantage for a recruit, even the poorest recruit could accrue recognition and eventually wealth by distinguishing himself in the service of the emperor."

"A Roman legion numbering between seven to ten cohorts, 3,500 to 6,000 men, had been stationed near Jerusalem since 35 B.C. Herod employed and supported the Roman legion himself. Herod's force was put together in the tried and true Roman fashion based on the operative unit of the cohort, which itself was composed of six companies of 80-100 men each. In addition to cavalry, infantry and artillery branches, Herod's forces even included navy based at his new city of Caesarea and an intelligence branch. Many of the troops in Herod's standing army were foreign mercenaries which included Thracians, Germans, Gauls and others. Many members of Herod's army were of his own Idumean ethnic background. He often settled these troops in villages where they would live an ordinary village life, farming plots of land awarded them but maintaining patrol and battle readiness."

The life of a Roman soldier was disciplined and brutal. In all probability, at the time of Jesus' trial, they were simply performing as was expected, living up to what had been done in the past as part of the military crucifixion squad. They seem despicable to us, abusing Him this way, spitting on Him and hitting Him and putting that terrible crown of thorns upon His head. Being crowned with thorns caused Him pain that He few people could endure. The soldiers behaved badly, but they weren't all bad.

Consider the Centurion mentioned in Luke 7:1-10. The Bible says, "Jesus entered Capernaum. There, the servant of a Centurion, whom his master valued highly, was sick and about to die. The Centurion heard of Jesus and sent some elders of the Jews to Him, asking Him to come and heal his servant. When they came to Jesus, he pleaded earnestly with them. 'This man deserves to have you do this because he loves our nation and has built our synagogue.' So Jesus went with them. He was not far from the house when the Centurion sent friends to say to Him, 'Lord, don't trouble yourself, for I do not deserve to have you come under my roof. That's why I did not even consider myself worthy to come to you, but say the word and my servant will be healed, for I myself am a man under authority with soldiers under me. I tell this one 'Go' and he goes. And that one 'Come' and he comes. I say to my servant, 'Do this' and he does it.' When Jesus heard this, He was amazed at him and turning to the crowd following Him, He said, 'I tell you, I have not found such great faith even in Israel.' Then the man who had been sent returned to the house and found the servant healed."

I have been to Capernaum and have seen the remains of the majestic synagogue he built for them. Not all Roman soldiers were evil. Certainly, the group around Jesus was acting like it. They were used to brutality and abuse with anyone sentenced to the cross.

We, too, are witnesses to many kinds of abuse, some on the evening news or others on the front page. The recent incident of the American soldier killing civilians in Afghanistan comes to mind. Or Mexican Drug Cartels killing thousands of people there. Or a convicted sex offender being released from prison and immediately holding some women hostage. Or children being used in the Middle East as homicide bombers.

Being part of a family whose members have served in the armed forces, I am especially aware of what pressures our soldiers, sailors and airmen have placed on them. It is amazing that our highly trained soldiers do as well as they do in this confusing time of modern warfare. Imagine what it was like when all warfare was hand-to-hand, face-to-face and sword-to-sword. What horror, what bloodshed! And without being able

157

to marry they were forced to wait around during peacetime. Perhaps the hardest thing a soldier faces is being trained to fight and then not being able to do it. Thus, crucifixion detail was always bloody and brutal.

How can we avoid being like the soldiers? How can we avoid being like those so abusive to Jesus? Psalm 119:9 gives us a great answer, **"How can a young person stay on the path of purity? By living according to Your word, O God."** By leaning on God's word, reading it, thinking about it, praying it, believing it, and living by it. God's holy Word is living and active, sharper than any two-edged sword. It is God showing us His heart, guiding us on the right path, keeping us from evil, guarding us from temptations, even holding our hand as we walk the hard path of life.

Always remember that through God's Word, the Holy Spirit speaks to us. He tells us of Jesus our Savior, as well as when things aren't right. When opening the Bible gets awkward or unsettling, that's when we need it most. Sometimes you and I are tempted to join the brutal crowd. Then we must step back from the crowd, and prayerfully ask what God would want us to do. But if possible we need to get away from the bad things first. We need to find courage to walk according to God's way, not man's way. We need to get away from the things that would hurt us or others.

But what if we stumble? What if we do get caught up with the crowd? What if we do listen to that voice tempting us and urging us to do what we know is wrong? How do we get back on the right road once we've strayed? 1 John 1:9 says, **"If we confess our sins, He is faithful and just and will forgive us our sins and purify us from all unrighteousness."** Confess and ask God's forgiveness. He will forgive us. He can even forgive people who behave as shamefully as the Roman soldiers did.

The apostle Paul saw the brutality of the Roman soldier, and yet he gives us one of the best examples of how to live through a military word picture. In Ephesians 6:13-18 Paul says, **"Therefore take up the whole armor of God, that you may be able to withstand in the evil day, and having done all, to stand firm. Stand then, having fastened on the belt of truth, and having put on the breastplate of righteousness, and, as shoes**

158

for your feet, having put on the readiness given by the gospel of peace. In all circumstances take up the shield of faith, with which you can extinguish all the flaming darts of the evil one; and take the helmet of salvation, and the sword of the Spirit, which is the word of God, praying at all times in the Spirit, with all prayer and supplication."

In today's modern world, the "wise people" would have us believe all soldiers are either 1) brutal thugs, or 2) completely unnecessary. But we know today's soldiers aren't all brutal, and they certainly aren't all thugs. And they are, however, still needed, because the world is full of thousands of brutal thugs who would kill all Christians, and even blow up innocent women and children.

I don't know how God can still love this world today, but He still does. He is still the loving father waiting for the prodigal son or daughter to return home. He would even send His son to the cross a second time if that's what it took to redeem the world. But, thankfully, once was enough. Jesus did what was needed. He gave His life on Calvary just once, that all who believe on Him might not perish, but have eternal life.

Because of sin we all can be wicked and evil. If Satan had his way, he would turn us all into savages. We all are capable of crowning our enemy with thorns. And yet, God our loving Father, reaches out to us wherever we are and invites us to come back to the embrace of His grace. In Jesus He forgives our evil ways.

One day, God willing, you and I will stand before Him next to that stalwart soldier who said, **"Surely, He was the Son of God."** (Matthew 27:54)   And we'll see Jesus wearing a real crown, not of thorns or jewels, but a crown of righteousness in glory. He'll have one for each of us, too. Amen.

LENT SERIES TWO
"Were You There?"
Week Six

✚ ✚ ✚

"WERE YOU THERE WHEN HE WAS CRUCIFIED?"

So far on our journey this Lent, we've taken some big steps along the passion road. We've taken a few steps into a world of two millennia ago, a world ruled by Rome and also the Jewish Church. We've gotten a glimpse of Jesus being pitted against the crowds. We have heard from the people in charge, the liars and thieves, the priests and the politicians, the soldiers and the disciples. We've tried to put ourselves in the place of those people, seeing a little of what it was like to be there, and perhaps also seeing ourselves right next to them, not quite joining in, but surely feeling a little like we're part of that history.

Today we come to the crucifixion. Ever since the execution of Jesus of Nazareth, crucifixion has been a focus of attention down through history during Lent. It was a method of capital punishment as cruel as mankind could create. But despite what we knew, until recently there was little archaeological evidence to back it up.

But that changed in 1968. That year in Jerusalem archaeologists discovered the very first bones of a crucified man, and it shed new light on how it was done. Among the skeletal remains was the right heel bone, and in it was embedded a 4½ inch long iron nail with olive wood fragments attached. The angle and position of the nail showed the man's heels were nailed to either side of the cross. The hands and arm bones were uninjured, indicating they were probably tied to the cross piece with ropes.

Other remnants of other crucifixions have since been found, showing nails with a round disc that went through the wrist or hand of the convict. What has been deduced so far is that the convict carried his own cross bar to the crucifixion site. Then his hands and arms were tied in place and some were nailed on as well. He was then hoisted up the center beam and

161

attached to it several feet off the ground.

The convict was then left to die there in public. Since places of crucifixion were usually outside the city walls, the Romans placed them along the main roads, as a punishment for all to see. Behold the fate of these who have broken Roman law! Do you also want to break the law? Then this is what will happen to you. Punishment and deterrent wrapped up in one.

Death on the cross usually took hours or even days. Death came by asphyxiation caused when the convict's legs could no longer support him (women were not crucified). Thus we read in the Bible that the legs of the thieves were broken so that their death would be hastened. The soldiers were surprised when they came to Jesus and found He was already dead. But they still struck Him in the side with a spear just to be sure.

One Jewish source reveals a little known fact. A crucified man could be redeemed by a wealthy passer-by. Even if the victim was near death, some guards could be bribed to let the man down from the cross. The only problem was that if there was no one below to help the convict, and there rarely was, he could surely die there on the ground anyway. There were no EMTs in ambulances ready to take him to a hospital. Crude medications could have been offered, such as the myrrh mixed with vinegar and aloes, a liquid that would have acted as both pain reducer and antiseptic. A pail of this mixture was usually there, even for the soldiers to wash their bloody hands.

But we're getting ahead of ourselves. History tells us Jesus of Nazareth was crucified at noon, and that He hung there three hours until dying at 3 PM. During that time the Gospels record that He spoke seven times, forgiving the people below, offering paradise to the thief, taking care of His mother, praying to His father, expressing His thirst, saying all was finished, and finally imparting His life to God. The "Seven Last Words from the Cross," we call them.

The words Jesus said from the cross are forever etched into the soul of Christianity. Throughout the ages the church has recalled these words to burn into its conscience the truth of His death on Calvary. This was no play-acting. It was not a staged event, as the Moslem Koran says, where Judas died in place of Jesus. Jesus' death on the cross was what it was, His very death.

He really died. The Roman spear jabbed in His side brought forth a flood of blood and water, genuine proof He had died a couple of hours before. Doctors tells us that when a person dies, the red blood cells immediately begin separating from clear plasma. That's why it looked like blood and water. He was dead and no one who was there would have disputed this. Roman soldiers knew their business, and they made sure He was dead.

Many things happened while He hung there those three hours. The soldiers gambled away his clothes. The disciple John and some women, including His mother, stood below watching. They knew this might last a long time, but they waited. People taunted Him during the wait. It was a grizzly scene.

Passers-by would jeer and even throw rocks at the condemned men on the cross. His accusers may have stayed awhile, but they would eventually have grown tired and left. They'd been successful. He would not escape now. Other friends may have been there. We hear of two, Joseph and Nicodemus, who were there. But again we're getting ahead of ourselves.

Years later, one of His apostles, Paul of Tarsus, would state an interesting perspective when he wrote in Galatians 2:20, **"I have been crucified with Christ. It is no longer I who live, but Christ who lives in me. And the life I now live in the flesh I live by faith in the Son of God, who loved me and gave himself for me."**

Crucified with Christ. Not literally, of course, but Paul could say it truthfully. Paul says Christ's crucifixion involved him, even though he wasn't there. He means Jesus' crucifixion envelopes him, surrounds him and absorbs his sins. He may not have been there, but his sins were, so Paul, too, was crucified on Calvary. Not easily understood, but true.

Were you there when He was crucified? In that sense, yes, because the sins of all people were there. We and the sins of mankind were crucified with Him. And because we, too, were crucified, we have the chance to become dead to sin and alive to Christ.

Christ now lives within us. His purity and perfection replace our sin and death. He arose from the dead, and He gives us His resurrection. He lives in us, and that means we can now

163

live for Him. That's why Paul could say, **"The life I now live in the flesh I live by faith in the Son of God, who loved me and gave himself for me."**

This new life is all for us. I guess we could say it's all about Him, but it's all for us, all the punishment, the betrayal, the denial, the accusations, the trials, the condemnation, the beatings, the crown of thorns, and the horror of crucifixion – it's all for us. It's all about Him, but it's all for us. Jesus did all this so you and I could get the blessings. It's not just story, it is reality!

This is all for us, you know, this church, these services, the hymns, sermons, Bible studies, potlucks, Confirmation, Holy Communion, mission work, service projects, everything. It's all for us. God doesn't need this stuff, but we do. God can get along just fine without all this. He doesn't need cathedrals or ceremonies or denominations or Lent or Easter or anything.

Those are all things we need. God sends His Son into the world because we need Him. He allows His only Son to die because we need the forgiveness Christ earned for us. God gives us Easter because we need to know and believe Jesus is alive. He's not just some unfortunate prophet who was innocently condemned, or some good guy killed unjustly. It's all part of God's plan. We all need Jesus because of what God gives us through Him.

So the Gospel today, the Good News that gives us life, the message that I want you all to take home today, is that all of this that we get from God in life is for us, for our benefit. If we didn't need it, God wouldn't have gone to all this trouble.

All this Lent during these Wednesday services, we have been singing the same song, asking the same question: *"Were you there when they crucified my Lord?"* By now you're probably tired of those words and that melody, and I don't blame you. Maybe you're even a bit tired of being asked if you were there, when you're not quite sure what it all means. If so, then remember – it's all done for us. And thank God it is! Amen

LENT SERIES THREE
"Seven Last Words"
Week One

"Father, Forgive Them, For They Know Not What They Do"
(Luke 23:34)

✠ ✠ ✠

Eternal God and Father of our Lord Jesus Christ, give us Your Holy Spirit who writes the preached Word into our hearts. May we receive and believe it and be cheered and comforted by it in eternity. Glorify Your Word in our hearts and make it so bright and warm that we may find pleasure in it, through Your Holy Spirit think what is right, and by Your power, fulfill the Word, for the sake of Jesus Christ, Your Son our Lord. Amen. (Luther's Prayer Before the Sermon)

These few words were prayed by Martin Luther often when he began his sermons, so I will begin my sermons during Lent with this prayer also. The sermon is a mighty gift from God, an important way to learn God's Word. Luther revived preaching during worship services so the people could learn. The sermon had been abandoned by the church around 500 AD, replacing it with some liturgical parts that were not as helpful. Many people today think the sermon is just the pastor telling people what's on his mind, sharing his ideas. But the sermon's real purpose is to explain God's Word and to encourage people to live a worthy Christian life. Above all, the sermon is given to share the Gospel of Jesus Christ, the Good News that Jesus is our risen Lord who loves us, wants us to trust Him and live with Him eternally.

Tonight we begin our annual midweek Lent services. The word "Lent" comes from the Latin word for "spring," and since 325 AD and the Council of Nicaea Christians have tried to observe six weeks during the spring to prepare for Easter. Christians over the ages have made preparations by reminding themselves why there was a need for the resurrection.

In Lent we hear again the Passion Story, the final events in the life of our Lord Jesus that caused Him to suffer and die on the cross. This year in our Lent sermons we will consider the seven final phrases Jesus said as he hung from the cross. The Bible records He spoke seven times during those six hours of

165

suffering. Hence, **"The Seven Last Words from the Cross."**

Our midweek Passion History readings this year will be from the Gospel of Mark. We will also hear Old Testament readings from 2 Samuel which tell the sad story of King David and his rebellious son Absalom. David has been called a "type" of Christ, meaning that some of David's character and actions in the Old Testament correspond to Jesus' character and actions in the New Testament. As David was saddened and threatened by his rebellious son Absalom, so Jesus was saddened, threatened and eventually killed by His rebellious sons and daughters of the world. As you hear the story of Jesus' suffering and death, you will also hear how David suffered through family pain and turmoil.

Jesus' first word from the cross is all about forgiveness: **"Father, forgive them, for they know not what they do."** Who is Jesus asking the Father to forgive? Some think Jesus must be praying for the Roman soldiers who nailed Him to the cross, but surely they are not all. He must also be speaking of those who moved the soldiers to act.

In Isaiah 53:12 it is prophesied of the Messiah, **"He poured out his life unto death, and was numbered with the transgressors. For he bore the sins of many, and made intercession for the transgressors."** As fulfillment to those words, we hear that as Jesus hung from the cross, He pleaded for mercy on behalf of those who committed the atrocities that put Him there. All this follows because Jesus himself had already instructed people in the Sermon on the Mount, saying, **"Love your enemies and pray for those who persecute you."** (Matthew 5:44) Jesus was practicing what He preached.

"Father, forgive them." During Lent, you and I need to ask, *"Who were the people who had brought about Jesus' crucifixion?"* Was it the Jewish leaders who put Him on trial? Was it the crowd that yelled, **"Crucify Him!"?** Was it Pontius Pilate who washed his hands of the whole thing and let soldiers do their crucifying? Or was Jesus praying for all of those people, and also for all of us, we proud humans who so well have followed the footsteps of those before us in sinning against God's holy commandments? You and I must admit that we sin against God as we live lives our own way and find every way to justify sin.

166

Jesus also said, "...for they know not what they do." So this prayer could not have been only for the soldiers. They knew exactly what they were doing and were very good at it. They were doing the job they'd been trained for, executing prisoners. They, of course, couldn't know they were crucifying the Son of God, and if they had, wouldn't have cared. In their wildest dreams they couldn't have known their actions would help bring about the salvation of the world. This One Man's death would forgive even their own sins.

The soldiers were not the only ones who did not know what they were doing. The crowds didn't either. They had been recruited to shout and demand His death. Possibly some of them had cheered His arrival at Jerusalem the Sunday before, but certainly Jesus' enemies had recruited most of them that day. So, did the Jewish leaders know what they were doing? Were they to blame for the death of Jesus of Nazareth? While they surely knew the God of Abraham, Isaac, and Jacob, their actions here were not for anything good. Probably they were just hoping to get rid of a rabble rouser and calm things down.

Then there was Pilate. Did he know what he was doing? He had a hard job in a difficult territory and the last thing he needed was a riot. Yes, Pilate could have saved Jesus, but he was a politician. He wanted the people and Jesus to go away. He wanted peace, not justice. I wonder if he his work kept him up nights. We know his wife hadn't slept well the night before. Maybe Friday during the darkness she reminded her husband he should have listened to what she said. I'm told wives often do that. It's true, you and I don't always know what we're doing in life. Then God must do for us what we cannot do for ourselves.

When I was seventeen, I had an accident with my Dad's '53 Pontiac. I stayed out late one night and sideswiped an oncoming car. The other driver and I were unhurt, and the cars were damaged but we were still able to drive them. Because it was late, we took each other's information and drove home. I woke Dad up after midnight with fear and trembling and told him what had happened. "Are you okay?" he said. "Yes, but the car isn't," I replied. "We'll see to it in the morning. Go to bed." He said. No anger, no yelling, just a Dad who went back to sleep. The next morning looking at the car he said to me, "I was wondering when you'd do something like this. All the other boys did, and I figured you would, too." Dad didn't lecture me and I never paid for the repairs. *Looking back, I realize my father had expected me to have an accident, and in his mind was ready when the time came. He figured it would happen, so he already had a plan to deal with it.*

Our Heavenly Father has done the same. He has a plan of forgiveness worked out for us even before we sin. Romans 5:8 says, **"While we were still sinners, Christ died for us, the Godly for the ungodly."** That's God, His way of grace, love we don't deserve. God provides what we need, even before we need it. That's what makes His grace so amazing.

There are many to blame for Jesus' crucifixion. Because of sin, neither they nor us always know what we are doing. We all had a hand in Christ's crucifixion. We all share the blame and we all should be punished. *Like the kid who said to the old gunfighter after the shooting, "But he had it coming, didn't he?" And the old gunfighter said, "Kid, we all got it coming."* Yes, because of sin, we all have it coming. **"Father, forgive them, for they know not what they do."** Not everyone believes it, but it's still true.

These words also speak to the story of David and Absalom. King David was blessed by God so very greatly, but that didn't stop him from committing adultery with another man's wife. God had given him victory, money, fame, sons and daughters, adoring subjects, good friends and advisers. God even gave David musical and athletic abilities. David had it all, but still he wanted more. Psalm 51 which we spoke in worship earlier in the service was written by David after he was caught with Bathsheba. David asked for forgiveness, and God did forgive him. But the child he had fathered died, and his children began to rebel, especially Absalom, his favorite son. You see, sin does have its consequences.

We parents can't always understand what motivates our children to do the things they do. We know our children are all individuals. Some are compliant, others rebellious. Some use common sense, others take a long time to learn it. Some are easy to love, others require more effort. Some kids seem most gifted at giving their parents high blood pressure. Why did she do that? Why didn't he listen? Why did he marry her? **"Father, forgive them, for they know not what they do."**

If during this Lent you are unsure you need forgiveness, if you aren't sure you're really all that bad, then look at the cross! That's God's plan to forgive us. It doesn't matter whether we've killed someone, or taken another person's spouse, or stolen or rebelled against our parents. What's important is whether we know Jesus. Do we realize we need the cross? If so, pray personally His wonderful words: **"Father, forgive me, for I know not what I do."** And our Father will answer our prayer saying, *"Child, I already knew you'd sin, so I have forgiven you. My Son has taken your punishment."* May God strengthen us in the faith, and may we give Him thanks for all the second chances He gives us. Amen

LENT SERIES THREE
"Seven Last Words"
Week Two

"Today You Will Be Me In Paradise" (Luke 23:43)

Eternal God and Father of our Lord Jesus Christ, give us Your Holy Spirit who writes the preached Word into our hearts. May we receive and believe it and be cheered and comforted by it in eternity. Glorify Your Word in our hearts and make it so bright and warm that we may find pleasure in it, through Your Holy Spirit think what is right, and by Your power, fulfill the Word, for the sake of Jesus Christ, Your Son our Lord. Amen. (Luther's Prayer Before the Sermon)

As the Son of God hung from the cross on that terrible Friday we call "Good", He was given no respect. The religious rulers, grateful a troublemaker was finally getting duly punished, scoffed at Him and said, *"He saved others, so let's see Him save Himself, if He is really God!"* The soldiers who did the nailing mocked Him out of boredom, offering Him sour wine and shouting, *"Hey, Mr. King of the Jews, show us your stuff!"* Even one of the criminals hanging next to Him on another cross made fun of Him:, *"Aren't you some bigshot Savior? Then save yourself – and us, too!"*

Jesus wasn't hanging there alone on Calvary. The Roman Cohort, like all good soldiers, were efficient. Why crucify just one? Let's hang several. Any more scheduled to walk the "Green Mile?" They'd probably crucified a dozen before, so they could make it a party. You see, crucifixion detail was neither fun nor exciting. It was bloody, brutal and boring. Soldiers had to drag stinking, screaming prisoners to the cross. They had to tie them to the crossbars and lift them up on the posts with ropes. Worst of all, they had wait around until the criminals died. So let's do it fast and let the dice games begin! No court appeals, no time on death row, no activists, just swift and lethal action, and it probably led to many innocent deaths.

It's at this point we encounter the second word Jesus spoke from the cross, and it begins with that other criminal hanging beside Jesus, the humble one. No taunting from this guy, no hateful words, just a grasping for hope. **"Don't you fear God?"**

171

he said to the other scoffing criminal, **"We are under the same sentence of condemnation. We're getting what we deserve for our deeds; but this man has done nothing wrong."** Then without waiting for the other guy to respond, he said to Jesus, **"Remember me when you come into your kingdom."** And Jesus did remember him.

The Bible says, **"Cursed is every one who is hanged on a tree."** Besides execution, the purpose of crucifixion was to revile and mock the condemned person. The condemned were to be scorned and hated by man and God, so they should suffer wrath and punishment. But Jesus, the only truly innocent person ever executed, said to the humble thief, **"Today you will be with me in Paradise."**

For most of recorded history, those sentenced to capital punishment were the worst of criminals. The Bible says the other two being crucified that day were thieves. It may seem harsh to us since no state in our nation today would condemn someone to death just for stealing. But this isn't a time to debate capital punishment. We'll leave the debate to the wise people of this age.

These other two men had no future on earth. They'd stolen, maybe beaten or killed people in their theft, so they were as good as dead when caught. The Bible tells us in Jeremiah that evil deeds earn the wrath and punishment of God. Jeremiah 21:12 says, **"Execute justice in the morning, and deliver from the hand of the oppressor him who has been robbed, lest my wrath go forth like unquenchable because of your evil deeds."** And again Jeremiah says, **"I will bestow punishment on you for the evil you have done."**

But Romans 6:23 says it most plainly, **"The wages of sin is death."** Sin always brings consequences. No matter what we think, we cannot get by with the wrongs we do in life, because sin always catches up with us. We cannot outrun our sin. We can deny it really is sin, but that doesn't change the fact or remove the consequences. Modern people like to deny there are absolutes, that there is no such a thing as true right and wrong. But when you're dealing with God, denial never works. That is why we need continually to ask God's forgiveness and mercy.

Think of it: **"The wages of sin is death!"** That's harsh!

172

Does God need to go that far - death? That seems pretty extreme. Can't He just paddle us, smack us around a little when we do wrong, deprive us of some things, put us in some kind of "Time Out," or maybe grab us by the collar and shake us up so we'll straighten out? That used to work with a teacher or two I've had. But death? What's so bad about sin that deserves death? Doesn't God have some other choices?

In Romans 1:18, Paul wrote about the true nature sin. He said, **"The wrath of God is being revealed from heaven against all the godlessness and wickedness of people."** Then Paul lists what he means, and the list is ugly:

"Wickedness, evil, greed and depravity; envy, murder, strife, deceit, malice; gossips, slanderers, God-haters, insolent, and arrogant; disobedience, unfaithfulness, lovelessness, mercilessness, hatred, unrighteousness and covetousness." Then Paul gets to the really bad stuff! *"Perverse sexual lust, godlessness, idolatry, and hearts filled with darkness."* Romans 1 has the full list.

In 2 Samuel, our Old Testament lesson today, we hear about some of this. Incest: Amnon raped his half-sister. Murder: Absalom killed Amnon. Treachery: Absalom lied to his father. Rebellion: Absalom wins the people's loyalty away from his father, and the list goes on. But seeds of this family warfare started when father David seduced a woman who wasn't his wife. Most of the time David was a good king. His armies whipped everybody, he was handsome and a singer. Most everybody loved David, except Absalom his son. David had much and wanted more, so trouble came to his house. Moralist John Acton once said that power corrupts and absolute power corrupts absolutely. That happens today, too.

The man on the cross next to Jesus knew all about this. **"Don't you fear God,"** he said, **"since you are under the same sentence of condemnation?"** Sin pays a deathly wage that will come to all. Unless we trust in Jesus there is no way out. We can't explain our way out of what's ahead, unless Christ comes into the picture. The second thief learned this, as Jesus said to him, **"Today you will be with me in Paradise."**

All who trust in Jesus will have paradise. *Paradise* is our version of a French word derived from a Greek word, which has its root in a Persian word, which all pretty much mean the same

173

thing, a place where everything is wonderful and harmonious. I think we all have our definition of *Paradise*, and we'd all like to go there. Paradise the opposite of this world with all its trouble and woe. For Christians, Paradise is where we can all be at our life's end through Jesus. It's like getting back to the Garden of Eden, getting back the perfect relationship we lost, the condition with God where we're not afraid of Him or each other.

The repentant thief said, **"Lord, remember me when you come into your kingdom."** And Jesus said, **"Today you will be with me in Paradise."** As simple as that!

Back in the 1950's, songwriter and radio host Carl Hamblen was noted for his hard partying. One of his bigger hit songs at the time contained the line, "I won't go hunting with you, Jake, but I'll go chasing women." That fairly well summed up Hamblen's philosophy of life. One day a young preacher was holding a revival in the area. Hamblen invited him on his radio show to poke fun at him, but decided first to attend one of his revivals. Early in the meeting the preacher said, "There is one man in this audience who is a big fake!" Hamblen was convinced the preacher was talking about him and left. Late one night he showed up very drunk at the preacher's hotel, demanding he pray for him. He said, "This is between you and God, and I'm not going to get in the middle of it." But they did talk all night until finally Hamblen, the "Big Fake," accepted Jesus.

After that, he quit partying. As a result, he lost his party friends and was fired by the radio station for refusing to accept a beer company as a sponsor. He tried writing Christian songs but his only success was, "This Old House," made popular by his friend Rosemary Clooney. One day his friend John took Hamblen aside and said, "All your troubles started when you got religion. Don't you ever miss the booze, women and fun?" Hamblen answered, "No." John said, "How you could give all that up so easily?" Hamblen replied, "It's no big secret. All things are possible with God." John replied, "That's a catchy phrase. You should write a song about that." The rest is history. "It Is No Secret What God Can Do" became his biggest hit. That young preacher who led Hamblen to Christ? It was Billy Graham. His friend John eventually quit partying, too, and was baptized just before he died. But we'd expect that from John, John Wayne, a guy who always did things his own way.

174

As you and I journey through life, there will be days when death stares us in the face, days we wonder if we are worthy of life. *In the movie, "Saving Private Ryan", decades after the war is over, the older man Private Ryan kneels over the grave of one of the soldiers who died saving him in WWII. This officer had said as he died "Earn this!" That day Ryan tearfully asked his family, "Have I been a good man? Have I lived my life well?"*

We all wonder that, whether we're good enough, or if we have lived well enough. Friends, we're not good enough! We haven't lived well enough, but Jesus has. He took care of everything on the cross. That thief wasn't good enough, but Jesus was. **"Today you will be with me in Paradise."** Jesus earned him a place in paradise. He's earned us a place there, too. Thanks be to God! Amen.

LENT SERIES THREE
"Seven Last Words"
Week Three

"Woman, Behold Your Son! Behold, Your Mother!"
(John 19:26-27)

Eternal God and Father of our Lord Jesus Christ, give us Your Holy Spirit who writes the preached Word into our hearts. May we receive and believe it and be cheered and comforted by it in eternity. Glorify Your Word in our hearts and make it so bright and warm that we may find pleasure in it, through Your Holy Spirit think what is right, and by Your power, fulfill the Word, for the sake of Jesus Christ, Your Son our Lord. Amen. (Luther's Prayer Before the Sermon)

Think back to when Mary and Joseph brought the baby Jesus to the temple in Jerusalem. At that time old Simeon blessed them and then said something rather ominous to Mary: **"Behold, this child is appointed for the fall and rising of many in Israel, and for a sign that is opposed and a sword will pierce through your own soul also."** (Luke 2:34-35) Over the years Mary may have wondered what Simeon meant. But when she saw her son crucified on Calvary, when nails pierced His hands and feet and a sword pierced His side, she may have remembered those words. The crucifixion certainly pierced Mary's soul. What mother should have to bear seeing her Son die such a shameful death? What mother should need to see her child suffer needlessly, innocently? Parents have asked themselves that question for centuries when they have watched helplessly as their children died for any reason.

There were two other men crucified there that day. Were their mothers present? Did they come to Calvary to weep over their sons? Or did they stay away in shame and fear? Parents for centuries have seen sons and daughters do shameful things, and despite their best efforts, have had to bear the pain of regret and self-blame. They have felt the enormous sadness of knowing their children did what was wrong, despite their being taught otherwise, and now they were receiving their punishment.

Mary was not ashamed to be there that day. She knew her Son was innocent. Nothing He'd done deserved this. Surely she

177

felt love seeing that even dying innocently would not bring her son to curse His captors. But not everyone, including some who call themselves Christians, believe that her son Jesus of Nazareth lived His life without sin. Even non-Christians think Him a good man who died a criminal's death. History has always wondered at the great injustice done that day

As Mary stood near the cross, I wonder if she remembered visiting Elizabeth during her holy pregnancy. Did she recall telling her cousin what the angel had said? As she watched Him suffer, did she realize that the man dying there was not only the promised Messiah, but her own personal Messiah? As the lovely Christmas song asks, *"Mary Did You Know, this child that you delivered would soon deliver you?"* Or did she just feel the pain and sadness of a mother looking up at her dying son?

Whatever the case, Jesus looked down and saw His mother. He knew she felt emptiness in her loss, so He gave her the only thing He could to fill it – someone else to care for her. He said to her, **"Woman, behold, your son!"** Then he said to the young disciple John standing with her, **"Behold, your mother!"** We know John took her to his own home. History records John cared for her and together they eventually moved to Ephesus where John was a good son all her remaining days.

Jesus addresses her, **"Woman, behold your son!"** Woman? He calls His dear mother, woman? Seems pretty cold. Yet the tender heart of God is in these words. Mary is a woman. Some think she embodies the women of all time, and perhaps in some way she does. But right then, she was a woman in need, and Jesus did for her what a dying son could. He gave her into the care of his special friend and disciple.

Little could be done to assuage her anguish. He had loved His mother and she had loved her son, and separation was imminent. The Fourth Commandment tells us to **"Honor your father and your mother,"** and Jesus was doing that. His love was shown towards both His mother and her new son. He knew a sword was piercing her soul, that she was drinking the bitter cup of foretold by Holy Scriptures. But He was destined to die! For her sake and for all the world He needed to make the divine sacrifice for the sins of mankind.

Who better to entrust her to than the youngest of the

178

disciples, John. **"Behold your mother!"** eloquently transfers family care from the dying to the living. **"Behold, your mother!"** No list of duties, no suggestions, no details, just, **"Behold, your mother!"** John's mother was also there, and some say she was Mary's sister named Salome. That would make John Jesus' cousin, but we don't know this for sure. It wouldn't matter. Jesus gives Mary His mother into the care of John who was the only disciple there.

Family blood ties may be strong, but the ties of friendship can often be stronger. This is evident in the Old Testament story for today. Absalom had openly rebelled against his father David. Absalom had raised an army and plans were in place for him to take over. Father David, not wanting to fight his own son, decided to take his family and small army and run. In this lesson we also hear an interesting story about a man named that Ittai the Gittite. He showed that loyalty by a stranger can be greater than loyalty from a son. Ittai had joined David's army just the day before the retreat. David told him to go home, to save himself. Ittai said, no, he had pledged fidelity to the King and would keep his pledge. To keep one's promise is a mark of maturity. It would be good today for many world leaders to follow the example of Ittai the Gittite.

Jesus' suffering and death on Calvary show us the most important relationship, that blessed relationship of trust in our Heavenly Father through His Son. Jesus' action here with His mother point out the importance of the new family which all believers now have, the family of faith. In bringing Mary and John together for their mutual care, He shows us we are to be one new family, a loving family. In Christ, we are all mothers and sons and brothers and sisters to each other, a new family in the Holy Christian Church, all bound together with God as our Father.

This new family will not be without sin or conflict, but it will be a blessing to all who participate. Through the Church we educate the young, heal the sick, give aid to those in need, spread God's hope and love, comfort the afflicted, and afflict the comfortable. Through the Church we find new friends, some of whom remain with us for eternity. Through the Church we help people live here in hope and there in glory for eternity.

History records that John did care for Mary for at least a decade or two. As the Christian faith spread around, so also did persecution, so John took Mary to Ephesus in Asia Minor (modern Turkey) where tradition says they lived in a small house on a hill high above that prosperous city. Young John matured into a revered pillar of the early church and was present for the first Conference of Apostles in Jerusalem.

After Mary died, he remained in Ephesus for most of the rest of his life, teaching many others the Word of God. Among his students was Polycarp, Bishop of Smyrna, that Church Father and ancient man of God whose horrific martyrdom resulted in the conversion of hundreds who saw him die. John was the only one of the Twelve who died a natural death, in exile on the island called Patmos, having lived well into his 90s. All the other 11 disciples died a martyr's death. The future church grew in a land fertilized by the blood of the martyrs.

In giving Mary to John, Jesus has set an example for future generations. Christ cares for us eternally, and also temporally. Mary and John, those closest to the Lord, cared for each other. We now care for each other through Christian education, support of the needy, hospitals, care centers, disaster relief funds and the countless ministries of our churches. People of each generation share the Gospel with others.

We never know what good will come from our deeds of kindness. God can use the smallest kindness in the mightiest way. There was a poor Scottish farmer named Fleming. One day, while working his land, he heard a cry for help coming from a nearby peat bog. Running quickly he found a young boy mired in the bog, terrified and vainly struggling to free himself. Fleming saved the lad from a terrifying death in the muddy bog.

The next day a fine carriage came to the Fleming's humble home and a nobleman stepped out, introducing himself as the father of the boy Fleming had saved. "I want to repay you," he said, "for saving my son's life." But Fleming refused the offer, saying, "I cannot accept payment for what I did." Just then the farmer's oldest son came to the door of the family home. "Is this your son?: the nobleman asked. "Yes," the farmer replied proudly. "Then let me take him and give him a good education. If the lad is anything like his father, he'll grow to a man you can be proud of."

And that he did.Farmer Fleming's son graduated from St. Mary's Hospital Medical School in London, and went on to become Sir Alexander Fleming, scientist, doctor and winner of the Noble Prize for Medicine for his discovery of penicillin as a healing medicine. That same nobleman's son was later stricken with pneumonia. What saved him? Penicillin. The name of the man who was saved by penicillin? Sir Winston Churchill.

"Behold Your Son...Behold your mother." Wonderful words of Jesus! We who have been orphaned by sin have been called together into a new family, the church. Here we can care for one another and love each other with the love which has been given to us by Christ on the cross. May the church always be a strong refuge of healing and love. Amen.

LENT SERIES THREE
"Seven Last Words"
Week Four

"My God, my God, why have You forsaken me?"
(Mark 15:34)

Eternal God and Father of our Lord Jesus Christ, give us Your Holy Spirit who writes the preached Word into our hearts. May we receive and believe it and be cheered and comforted by it in eternity. Glorify Your Word in our hearts and make it so bright and warm that we may find pleasure in it, through Your Holy Spirit think what is right, and by Your power, fulfill the Word, for the sake of Jesus Christ, Your Son our Lord. Amen. (Luther's Prayer Before the Sermon)

The Bible tells us that on Good Friday at about the ninth hour, Jesus cried out loudly in His native tongue, **"Eli, Eli, lama sabachthani?" "My God, my God, why have you forsaken me?"** A man over-looking the wreckage of his home after it has been leveled by a tornado or earthquake looks heavenward and says, **"My God, why this now?"** A woman and her husband stand at the bedside of their 8-month old daughter who has just died, and cry, **"My God, how could this happen?"** A young man, walking out of the doctor's office, having just been diagnosed with a fatal disease, shakes his fist heavenward and rages, **"Why, God, why?"**

Remember Job in the Old Testament? He was a righteous, God fearing man who avoided evil. He had a fine family and a trusting relationship with God and used his wealth to serve God. Yet it was all taken from him – his wealth stolen, his children dead, and his health overtaken by a brutal disease. Job, who thought his relationship to God was good, asks, *"Why this? What have I done?"* All these echo the fourth Word of Jesus from the cross: **"My God, my God, why have you forsaken me?"**

Who here hasn't asked some form of this question, *"My God, why me? Why now? Why this?"* **"Why have you forsaken me?"** Who in our lifetimes hasn't felt God was a Holy all-powerful Being living far off and acting as if He doesn't care? He is the God way up there in heaven. Why can't He listen to us and answer our earnest prayers?

183

Think of those victims of the recent Japanese earthquakes and tsunamis, or the mud-slides in California, spring flooding in the midwest, or the hurricanes sure to come again this fall. Add to that American and Mexican drug problems, national insecurity, middle eastern countries on the edge of civil war, and our ever-increasing national debt. Then add your own sorrows or health issues, or family worries and it is almost impossible not to ask, **"My God, my God, why have you forsaken me?"**

In such times, it is easy to believe God has forsake us. Friends, neighbors, and even our own family live in fear and mistrust. How can a child trust in the heavenly Father when he cannot even trust his earthly father? How can a woman believe God won't forsake her when her husband of twenty years has forsaken her and her children?

So, like Job, we ask why. So did Jesus ask why. God doesn't answer our questions right away. Instead, He gets involved in answering them. His answer is simple: *"Trust me, I haven't forsake you."* It just seems so because life is hitting us hard, and disappointing or frightening us. He hasn't forsaken us. He sent His only Son to take upon Himself our sins, our pains, our hatred and fears, our misery and shame. That is why God's Son asks, **"Why have you forsaken me?"**

Ever wondered if God is real? Are we sure God is still up there? Have the events of life lately made you wonder if He even exists? A doctor was making a house call on a very sick man, and as he was preparing to leave, the man said, "Doctor, I am afraid to die. Tell me what lies on the other side." Very quietly, the doctor said, "I don't know for sure." "You don't know?" said the sick man, almost in shock. "You, a Christian man, do not know what is on the other side?" "Not exactly," the doctor said as he was holding the handle of the door. On the other side of the closed door came scratching and whining, and as he opened the door, a dog leaped eagerly into the room. Turning to the patient, the doctor said, "This is my dog. He's never been in this room before today. He didn't know what was inside, but he knew I was in here, and that was enough. When the door opened, he ran to me without fear. I do not know exactly what is on the other side of this life, but I know my Master is there and waiting for me, and that is good enough."

All of us have wondered what is on the other side of this life. We can't accurately describe heaven, but we still want to go there. As believers, we have the advantage of not fearing what's on the other side. Few of us want to die, but when we do, we know God will be there, and life with Him will be very good, far better than now. Just knowing that the Master is there on the other side is good enough.

"My God, my God, why have you forsaken me?" Jesus was quoting Psalm 22:1 in the midst of His pain. God's Word often comes to us in time of trouble. That's why we try to learn them, to memorize some of them so that we have them with us when we need them. God isn't just an observer of creation. He steps into creation by taking human form, because being human can be a difficult, even cruel, experience.

In tonight's Old Testament Lesson, King David saw human cruelty. As his family is retreating from Absalom's army, someone from his long ago past gets into the act. Shimei, from the house of Saul, curses David and throws stones at him. Even past King Saul's family was persecuting him. Our past sin has consequences. Just when things can't get any worse, they do. Voices of our unrepented past cruelly remind us we need God's forgiveness earned by Christ on the cross.

His soldiers wanted to kill Shimei, but David stops them. He sees Shimei as a messenger from God, reminding him of his need for God. David wrote those words of Psalm 22, and he already knows why. Tonight as you hear our Lord's loneliness and pain in these words, hear also His promise, **"I will never leave you nor forsake you."** (1 Peter 3:15)

We may feel forsaken, but we are not. God Himself says so. Why has God forsake us? He hasn't. He is still with us, on the other side of the door. We, His beloved, are never forsaken like Jesus was.

After World War One, Robert Watson-Watt invented a process called Radio Detection and Ranging, which was reduced to the word "Radar." Radar sends out electromagnetic waves that reflect off a target and are transmitted back to a receiver, accurately showing location, size and even speed of the target. Radar can see where humans cannot. If we have ever traveled by airplane, we probably didn't realize that our plane was being guided by radar. It gives a pilot

185

the ability to fly no matter what the sight conditions, day or night, in clear weather, fog or storm. In the densest of clouds that would keep a pilot from seeing anything, radar shows what is ahead and all around. Radar penetrates clouds and fog and shows the pilot what is out there.

Faith in Jesus Christ is the radar that guides us through the clouds of our life. If we look only with our eyes, we will miss seeing God. The victory of Christ on the cross can be seen only with faith. Faith in Jesus looks through the clouds and perceives what is real. Our eyes, ears and all our senses are limited to time and space, but faith in Christ punches through all our fears and troubles and points us to God. Faith's holy radar looks past our trouble and heartache so that we can see Jesus and know He is with us, and will guide us through the storm.

Human wisdom alone is usually a poor guide. Human pride and vanity blind us to trust only in ourselves. When you fly, know that your pilot is being guided by radar. When you face troubles, let yourself be guided by Jesus Christ.

There will be times when we all will ask, **"Why have you forsaken me?"** Remember that Jesus asked that question first. One day we will all hear the Father in heaven saying, **"Never did I leave you, never did I forsake you."** I gave you my only begotten Son that you might be with me in eternal joy, forever, Amen.

LENT SERIES THREE
"Seven Last Words"
Week Five

"I Thirst!" (John 19:28)

✠ ✠ ✠

Eternal God and Father of our Lord Jesus Christ, give us Your Holy Spirit who writes the preached Word into our hearts. May we receive and believe it and be cheered and comforted by it in eternity. Glorify Your Word in our hearts and make it so bright and warm that we may find pleasure in it, through Your Holy Spirit think what is right, and by Your power, fulfill the Word, for the sake of Jesus Christ, Your Son our Lord. Amen. (Luther's Prayer Before the Sermon)

As Jesus hung from the cross, He uttered two very human words, **"I thirst."** Dying can be a thirsty business, especially dying on a cross. When you have been deprived of sleep, beaten with fists, whipped with the deadly scourge, tortured with thorns and finally had nails pounded through your flesh, you will get thirsty. I wonder how the soldiers could do this? Did they get thirsty doing what they did? How did the crowd feel after watching a few hours? Did they sit down? Did anyone send out for lunch? Did a person bring his own lunch to a crucifixion in those days? Besides family and the soldiers, what kind of a person could stand and watch something like that?

The night before in the Garden of Gethsemane Jesus wanted His disciples to watch with Him, but they fell asleep. *One night years ago some dear friends from a former church had come to visit us. We missed them so, and were glad they had come, but the next day they were leaving. I had planned to talk to them a lot that night, but I fell asleep. I felt such sadness the next morning as they drove away because I had wanted to tell them how much they meant to me. But we didn't talk because I fell asleep.*

Another time we were invited to a "Going Away" party, and in the middle of that party held in my honor, I sat down in a rocking chair by the fireplace. And right there among my guests, I fell asleep. The night my newborn son came home from the hospital, I sat with him so proud a father to hold my baby son. And I fell asleep. When I woke up my wife had taken little Charles to the cradle I had made for him. Last Sunday afternoon little Charles, now 37 years old and father

187

of three small children, came to visit us. And as we were playing with the children after lunch, he fell asleep.

But Jesus didn't sleep. He was awake every miserable moment from His bloody prayer in the Garden on Thursday until Friday afternoon and that moment when He was dying of thirst. No, Jesus didn't fall asleep, at least not until He slept in death. No amount of water could slake His thirst but weariness from bearing the weight of the world's sin was more than He could take.

Do you recall what Isaiah the prophet foretold of the Savior? Here is what Isaiah 53 tells us from the Contemporary English Version: **"He was hated and rejected; his life was filled with sorrow and terrible suffering. No one wanted to look at him. We despised him and said, 'He is nobody!' He suffered and endured great pain for us, but we thought his suffering was from God. He was wounded and crushed because of our sins. By taking our punishment, he made us completely well. All of us were like sheep that had wandered off. We had each gone our own way, but the Lord gave him all the punishment we deserved."** (Isaiah 53:3-6)

All that despising and wounding and crushing and punishing cost Jesus a lot of blood. The Old Testament required that blood be shed in order for people to be forgiven. Whether it was blood on the altar during an animal sacrifice, or blood sprinkled on the people after the sacrifice, or whether it was Jesus Himself saying, **"Take drink, this is my blood of the covenant, which is poured out for many for the forgiveness of sins"** (Matthew 26:28). Jesus shed His blood on the cross, that we might have forgiveness, a second chance in life with God.

Everyone gets thirsty, especially here in the desert. Sometimes I need to take a drink of water during my preaching. I never thought I'd have to do that during a church service. But when you're dry, you need to slake your thirst. Jesus' thirst came from the pain and anguish of bearing our sins. When He said, **"I thirst,"** the soldiers raised a stick with a sponge on it and give Him sour wine mixed with gall, a pain reliever. They did this more to quiet Him than to help Him, and it didn't help Him much. **"I thirst"** meant His thirst was simply too great.

Jesus wasn't playing a role, He was human being and He

was really dying. He needed to be human to be one of us and endure all the temptation that comes to us. To fulfill the holy Law of God for us, Jesus lived under that Law, and then did what no one else would ever do. He kept that Law, all Ten Commandments, perfectly without committing a single sin. He did this as our substitute. Jesus placed Himself under the demands of the Law so that His perfect life could be applied to us by God the Father. He did all this for each one of us.

At any time, Jesus could have walked away. He could have called down legions of angels to free Himself and stop the whole bloody mess. You almost wish He would have, just to get even, but He didn't. Instead, as Isaiah continues, **"He was painfully abused, but he did not complain. He was silent like a lamb being led to the butcher, as quiet as a sheep having its wool cut off. He was condemned to death without a fair trial... His life was taken away because of the sinful things people had done, and he was buried in a tomb of cruel and rich people."** (Isaiah 53:7-10) Isaiah wrote this 500 years before Jesus.

A thousand years before Jesus, our Old Testament lesson tells us King David had stopped running and started fighting. The Bible says he organized his army because the time for running and being abused was over. David the warrior turned to face his enemy, his son Absalom. And Absalom's mighty army turned and ran, leaving their leader hanging from his long hair in a tree. It all happened so quickly. King David had first run like a coward, then suddenly turned and fought. The rebel Absalom had a big army, but they abandoned him. Absalom didn't even have a chance to fight. God used his vanity against him and tangled him in a tree branch. We will hear next week what finally happened in this dramatic story. Meanwhile, we wait at the foot of the cross, hearing our thirsty and dying Lord.

An anxious old man came to the information desk asking about a young patient to whom he was related. A nurse escorted the man to the bedside of the young man. "Your father is here," she whispered to the patient who was bandaged and heavily sedated from a terrible auto accident. He reached out and squeezed the older man's hand. The nurse brought in a chair and all through the night the old man sat holding the young man's hand, whispering gentle words of hope, and maybe a prayer. The dying man held tightly to the old man's hand.

As dawn approached, the young man died. The old man wept as he placed the lifeless hand back on the bed, and went to call the nurse. She did what was necessary and offered her sympathy to the old man, but he interrupted her. "Who was he?" the old man asked. Startled, the nurse replied, "I thought he was your son." "No, he wasn't my son. I've never seen him before. I was looking for someone else and you brought me into this room." "Why didn't you say something when you realized the mistake?" the nurse asked. The man replied, "I was here maybe ten minutes before I realized this wasn't the young man I was looking for. But he was so badly injured and so sick, so I just stayed. I think he needed a father by his side."

And, friends, so do we. We all need a father by our side, someone who cares. Our most basic need is to be loved and approved of, to be valued and cared for. We can tolerate a mountain of pain if we know someone is beside us who cares. Our Heavenly Father cares. He is by our side, and will never leave us nor forsake us. He holds our hand when we're sick and quiets our heart when we're troubled. He whispers to us through the voices of those we love. He even asks us to be His hands to hold the hands of others, and His voice to softly tell others of His love.

Jesus was true man and suffered as we suffer. He knows what it's like for us. That's why He promises to be with us always, to the very end of the world and even beyond. Jesus is not merely an Unknown God, or a Prime Mover, or First Cause or Divine Spark or any of the humanistic terms we come up with. He is God's Son! Jesus is the son of Mary, but He is also Son of the eternal God, who died on a cross to forgive all who trust Him and what He has done.

Jesus thirsted, so He knows our thirst. He was forsaken by the Father, just as we have felt. We may thirst after the wrong things in life, but Jesus quenches our thirst with what is right and good. He poured Himself out as an offering to God for us, then gave us Himself in the Lord's Supper. May we hunger and thirst after righteousness and then have our thirst quenched by the One who promises us rivers of living water. Amen

LENT SERIES THREE
"Seven Last Words"
Week Six

"It Is Finished!" "Father, Into Your Hands I Commit My Spirit!" (John 19:30, Luke 23:46)

> *Eternal God and Father of our Lord Jesus Christ, give us Your Holy Spirit who writes the preached Word into our hearts. May we receive and believe it and be cheered and comforted by it in eternity. Glorify Your Word in our hearts and make it so bright and warm that we may find pleasure in it, through Your Holy Spirit think what is right, and by Your power, fulfill the Word, for the sake of Jesus Christ, Your Son our Lord. Amen.* (Luther's Prayer Before the Sermon)

Today we consider the last two words of Christ from the cross. We must do two because the numbers don't match – Seven Words of Christ in six weeks of Lent. But most of us have probably considered these two words together as one. John's Gospel records Jesus as saying, **"It is finished!"** And St. Luke records that Jesus said with a loud voice, almost a shout, **"Father, into your hands I commit my spirit!"** Then He dies.

It's surprising Jesus still had enough strength left to shout. A dying person can rarely be heard uttering last words. As death approaches, the body gets weaker and strength to speak any word is lost. Still, Jesus has enough strength to say loudly, **"Father, into your hands I commit my spirit!"** It's almost as if He wanted to make sure those all around, including His father, would hear him.

This is why Jesus came. His entire purpose was to die, to give His life for us, to be our substitute, to forgive us. Jesus once told His chief critics, the Pharisees, **"For this reason the Father loves me, because I lay down my life that I may take it up again. No one takes it from me, but I lay it down of my own accord."** (John 10:17-18) If they thought they could stop Him, they were wrong. He is in charge of His life, not the church leaders or the Romans.

These words of Jesus from the cross have important meaning for you and me and every Christian. They also have eternal meaning to all who are not Christian, for without faith in the One who spoke these words, there is only hell and the torment of separation from God awaiting us.

"It is finished," He says. "Father, into your hands I commit my spirit!" Jesus has fulfilled the Scriptures. He did all that was foretold of Messiah. In Peter's first sermon on Pentecost, he said, "What God foretold by the mouth of all the prophets, that his Christ would suffer, he has thus fulfilled." (Acts 3:18)

Jesus, knew that He had accomplished all that the Father required of Him. He was born of human flesh to be a man. He was born at a specific time in history, not some legendary date. He endured all that was required to make satisfaction for your sin, for my sin, and for the sins of the whole world.

Jesus knew what was coming, long before it happened. He went to Jerusalem knowing they would get Him. He knew the steps He'd have to take to get it done. When He says, "It is finished," He's saying it has all been done. He had fulfilled all the requirements and suffered all the punishment. He had done everything so that all those who trust in Him might be saved. No one needs to suffer in payment for sins with God. We may suffer for the sins we commit, for sin has its consequences. But no one need suffer to satisfy God any more. Jesus has done that. It really **IS** finished.

Ken Follett's epic novel, Pillars of the Earth, is about the struggles to build a cathedral during the Middle Ages. Without modern machinery, everything must be done by hand, every stone quarried, hauled, cut, measured, shaped, lifted and set in place by human hands or crude machinery. Without (sometimes even with) the protection of God or Church, king or nobleman, the builder is opposed by someone who doesn't want the job done. So the cathedral is started then burned, rebuilt then smashed, rebuilt and destroyed, and then rebuilt again. The book's cathedral takes fifty years to build. History tells us some European cathedrals took five hundred years to complete, and in the process they often impoverished the people with conflict and constant financial demands.

When Jesus said, "It is finished!" His work was done, over. His years on earth, His ministry among the people, His establishing the New Kingdom, His keeping the Holy Law, His atoning for the sins of the world, all these monumental things were over. **"It is finished!"** meant achievement not defeat, completion not quitting.

A mother who has raised a large family, a man who has finally paid off his house, a doctor who has studied medicine at the university for ten or twelve years, a middle aged woman who is finally getting married, or a man who finally retires after working fifty years, all these know the meaning, **"It is finished!"** Yet not all is finished. A parent's task is not over, the house needs maintenance, the doctor needs patients, the marriage needs work and the retirement is just beginning.

"It is finished!" may mean more to come, but with Jesus His task truly was done. **"It is finished!"** for Jesus means nothing else is needed for salvation. No human effort, no sacrifice, no obedience, no act of mercy can add to what Jesus has already done. We cannot make His perfection more complete. Our faith will benefit us, but it won't change what Jesus did. He endured the cross victoriously, and in three days, the world would know it. He finished the task, and all people for eternity would be the beneficiaries. **"It is finished!"**

In this season of Lent, we have considered the last words in the Good Friday drama which Jesus spoke from the cross. At the start Jesus said, **"Father forgive them."** Then He gave His mother into the keeping of another disciple, then He assured the condemned but humble thief that he also had a place in paradise. Then Jesus cried out words of the desolation of being abandoned by God, and the He spoke the thirst of a dying man. Finally He said, **"It is finished"** and cries out, **"Father, into your hands I commit my spirit!"** It was over.

Our Old Testament drama also concludes today. When Absalom ran away and caught his hair in a tree, his days were over also. Joab the General found the young man and did what King David couldn't do, he killed the rebel son. He knew His Father's mercy would spare the son, so he took matters into his own hands and killed the rebel. David's words of great sadness have resounded through the ages, **"Oh Absalom, my son, my son! If only I could have died for you, Oh Absalom, my son, my son."** Such heart rending words to say!

Jesus did what no one else could do – He gave up His life, hanging on the tree of the cross. He cried out and He died, of

His own will, His own decision. He died for us rebellious Absaloms and proud Davids. He died for the Joabs who take matters into their own hands, and the weak Bathshebas who can't resist temptation. In this one act, Jesus Christ died for us, and the Heavenly Father would have wanted it no other way.

Dr. Joe Morgan had been stationed at Pearl Harbor. At 7:55 am on December 7, 1941, he heard planes overhead as the bombing began. This nineteen year-old Texan, who had joined the Navy to "see the world," was confused as machine gun bullets rained down. As he watched his fellow sailors fall, hit and bleeding around him, his confusion turned to a fear and then to hatred as he saw the symbol of the rising sun pass overhead on plane after plane. His first tried to hide, but seeing the other men around him scramble for weapons, he settled into a machine gun nest and managed to shoot down several Japanese planes.

Although Joe was a Christian, he found himself hating a nation and its people that in the end, killed 2,403 Americans, including 68 civilians. Joe promised God that if he survived that war, he would become a preacher. And although he kept his word to God, he never quite got over his hatred towards the Japanese. In 1954, Joe became a pastor in Maui. Two years later, he heard that Mitsuo Fuchida, commander of the Japanese naval air forces that attacked on Pearl Harbor, was coming to Maui, so Joe went to hear him. He listened with awe as Fuchida told of his becoming a Christian. After Fuchida's talk ended, Joe went up and introduced himself to this man who had changed his life. Mitsuo Fuchida immediately bowed to him and said one word in Japanese. "Gomenasai." "I am sorry." What happened next was as an important moment as any other in history. Joe Morgan said, "I forgive you," and felt all the anger toward the man and his country leave. God had replaced anger with the peace of forgiveness. Morgan and Fuchida, former enemies, were now brothers in Christ.

Forgiveness is a gift you give. It does not need the other person's contrition or sorrow, just your willingness to let go of what has hurt you. God gave us the gift of His forgiveness, even when He knew most people would reject His gift. We, too, can do no less than forgive others who have failed us. Forgiveness is good for the soul, and it helps our peace of mind as well.

You and I are all brothers and sisters in Christ, and so, in these words, knowing that He is making atonement for your sins, Jesus is committing you as well, into His Father's hands. **"Father, into Your hands I commit my spirit."** Having said this Jesus breathed His last. You and I know the rest of the story. It will be continued on Easter Sunday. But the work of salvation by Jesus Christ on the cross is finished, committed to the Father's hands. Trusting in His mercy, you and I will live, even as Christ lives. Christ's faith in the Father was not in vain, nor is yours. As Christ was raised, by the glory of the Father, so also you and I will live a new life, confident that you will share in His resurrection.

In baptism, we are united to Christ. By hearing of the Word of Christ, we are strengthened in faith and enabled to forgive. Christ's Last Words from the Cross show us His love, His power and His mercy. **"It is Finished!"** **"Father, into your hands I commit my spirit!"** Thus we have a future with Him in His kingdom, both here and hereafter in heaven. Amen.

LENT SERIES FOUR
"Miracles of Good Friday"
Week One

Matthew 27:45-46   "Miracle of Darkness"
"Now from the sixth hour there was darkness over all the land until the ninth hour. And about the ninth hour Jesus cried out with a loud voice, saying, "Eli, Eli, lema sabachthani?" that is, "My God, my God, why have you forsaken me?"

This year's Lent theme is "The Miracles of Lent." We'll examine some amazing events that happened Good Friday, and see how they apply to all of life, not just Lent or Holy Week. Today, Ash Wednesday, we consider "The Miracle of Darkness" which occurred on Good Friday during those three hours in the afternoon before Jesus died.

I never knew what real darkness was until one October night in North Dakota. I had scheduled a German Reformation service and my church was filled. Lutherans, Baptists, Methodists, Catholics and even some Adventists all came because they wanted to sing German hymns and see if that new preacher really could speak German. The first part of the service went well, as we prayed and heard the lessons "auf Deutsch." During the sermon hymn, I stepped into my front office, and when I opened the door to return all the lights went out! Every one of them! It had been a cloudy, moonless night and it was dark!

For a few moments all was silent. Then my organist asked quietly, "What happened?" A flashlight came on, and another and then a lighter. "We are in blackout." said someone. "The whole town has no lights." I told the people to remain calm and we'd think of something. Then I remembered the box of Christmas Eve candles in the office. I asked for a flashlight, we passed out the candles, and I went into the pulpit to preach my German sermon with a flashlight. Halfway through, the lights came back on. A snowmobile had struck a support wire on a light pole, knocking out the transformer. Half the town was in blackness, but now the lights were back on.

People are afraid of the dark. It doesn't matter where we live or what period of history, we all seem to be "hard-wired" to fear total darkness. It's because we fear what we can't see. Light is good, but darkness is bad. Why? Because we feel helpless in the dark and completely defenseless. We can't see anyone or anything. Darkness takes away our sense of control and douses us with fear of the unknown.

Tonight, as we begin the penitential season of Lent, it's still fairly light outside, and yet knowing it's Lent, there is a sense of darkness and solemnity that wasn't here before. Maybe it's the dark stain of the ashes on our foreheads. Or may be the black color of the altar paraments. The Gospel reading adds to it. It's night time on the Mount Olives and Jesus is talking about them denying Him and running away. Jesus prays for them like there's no tomorrow. Then soldiers come to arrest Jesus and the disciples do run away. Everything takes place in the dark, with only a few torchlights, or maybe moonlight. They didn't have street lights back then. Lent is quick to bring us a sense of darkness.

Yet we've gathered to hear about the "Miracle of Darkness." Maybe "miracle" isn't the right word. "Miracle" doesn't cause me to be scared, or to look nervously over my shoulder or pull the covers up a little higher. "Gloom" is a more accurate word. "Miracle" seems like a good word. "Miracle" is something to anticipate, not something to fear.

So, will it be the "Miracle of Darkness", or the "Gloom of Darkness?" Most Christians consider those three hours of darkness a sign of God's wrath and anger over our sins. And God is angry about the sins laid on His Son. Darkness shows Jesus was truly forsaken. Good Friday is Jesus forsaken by His Father. There's just something about calling darkness a "miracle" that's not quite right.

We will see many "miracles" in the coming weeks, so let's look at what we mean by the word. In the Greek New Testament, miracle is "thauma" which is a wonderful, miraculous event, a "sign" from God. We hear of this at Jesus' birth when the angels told the shepherds, **"This shall be a sign (thauma) for you. You will find the baby wrapped in clothes and lying in a manger."** The word used is "miracle," It could have been translated, "This shall be a miracle for you."

Jesus' first miracle was at the wedding of Cana when He

turned water into wine. The Bible says, **"This, the first of His "signs" (miracles), Jesus did at Cana in Galilee, and showed His glory, and His disciples believed in Him."** (John 2:11) Did you catch that? A sign—a miracle—that's how God shows Himself to the world and mankind, demonstrating that He is God living on earth.

Jesus came to earth in a real and tangible way. I've never seen human birth, but I'm told it's about as real – and gory – a thing as you can see. Jesus was born human, truly one of us, and He did something miraculous about our sinful state. In miracles, God is breaking out of being separate from us and breaking into our history. Jesus is God being part of our lives.

That's important to remember, God being part of our lives. People often look at the miracles in Scripture as heavenly entertainment. Things would get dull in His ministry, so Jesus healed someone, or raised someone. But "miracle" is not pulling a rabbit out of a hat. A miracle is a powerful sign to get our attention and wake us up to God's mighty power, here on earth, in our midst, and for our eternal benefit. The miracle of darkness is the sign that God is among us.

My wife and I once visited a new cave in Southeastern Minnesota. The young guide took us far inside as we walked along a lighted path. Then he asked us to stop where we were while he turned out the lights. I've never been in darkness like that. An unlighted cave is as dark as it gets. The young guy joked about the cave collapsing on us, but no one laughed. Being underground in total darkness is no laughing matter.

Life can be like that cave. We're going along okay when suddenly the lights go out. Someone we love dies, or we lose our money, or we get into trouble with the law, or the tests come back "cancer." The evils of the world have a way of taking us underground and scaring the life out of us. If we don't understand how evil can turn the lights out, we haven't been watching the news. There are people all over out there who think they have a perfect right to put all Christians to death. I don't know the whole solution, but it's more than our elected leaders are doing for us right now.

Jesus hung on the cross during those three hours of darkness on Calvary. In that darkness He paid the price for every sin we've committed and every sin our enemies have committed. The miracle of Christ in the darkness is the fact that God had truly forsaken His own Son, so that we might not perish, but live with Him. God forsook Jesus so that He didn't need to forsake us. No matter how bad our life has been, God has never forsaken us. It doesn't matter how rotten or vile or mean or crude or nasty a person we may be now or has been in the past, Jesus can still forgive us when we repent. As long as we have a sky over head and air in our lungs, we have a chance to repent and be forgiven, to turn back to Him in faith and trust Him to forgive us.

Jesus paid the price — in full — for us. He was our complete substitute. **"It is finished!"** (John 19:30) means the wages of our sin is paid in full. The debt has been satisfied with the blood of the Lamb of God. I do not fully understand how God has that worked out, but I'm glad He does. I don't have to know how electricity works, I'm glad it does. God knows what He's doing and that's enough for me.

"Paid In Full." Now there's something that sounds good. This summer I am going to enjoy something I've not for a long time. After thirty years, we're going to make our last mortgage payment. Our house loan will be "Paid In Full." I used to think my Dad took too long to pay off his farm, but it has taken me just as long to pay off my little house. But a paid-off mortgage with the bank is small potatoes next to a paid-off life with God. When we hear that our lives are "Paid In full," it won't be from any payments we've made. It will happen because Jesus paid the price for us. Calvary means "Paid In Full" by God's love.

I want you to think for a moment about the dark smudges of ash on our foreheads. It's not just some random dark blot or smudge. It symbolizes our sins, and it reminds us of the cross. That smudge of darkness on our foreheads shows that the miraculous is still with us tonight. The ashes remind us of our unworthiness. We are not "little gods." People are not a chip off the divine block. We are not in control of everything, though we'd like to think we are. That fear of the dark, of not being in control, ought to prove there's the darkness of sin within us. That's why we see those dark, ashy crosses of foreheads tonight.

We've all sinned and fallen short of the glory of God. We all deserve nothing but darkness and separation. But praise God that Jesus bridged the gap. His cross on Calvary is evidence our sins have been paid in full. The darkness of sin no longer separates from God. With faith in Jesus, we are united to the Father, and that's Good News! That's Gospel in it's simplest form. Praise God for the miracle of darkness that has shown us Jesus, the Light for the world. Amen

LENT SERIES FOUR
"Miracles of Good Friday"
Week Two

Matthew 27:51   "Miracle of the Torn Curtain"
At that moment the curtain of the temple was torn in two from top to bottom. The earth shook and the rocks split.

✚ ✚ ✚

One of the things my wife and I have in common is that if we find something we like, we hang onto it. She's always been like this, and I've become more this way in recent years. Both of us completely wear out some things such as favorite clothing. I've had pairs of shoes for over 20 years. I have a few "holey" T-shirts that some day are going to disintegrate in the wash machine. Last week Carol showed me one of her shirts where the elbow had worn through. Yes, we can afford to buy clothes, and we do shop. We just keep some old things around a bit too long. "Ashes to ashes, dust to dust," as we said last week.

But then, I did get rid of a black clerical shirt nearly 20 years old, worn so thin I could almost read a newspaper through it. Remember how I said the word for "miracle" also meant "sign"? When an armpit finally tore, I knew it was a sign from God, so I retired. I did get a new one, but it's already 8 years old. I got another one case that one tore.

Tonight in our series, "The Miracles of Lent," we will consider the "Miracle of the Torn Temple Curtain." Did it really happen? Why did it happen and what did it mean? Of all the Miracles of Lent we shall consider during Lent, this one puzzles me the most.

And yet, after knowing what happens to old clothes, maybe we could say, "Maybe it was time they got rid of that old curtain!" Temple worship was still good, but some of the customs surrounding it were old. For centuries the Jews had centered their worship around how God rescued them from Egypt by the Angel of Death in the Passover. The curtain was put in the Temple to keep ordinary people from being with God. That was the job of the High Priest. Once a year he moved the curtain aside and went in the Holy of Holies and prayed and burned incense. Otherwise that curtain just hung there getting old.

But I don't believe the temple curtain tearing at the moment of Jesus' death was just a coincidence. I've never heard anything about it in old Jewish stories. Maybe the curtain tore because it started swaying during the earthquake. Maybe it tore because it was old and sagging and decayed. Like an old shirt, maybe there was too much stress for its frail fibers to handle and it surrendered itself to its age. Then again, maybe the torn temple curtain tearing was more. It was probably a miracle, a "sign" from God, meant to get people's attention and give them a message from God.

I believe the "sign," the message from God, was to say it was time to put the Old Covenant out and bring the New Covenant in. Like getting rid of the old hymnal, or bringing new chairs or a contemporary worship service. That curtain had been put up a couple of hundred years before, and the priestly duties of worship were there long before that. Until the death of Jesus, only the priest could come to God in worship. After Jesus's death, the curtain is torn down and anyone can go in.

Matthew, Mark and Luke, all mention the torn temple curtain. Matthew connects it with the earthquake: **"At that moment the curtain of the temple was torn in two from top to bottom. The earth shook and the rocks split."** Luke adds that it happened after the sun shopped shining (Luke 23:45). Mark says it with the fewest words, **"The curtain of the temple was torn in two."** (Mark 15:38) All three said the curtain was torn in half. I remember my Confirmation pastor telling us, that curtain was fifty feet high and a couple of inches thick, so it would have weighed a couple of hundred pounds. The old, worn out way of temple worship finally ripped in half under its own weight.

It really was a miracle. Remember the two meaning for the Greek word, "thauma" - "miracle," and "sign"? The torn curtain was a miracle and also a sign from God. It was a mighty display, a demonstration of God's power to change things. It wasn't just time for new curtain, it was time for NO curtain. It was time to get rid of whatever separated people from God. It was time for Jesus to be the new bridge or pathway to God.

That curtain had a special purpose. In front of it was the

Holy Place where God's people could come to worship Him. Behind the curtain was the Holy of Holies, something like the throne room. God had told His people back in the wilderness that the day would come when they should construct a temple to His exact specifications. It included a large, heavy curtain hung to separate the Holy of Holies from the Holy Place. God kept that separation because it's what His people needed then. It sounds strange to us today, but God needed to veil Himself from the people for their own good. "No one can see God and live." Moses said. Only the High Priest could enter into that holy throne room and be with Almighty God. Everyone else would have faced sure and certain death.

But all that changed with Jesus. His death finished all the sacrifices. That is what God was telling the people with the torn curtain. Jesus is now our great High Priest, and through Him we now boldly and confidently can approach our God and Father. Because of the priestly sacrifice of the spotless Lamb of God, we're now brothers and sisters in Christ. We even become priests as well, in something the church calls the "priesthood of all believers."

What did the OT priests do? They sacrificed. They interceded with God. They prayed and gave the people God's messages. My fellow priests, we can do the same. We can sacrifice of time, talents and treasures. We can intercede for others in prayer. We, too, can tell others what Jesus means to us. Our best sacrifice is being thankful. That's what we, NT priesthood of all believers, can do. Give Him thanks! Show Him we're grateful.

That's how we serve. We build churches, or we repair homes for Habitat for Humanity, or we give food to the hungry, or clothes to the poor. We come to the altar of thanksgiving in the house of God, and offer Him our sacrifice of praise and thanksgiving for what Jesus did. At the altar God feeds and nourishes us with His precious Body and Blood. In Communion we receive the Lamb of God Himself. He gives us His holy gifts and, in response, we give Him our humble sacrifices of thanksgiving.

Unfortunately this isn't easy to believe. Our sinful heart has a real problem with this. By nature we want to do something to earn it. We want to do our part. Surely there must be something that we need to do on our end in order to help get ourselves to heaven. There must do something to make up for our sins. But no - it's all been done for us in Jesus.

When Jesus said, **"It is finished!"** God finished it, and then He tore down the curtain. It was His miracle, His sign. In the torn curtain God gave us real and tangible proof that Jesus' had done it all. It is all finished, then, now, and forever!

The very fact that we all can see the altar right now shows that Christ's sacrifice did it all. The barrier that separated us from God was torn apart and cast aside for all times when Christ died. The death and resurrection of Jesus forgives all our sins.

May God grant us the faith to believe and trust in our Lord Jesus. And may we continue in that faith all our days, no matter how many or how few we have left. Amen.

LENT SERIES FOUR
"Miracles of Good Friday"
Week Three

Matthew 27:51   "The Miracle of Earthquakes"
"At that moment the curtain of the temple was torn in Two from top to bottom. The earth shook, the rocks split."

✠   ✠   ✠

Did you feel the earth quake last Saturday about noon? It happened when I hit a drive about 350 yards almost onto the green. Of course I had a huge tailwind and it ran up to the green on hard clay. Another one happened when my team came in last – 32nd out of 32! For that we won a golf lesson! We continue our Lent series on the "Miracles of Lent" and tonight we consider "The Miracle of Earthquakes."

I will never forget my first earthquake. I was going to pick up a man who had just finished his sentence in a California prison and was going home to his family for the first time in ten years. He could leave the halfway house at midnight and his wife had asked me to pick him up since her car wouldn't start. At midnight just as I was getting into my car, my driveway and garage floor rolled under my feet. I almost decided not to go, but I did. The voice on the radio said, "Yep, folks, that was a little roller, a 3.1, just north of Riverside." A few years ago I noticed our mini-blinds quivering in Palm Creek, and discovered it was due to a 3.3 rumbler in Yuma.

There is a website called usgs.gov that's connected with the US Geological Offices in Boulder, Colorado. Every moment of every day it shows every earthquake on earth, within seconds after it happens, where it happened, how big it was, and how deep in the earth. Most earthquakes happen around the "Rim of Fire" in the edges of the Pacific Ocean that include North and South America on the east, Russia, China and Japan on the west, and Hawaii right in the center. Many earthquakes happen also in the Middle East, Afghanistan and eastern Europe. You might be surprised to know of the number of earthquakes that happen inside the United States in Nevada, Oklahoma, Kansas and even Missouri. No, they didn't start with "fracking." They've been rumbling around the earth for as long it has been here.

An earthquake is caused by something called "plate slippage." As the molten center of earth moves ever so slightly, the earth's thin crust slips over or under itself. This causes the earth above to quiver, shake or even crack open and move. Most earthquakes are so small they aren't noticed. Each day, about 2,750 earthquakes happen around the world. That's one million quakes a year, but only about a tenth, 275 a day, are felt by people. That's still a lot!

I wonder how high on the Richter Scale the earthquake would have been the day Christ died. Probably it was small, despite graves opening (We'll talk of that next week). We have only a small reference to this in Matthew. Some earthquakes can result in great change, most of which isn't noticed until later. In recent years our American earth was shaken: Pearl Harbor on December 7, 1941, and Pres. Kennedy's assassination on November 22, 1963. Who can forget September 11, 2001, when terrorists attacked the United States?

Worldwide, another earthquake that happened June 8, 632 AD, when Mohammed died and his followers began their Jihad of killing Christians that continues to this day. Another earthquake happened October 31, 1517, when a priest named Martin Luther nailed 95 Topics for Debate to a Wittenberg church door.

But the biggest one in all of earth's history was barely a crack in the earth. It was the day Jesus of Nazareth died on a cross on an obscure, small patch of earth on the eastern side of the Roman Empire. The death of Christ on Calvary changed everything in history. The small cracks in the ground on the day were nothing compared with the cracks that would spread throughout human history and change the world forever.

A physical earthquake will effect people and its surroundings based on how deep it is in the ground and how far away it is. Even a medium earthquake in Yuma will not affect us much here in Casa Grande. But if you're standing right on top of it in Yuma, you knew something big just happened. And if that earthquake happened 20 miles underground, it won't be noticed nearly as much as one just five miles below. When Jesus died, few people, even those nearby, noticed its effect at that moment. But looking back at it 20, 50 or 100 years later, they and their descendants saw how His death affected

208

the known world at the time. Eventually, every part of the world, east and west, north and south, would hear of the death of a Rabbi called Jesus who gave His life for the sins of the world.

Earthquakes are necessary for human life. They happen as a part of a process of recycling the earth's elements so that we people can live on the earth. If we didn't have earthquakes, there'd be no life on earth. Two years ago on the USGS website a series of earthquakes rattled the South Pacific most every day for months. Tonga, Fiji and Samoa had enormous ones deep under the ocean 40-50 miles down. But the people there are used to the ground shaking. They used to think it was gods being angry. Now most of that area knows about Jesus now, and many believe is God who helped create the earth.

It is necessary for all people to know about Jesus and the earthquake He launched on Good Friday. His quakes are spiritual and eternal. Their effects are felt everywhere. In 1964 the state of Alaska was almost torn apart with a terrible 9.0 earthquake. It set off tsunamis thousands of miles away and killed hundreds of thousands of people in Indonesia, the Philippines and New Zealand. The earth "recycles itself" in those events. In a similar way, on Good Friday God shook up the world so we could be forgiven, spiritually recycled if you will, so that we can be redeemed and saved from our sinful ways.

Did you know the Bible speaks of six different earthquakes? 1) On Mt. Sinai with Moses (Exodus 19), 2) On Mt. Horeb with Elijah (1 Kings 19), 3) During the reign of Uzziah (Amos 1), 4) At the Crucifixion (Matthew 27), 5) At Resurrection (Matthew 28), 6) When Paul and Silas were freed from prison (Acts 16). Despite the fear they provoke, earthquakes have a purpose.

The author of Hebrews speaks of a time when another shaking will happen. In 12:26-28, he writes, **"At that time His voice shook the earth, but now He has promised, 'Once more I will shake, not only the earth, but also the heavens.' 'The words 'once more' indicate the removing of what can be shaken—that is, created things—so that what cannot be shaken may remain. Therefore, since we are receiving a** kingdom that cannot be shaken, let us be thankful, and so worship God acceptably with reverence and awe."

In Jesus Christ, we are receiving a kingdom that cannot be shaken. As we gather this evening to meditate on the miracles of all earthquakes as well as the Greatest Earthquake at Jesus' death, let us look back on these events. Let's see them, not through the eyes of geological history, but with the eyes of faithful hindsight. You see, faithful hindsight recognizes them for something from God. It helps us realize an answer to an important question: What is God telling us and showing us in these events? How is His glory made known in events today?

These Passion miracles are God's way of telling us that it is really finished! The old has gone and the new has come. The beginning is over and the end has begun. The labor pains begun on Calvary and will continue until Christ comes again. The Bible isn't just a story of Jesus and the end coming later sometime. It's all connected. But "It is finished" means just that—it is done. Game over. That's why Scripture tells us that the devil roars and rages. He knows he's done. All that's left is the return of Christ and separating the grain and chaff.

That's what this miracle is all about. Salvation is finished and the End has begun. But we have nothing to fear. Like Paul says, **"Salvation is nearer to us now than when we first believed."** (Romans 13:11) Therefore we can join in praying, "Come Lord Jesus." Amen!

LENT SERIES FOUR
"Miracles of Good Friday"
Week Four

Matthew 27:52-53   "Miracle of Resurrections"
"The tombs also were opened. And many bodies of the saints who had fallen asleep were raised, and coming out of the tombs after his resurrection they went into the holy city and appeared to many."

✢ ✢ ✢

This season of Lent we are considering the "Miracles of Good Friday." Everything we speak of here relates to that fateful day when Jesus of Nazareth was executed, killed by bored Romans and fearful Jews. And of the six miracles associated with Christ's Passion, none is more mysterious than today's which spotlights the resurrection of some deceased Jewish believers people right at the moment of Jesus' death.

We know that the Easter Sunday resurrection of Jesus Himself is the most glorious of all, the "grand-daddy" miracle of His ministry. His resurrection showed He truly was the Messiah. No Christian disputes that. However, this much smaller Good Friday resurrection miracle seems strange. Who were these dead people who were raised? Why did it happen? How did it happen? Did it really happen? What happened to them later on? Who? What? Why? Where? How? All questions of an investigation. The only one not asked is "When?"

Matthew is the only Gospel writer to mention this, and like the time period around Jesus' childhood, he says very little. Only a few words are given about some people who were resurrected when He died. I am sure this is because Matthew did not want to detract from the resurrection of Jesus, the foundational act that shows He was the Son of God.

Later on, Peter, Paul, James and all the other disciples died for their faith that was centered on Jesus' resurrection. They weren't burned at the stake or fed to the lions because they insisted He cured lepers or the blind. They didn't get murdered for centuries because they believed He fed 5,000 people with a boy's lunch. They believed in Him because they saw Him alive

211

after He'd been crucified, died and buried. They believed He was who He said He was, the Son of God, and He proved that by returning from the dead. Paul's entire ministry was centered around His resurrection. Everything else was secondary. That is why he said in 1 Corinthians 15, **"If Christ has not been raised, then our preaching is in vain and your faith is in vain."** Listen to Paul's whole reasoning:

"But if there is no resurrection of the dead, then not even Christ has been raised. And if Christ has not been raised, then our preaching is in vain and your faith is in vain. We are even found to be misrepresenting God, because we testified about God that He raised Christ, whom He did not raise if it is true that the dead are not raised. For if the dead are not raised, not even Christ has been raised. And if Christ has not been raised, your faith is futile and you are still in your sins." (1 Corinthians 15:13-17)

Jesus' bodily resurrection really and truly is the most important belief in the Christian faith. It's the Standard, the Core, the Fulcrum that balances it all. Without resurrection, Christianity is not true. Let me repeat this again, Without the resurrection, Christianity is not true. It is then merely an idea based on the words of one good man who lived an amazing life and nothing more. Without Jesus' resurrection, Christianity is just a slightly better version of every other false religion.

This is why, I believe, Matthew interjects, only briefly, the news that spread around Jerusalem, news that graves were broken open by the Good Friday earthquake, and some dead people were recognized walking around town a few days later.

When the earth opens, the dead come forth. That's been a basic Jewish belief for centuries. Matthew, we know, was a Jew, and he had one main purpose in writing his book, to show his fellow Jews that Jesus really was the Messiah they had been waiting for. That's why he quotes the Old Testament so much. The Old Testament was the Bible of the Jews, the only thing they'd understand and accept when discussing the Messiah. It told them the Messiah was coming, so Matthew wrote his long and wonderful story, proving to the best of his ability, that Jesus was who He said He was – the Son of the Most High God.

I say this first because it's the most important fact. As far as the other details of this "mini-resurrection" are concerned, we don't know much. Students of the Bible have asked many questions, most of them unanswerable: "What did the people look like? Did they have grave wrappings on them? Did they look like they did when they were alive, or did they have new and glorious heavenly bodies? Why did they wait until Sunday to go into town?" Some questions show doubt: "Could Matthew be mistaken? Were the people just spooked and 'seeing things'? Could Matthew have made this up?"

Such questions satisfy some people, even if they don't get the answer. Questions show they are 'thinkers', modern people who need proof. That Matthew made this all up would make more sense, right? He probably heard about it and accepted it as fact. But you see, we can only go with what the Bible text says. There is no other mention of this anywhere in Jewish writings or pagan historians. It just came from one loyal disciple named Matthew who reported this miracle.

Actually, that's not quite true. The Scripture is not totally silent on this. Remember what the purpose of a miracle is? An event to make known the glory of Almighty God? Miracles are signs from God. They happen because He wants to get our attention and tell us something. And guess what? There really is some references to this miracle in Holy Scripture.

Let's start with what the Old Testament has to say about the resurrection and the Messiah who is to come. It was a very common belief among the Jews (except for the Sadducees) that with the coming of the Messiah, the dead would be resurrected. This belief came from the Old Testament Scriptures. In Ezekiel 37 God gives life to a whole valley of dry bones. Remember the song? *"Them bones, them bones, them dry bones, now hear the Word of the Lord."* Why does God give the bones life?

Ezekiel 37:13 says, **"Then you shall know that I am the Lord, when I open your graves, and raise you from your graves, O my people."** Long before Ezekiel, a prophet named Job confessed, **"I know that my Redeemer lives, and at the last He will stand upon the earth. And after my skin has been thus destroyed, yet in my flesh I shall see God, whom I shall see for myself and my eyes shall behold, and not another."** (Job 19:25-27) Opening graves and raising them is

213

resurrection.

Then there was the prophet Daniel who prophesied about the reality that will face every one of us when Christ comes in all His glory on that final day of judgment. He said, **"And the many of those who sleep in the dust of the earth shall awake, some to everlasting life, and some to shame and everlasting contempt."** (Daniel 12:2) "Sleep – awake"? That's resurrection.

You see, the Old Testament has many faithful witnesses who looked forward to the resurrection of the body in the presence of the glory of the Messiah. But the people of Jesus' day didn't yet understand. It took time for them to see who He was (although some would never see). It's much like today. People know what "resurrection" means, but our logical minds can't wrap themselves around the idea. It's too easy to say, *"When you're dead, you're dead. They bury you and that's it."* Wise people of this age don't accept Jesus any better than they did when He walked the earth.

Another thing. What did Jesus do three times during His ministry? He raised three people from the dead: daughter of Jairus, widow's son, and Lazarus. Consider those three for a moment. The Old Testament scriptures said that for something to be considered true, there needed to be at least two or three witnesses. Courts will even accept that evidence today. So what does Jesus do? He raises up three witnesses from the dead to testify. What better witness do we need to show Jesus is the Messiah? And all the Gospel writers tell of Jesus raising people from the dead, not just Matthew.

The most important thing is that Jesus was raised from the dead. The martyrs didn't get killed because they believed He raised Lazarus, but because they believed He raised Himself! The Miraculous resurrections of Good Friday nudge us closer to believing the real one. Jesus of Nazareth really did die on Good Friday. Three days later He really did arise from the dead.

In spite of any uncertainties we might have, the message of the resurrected saints is clear: Jesus came back to life. He's the Son of God who will one day restore us to life and take us to the place He's prepared for us when we pass from this world. Praise God for the hope we have in Jesus through the "Miracle of the Resurrections." And all God's people said, "Amen!"

214

LENT SERIES FOUR
"Miracles of Good Friday"
Week Five

Matthew 27:54   "The Miracle of Faith"
When the centurion and those who were with him, keeping watch over Jesus, saw the earthquake and what took place, they were filled with awe and said, "Truly this was the Son of God!"

Today we continue hearing of the "Miracles of Lent," a narrative about amazing events that surrounded the suffering and death of Jesus on Good Friday. We began with "Miracle of Darkness," then "Miracle of the Torn Curtain," "Miracle of Earthquake" and last week "Miracle of Resurrection." Today we'll consider the "Miracle of Faith," faith of the people beneath the cross, those who were not connected to Jesus' ministry, only His execution.

Crucifixion was a gruesome method of execution, cruel to the victim and painful to watch. Yet there were always a few who came to observe, so soldiers weren't the only ones there. Crucifixion was public and could only be carried out by Roman soldiers. Soldiers were stationed in most larger cities and given various details of punishment or execution in their otherwise boring life. Jewish Passover time brought its own unique problems, so the soldiers made sure things were done correctly that there wouldn't be any more trouble than necessary.

Roman Army officer ranks were fairly simple. Like today with Lieutenants to Generals, there were Cadets, Centurions, Tribunes, Legates Consuls and Generals. A Centurion was a captain who commanded up to 100 soldiers, but also smaller details of men. Others were also present at Calvary, including Mary and John, but it was the Centurion's words that were recounted in the Bible.

When Jesus suffered in the darkness and died amid an earthquake, there was surprise from the spectators, including the soldiers. Matthew wrote that the centurion and those who were with him were filled with amazement and moved to say,

"Truly this was the Son of God!" Mark said, "When the centurion, who stood facing Him, saw that in this way He breathed His last, he said, **"Truly this man was the Son of God!"** (Mark 15:39) Luke took the legal view: **"When the centurion saw what had taken place, he praised God, saying, "Certainly this man was innocent!"** (Luke 23:47)

Mother Mary or Apostle John surely must have heard him say this. It may seem amazing to us that a Roman soldier would say anything positive at a crucifixion, but Roman soldiers, especially the officers, were not all cruel or without feelings. They had ears and eyes, and they'd seen and heard Jesus and His followers around the city. Jesus and His men were a force to be reckoned with, so they learned about Him. Some of what He said must have resonated with them. They knew Jesus was not guilty of a capital crime. The Centurion was amazed because he saw more than a man die on a cross. He saw enough to know this Jewish man was who He said He was, the Son of God.

It is amazing that a Roman officer should be moved to say something positive at a crucifixion. The events of Calvary were more than just an incidental execution, an trifling event expanded by followers with a creative imagination.

The Bible tells of another centurion in Capernaum who'd heard Jesus was in town and wanted Him to heal his servant. He said, **"Lord I'm not worthy to have to You come into my house. Just say the word and my servant will be healed."** Jesus said what great faith the man had. (Matthew 8:8)

We may forget that one of the first Gentile converts to the Christian faith was a centurion named Cornelius of Caesarea. Acts 10 tells us his prayer life, his good works among the Jews and his visit by Peter, who came to his house only after struggling with his Jewish conscience as to whether or not he should even set foot in a Gentile's house. It makes us wonder if one of them appears twice.

We're talking tonight about miraculous faith, notably the centurion's. He knew little of Jesus before that day, and he probably knew little more afterwards. Maybe he was Cornelius, but probably not. Whoever he was, his words have been recorded for us as an example of miraculous faith of someone who should have passed Jesus off as just another quirky Jewish

Rabbi, another rebel in a rebellious land called Judea. Yet the Holy Spirit moved the centurion past his ordinary skepticism and into miraculous faith.

There was another time before the start of Jesus' ministry, when the presence of Roman soldiers were entered into the New Testament record. In Luke 3 John the Baptist was preaching in the desert, and people were coming out to hear him. There were a few soldiers there to make sure this scruffy prophet wasn't creating problems. John was telling people to give evidence of their repentance. He told some to share what they had with the poor, and others not to cheat people. **"Soldiers also asked him, "And we, what shall we do?" And he said to them, "Do not extort money from anyone by threats or by false accusation, and be content with your wages."** (Luke 3:14)

I doubt those soldiers were speaking kindly or in genuine faith. They were probably mocking John the Baptist, but still their question has been remembered. What is the miraculous faith we should note here? Is it a miracle that a soldier should actually believe in Jesus? Yes and no.

Yes, it's a miracle that anyone can believe in Jesus Christ, and no, it's not a miracle that soldiers do. I have an idea there are very few non-believers in the Armed Forces, especially among those whose lives are on the line. Our soldiers, sailors, marines and airmen see the dangers in our world, and they acknowledge the need for God to combat the evil around us. Soldiers probably pray to God more often than non-soldiers do, because they see Satan alive doing his terrible deeds.

But it's still a miracle anyone can believe in God these days, the True God, Father, Son and Holy Spirit. I don't mean Buddha, Allah or Hare Krishna. There are hundreds of gods people can latch onto, today as well as in Jesus' day.

I mean it's a miracle anyone can believe in a Creator God of the universe and in His Son Jesus Christ. It's too easy to look at the scientific evidence and think religion is just something made up. Today we have so much knowledge about astrophysics and quantum mechanics, biology and cosmology, big bangs and black holes, that it's amazing people believe in God at all.

Knowledge is wonderful. It's a great gift of God that we

can learn by observing our world and ourselves. To understand about life and our universe is critical to our survival. But self-awareness can lead to self-pride. The more we learn, the less we may need God. It's a miracle that the centurion believed, but it's probably a greater miracle that so many people believe in Jesus Christ today, even inside the church. Faith is a gift from God, a miracle we don't appreciate.

It's too easy to rely on our facts and technology. Even Bible knowledge and doctrine can become a danger if we forget our need for a child's faith. Satan finds all kinds of ways to convince the brilliant and educated they no longer need God.

I believe a Christian should look himself or herself in the mirror every day and say, "I don't have all the answers." We need to keep learning, but faith isn't dependent on knowledge alone. There is a golden simplicity in believing, *"God the Father created us, Jesus died and rose again to save us, and the Holy Spirit helps us believe the whole thing."* Having faith is a miracle, and I am grateful that eternal life doesn't depend on me, but on Jesus who has forgiven me. It's amazing how God brings us to faith.

I once heard a Gideon tell the true story of a young man in college who was smoking marijuana. One day he was out of papers to roll his "joints" and all he could find was a Gideon's New Testament. Seeing now thin the pages were, he tore one out, rolled in some dope and smoked it. He did that again and again. After some days he got a little guilty – it was the Bible, after all. So he thought he'd read a little of what was on the page, so he read some of the page, and then he smoked it. But he didn't stop. In fact, he smoked his way through the entire book of Matthew, then Mark, and then Luke and into John, but always reading a little from the page. But then one night he came to John 3:16, and a little bell went off inside his head. He'd memorized that verse in Sunday School! And, and, and then he couldn't go on. His conscience bothered him so much, that he prayed that night for the first time in years. By the end of the week, he'd talked to a campus pastor about Jesus. He quit smoking and asked Jesus to forgive him.

For this man, faith came from hearing the Word of God even if it meant smoking its pages. Now that's a miracle! Praise God the Holy Spirit who can and will use any and every way to turn our hearts to the Lord. We'll talk about the "Miracle of Forgiveness" next week. And all God's people said, "Amen!"

218

LENT SERIES FOUR
"Miracles of Good Friday"
Week Six

Luke 23:34   "Miraculous Forgiveness"
"Jesus said, 'Father, forgive them, for they know not what they do'."

✚ ✚ ✚

We've come to the last of our midweek Lent services. Next week is Holy Week. Tonight we will consider the "Miracle of Forgiveness," earned by Jesus through His perfect life, His innocent suffering and death, and His resurrection that shows us He was who He said He was. Forgiveness is a very important event for our daily life and especially our relationship to God.

Forgiveness the "Big One" in relationships, the deliberate decision that can change a person's life. It can either be bad if we choose not to forgive, or it can be good if we do forgive. Forgiveness is not only something we can do for others. Sometimes that person we need to forgive is ourselves. Forgiving ourselves is as important as forgiving others.

During the decade of the 1990s, I conducted a dozen and a half "Divorce and Loss Recovery" workshops. Over a hundred men and woman of all ages came to these Friday night and Saturday workshops seeking peace and some useful tools to handle the emotional wreckage caused by their divorce or the death of their spouse. We discussed many topics, but always the difficult one was the same – forgiveness.

After an hour or so of discussion, I'd ask them to write a letter to their former spouse expressing words of forgiveness. In it I also suggested they ask forgiveness for their part in the marriage breakup. In the case of loss by death, they would ask forgiveness of the deceased person. Some participants wouldn't do it until I told them they did not have to mail the letters. At the end of that session, we'd all would tear our letters into pieces and perhaps burn them when we could do that or else place them into sealed plastic bags and throw them in the trash. Most of the participants said writing that letter was the hardest part of the workshop, but usually the most rewarding. Now and then someone just could not write the letter. Forgiveness can be hard to do.

Forgiving someone who has grievously harmed or offended you is one of the hardest things you will do in life. I believe this is because we don't always understand what forgiveness is, how it is done, and why it is necessary. Let's look at these three aspects – what forgiveness is, how it is done and why it is necessary. These can apply in all kinds of situations, but they are mainly for where major harm has been done.

WHAT IS FORGIVENESS? Forgiveness is not excusing what another person has done. Rather, it is giving up all claim on one who has hurt you. It is surrendering your right to hurt the offender back. Forgiveness means no retribution, no "eye for an eye." If healing is going to take place, there must be forgiveness. Forgiveness is a decision not to let the offender or the offense control you. It is choosing a new way to live.

HOW CAN I FORGIVE? Forgiveness is done by the person who's been offended. It does not need the offender's confession or repentance, only willingness of the offended. After the 1999 Columbine High School massacre, some parents forgave the shooters right away. Others were told, some even by their pastors, that they didn't need to forgive the shooters since forgiveness required repentance. But that's wrong. Forgiveness is a choice of the wounded. Ideally it would be great if we forgave only after hearing sorrow by the one who causes the pain. But sometimes they're dead, or they refuse to repent. Forgiveness is a choice by the wounded person towards the one who caused harm. It is done when the offended person grants it.

WHY FORGIVE? The answer is simple: to release yourself from the other person. Forgiveness frees you from the prison of anger and hate. It's a mistake to think forgiveness is a sign of weakness. It's really the opposite. Withholding forgiveness hurts the offended more than the offender. It takes courage and faith to forgive, and the reward is far greater than we think. Forgiveness is a conscious decision of release made so the hurt person can go on living. It is also a way to show mercy to the offender. Withholding forgiveness locks us into a prison that only hurts us.

A recent TV show was about a young woman who's family had been killed. She was only 6 years old when a drug-crazed many brutally murdered her parents and her older brother as she watched from a closet. The murderer was convicted and sentenced to life in prison. Twenty five years later he asked to see her and tell her he had "found God" and was terribly sorry. She was still rabidly bitter and told him she would never forgive him. The only way he could show he was truly sorry, she said, was for him to kill himself. She left the prison smiling because she'd finally told him what she wanted. She had hurt him back.

Watching this show, I was left with an empty feeling and disappointment. The writers gave us the view of forgiveness of a terrible crime. They were saying, "Don't do it!" But that's a mistake. Hurting the killer back will not give her relief. Of course I haven't walked in her shoes, but it seemed to me that evil somehow won that round. Satan made bitterness the solution. We were supposed to hatred would make the woman happier. She would be vindicated by her personal pronouncement of death on the murderer. But that's not true.

In today's Bible text, Jesus of Nazareth was hanging on a cross. After a night of being confined and a morning of betrayal and brutal beating, and after humiliation and harassment of the crowds, and finally the pain of being nailed to a cross, His first words were a prayer of forgiveness. "Father, forgive them, for the know not what they do." Despite all they had done to Him, Jesus knew forgiveness was needed now, and He did it. He forgave them and also us today, because we sin and don't always know what we're doing. He also told His disciples, **"Love your enemies and pray for those who persecute you."** (Matthew 5:44)

Jesus gave miraculous forgiveness to those who had placed Him on the cross, and also for all of us. He gave us a great lesson there. When you're nailed to a cross for things you didn't do, then go on the offensive – pray for them and forgive them. When someone has brutally hurt you, hit them back with forgiveness, not hatred. If you are guilty of some stupid or vile sins, confess them and forgive yourself, then pray for help not to do them again.

The history books are filled with terrible, vile things people have done to each other. What we're seeing today in the Middle East and Africa, atrocities against Jews and Christians, we must take care not to nurse hatred. When you hear of homicide bombers that kill dozens and wound hundreds, and then hear the enemy call them "Blessed events for Allah," do not store up hatred for them. The real enemy is Satan. We must resist his temptations, but we should pray for his followers, that they will be defeated and possibly change their minds about such senseless killing.

Forgiveness by Jesus is a miracle. Our forgiving each other is a miracle. How God could find it in Himself to forgive our sins is an absolute miracle. It's the reason for what Jesus did with His life. Forgiveness is why Jesus said, **"It is finished."** Trusting in Him makes His forgiveness ours. He has forgiven us, so now we can forgive others.

In WWII Corrie ten Boom and her sister Betsy were captured by the Nazis and sent to a death camp in Ravensbruck, a place of horror where Betsy died. Through a clerical error Corrie miraculously escaped and after the war spent all her remaining days telling people of God's love and mercy despite such terrible atrocities. But while she spoke of forgiveness, she confessed she held a secret anger in her heart towards the camp guards. One evening after speaking to a large group of people about Jesus, she recognized one of the camp guards walking towards her. While she wanted to go the other way, she said God wouldn't let her. Instead, she faced him. When the guard identified himself and said he believed in Jesus, she was skeptical. When he admitted he was wrong and asked her forgiveness, Corrie said she froze, unable to speak or act. But when he extended his hand to her, she took it and said God sent a shock of forgiveness into them both. That powerful moment was for them both a sign of God's forgiveness and Christ's love. She later wrote she had peace she'd not had since the war. A former enemy and a woman of God came to realize the miracle that comes with forgiveness.

"Father, forgive them, for they know not what they do," said Jesus. This Lent we have examined the miracles – the darkness, torn temple curtain, earthquakes, resurrections, a man's faith, and now God's forgiveness. As Lent comes to a close this Sunday and we enter Holy Week, may all of these miracles have a blessed effect in our lives, one that lasts through a glorious Easter and every day God grants us after. Remember, *"God the Father has created us, Jesus the Son has died and rose for our sins, and the Holy Spirit gives us faith in the whole thing."* May you be blessed all your days. Amen

222

LENT SERIES FIVE
"Living for the Lord"
Week One

Mark 14:3   "Risky Life"

"While he was in Bethany, reclining at the table in the home of a man known as Simon the Leper, a woman came with an alabaster jar of expensive perfume, made of pure nard. She broke the jar and poured the perfume on his head."

✠ ✠ ✠

Some acts are simple but their effects reach out through the years. The woman's gift of perfume poured on Jesus' head or a monk's nailing some words to a church door are among them. So simple at the time, yet they are forever remembered. Some acts of giving are great, but only a few know of them. All of them involve great risk.

A man named "Artful Eddie" gave a great gift. He was a lawyer who once had it all. He was the slickest of the slick, one of the roars of the Roaring 20's. He was one of Al Capone's lawyers who fixed the races at the Chicago dog tracks. He mastered the technique of overfeeding seven of the dogs and betting on the eighth. And so wealth, style, status - Artful Eddie lacked nothing. But one day he walked into a police precinct and turned himself in. He squealed on Capone's betting ring. Why? What was his motive? Surely he knew the consequences, certainly he knew the mob would kill him. Yes, he did know, but he did it anyway. So what did he have to gain? What could society give him that he didn't have? What could have moved him to do such a thing?

The answer was simple, his little son Butch. Artful Eddie had spent his life with the despicable. He had smelled the stench of the underworld long enough. For his son, he wanted more. He wanted to give his boy a name he could be proud of. And to do that Eddie would have to clear his own name. Eddie was willing to take a risk so that his son could have a clean slate. But Artful Eddie never saw his dream come true. The mob found him and silenced him with a shotgun blast. So, was it worth it? For his son, Butch, it was. Artful Eddie's boy lived up to the sacrifice his father made for him. His name became one of the best-known names in the whole world.

But before we talk about Butch, let's talk about the principle of risky life, and risky love. A risky life and a risky love are willing to take a chance. They go out on a limb for the one that's loved. This is life that makes a statement and leaves a legacy. This is true sacrificial love.

There is a kind of love which is expected and predictable. But there is also a kind of love which is unexpected, surprising and even stirring. This is the act of the love that steals the heart and leaves an impression on the soul. This is the act that's never forgotten.

Jesus experienced such a risky act of love during His final week. The woman, some say it was Mary Magdalene, gave a demonstration of devotion that the world has never forgotten. It was an act of extravagance and tenderness to the Lord.

A small group of people were gathered in a room. Jesus and a few of His friends were in Bethany at the home of Simon the Leper. Actually he was Simon the ex-leper. We don't know just when Jesus healed him, but we can imagine the change in Simon's life. Twisted, painful hands were now whole, sores and scabs were now healed, tattered wraps and isolation among strangers were replaced by clean clothes and friends. Jesus risked touching Simon and Simon was changed forever.

Simon may have been one of the 10 Lepers Jesus healed, maybe the one who came back to say thank-you. Or he may have been one of the dozens of others who begged for Jesus' healing touch. We don't know why, but we do know he invited Jesus to his house for dinner.

Simon's invitation must have meant a lot to Jesus. After all, He knew He didn't have many days left. He would soon crack His whip in the temple and the Pharisees would begin clearing out a cell for Him on death row. But for these few hours, Jesus enjoyed Simon's hospitality and his home.

Jesus would visit a few other homes before the week was out, but they will not be as gracious as Simon's. Before the week was out, He would be a guest at the High Priest's house, the one with the beautiful view of the valley. But Jesus won't see the view and He won't find hospitality there.

Jesus would also visit Herod's house, or rather his palace. Elegant chambers, plenty of slaves, good food. But Jesus won't be given any food. He was there to show Herod a few tricks, be a sideshow. **"Show me a miracle, country-boy,"** Herod said, and the guards laughed at Him.

Jesus also visited the house of Pontius Pilate. He would have the rare opportunity to stand in the Roman Governor's mansion and defend Himself. That should be a moment to remember, but it won't be. It's a moment the world would rather forget. Pilate had the opportunity to perform the world's greatest act of mercy, but he failed. God stood before him, and Pilate didn't see him.

One can't help but wonder - what if? What if the High Priest had come to the defense of a defenseless Jesus? What if Herod had asked Jesus for help rather than entertainment? What if Pilate had been as concerned with truth as he said he was? What if one of them had turned their back of the crowd and their face towards God and made a stand?

But they didn't. Their prestige was too important, their possessions too precious, their fall from power too great. They didn't, but Simon did. Risky life and love seize the moment. Risky love takes a chance. Risky love doesn't wait until the time is perfect, it realizes the only time is now. The woman knew that, too, so she opened the imported perfume and poured it on Jesus' feet. She anointed Him with precious oil and her cup of joy overflowed.

I wonder if Jesus thought of Mary's gentle act later on. I wonder if during the strokes of the whip He could still remember the fragrance or the smoothness of that perfume. I wonder if He thought of her faith as He carried the crossbar to Calvary. I wonder if He felt less alone, recalling this amazing act of extravagance and kindness. That kind of perfume cost a whole year's wages. It was an incredible gift. Some of His disciples complained at the cost. **"It could have been sold and the money given to the poor,"** they said. There will always be those with the practical, but narrow focus of how much something costs. **"Let her alone,"** said Jesus. **"She's done a wonderful and memorable thing."**

Jesus' message for us tonight is simple -- there is a time for risky love. There is a time for extravagant gestures in life. There is a time to pour out your affections for the one you love. When

225

the time comes, seize it – don't miss it!

The young boy watched as the students taunted the other kid, and his insides were churning. It's his friend they are laughing at. He knows he should step in, he knows he should stand up for his friend. But those laughing are the cool kids he wants to get friendly with. If he speaks up what will they think? And because it matters what they think, he walks away from his friend.

The young husband looks into the display case, he rationalizes, "Sure she would like that bracelet, but it's expensive, and she already has one. She is a practical woman and will understand if I just get her those towels. Someday I will get her a bracelet like that. Someday..." Years later the man was going through his wife's dresser after she died. In the bottom drawer he found a box with a pink negligee he had given her, unworn, still in the box. She was waiting for a special occasion or for the other one to wear out. One of her favorite expressions he remembers her saying was, "Someday, someday we'll do that." A few of those days came, but most never did.

Someday! Someday is the enemy of risky life and love. Someday is the snake whose tongue deceives us. *"Someday,"* he hisses into our ear. *"Someday, we'll go visit those folks. Someday, I'll take her on a cruise. Someday, I'll tell my parents I appreciate what they did for me. Someday, I'll do something special for my Lord. Someday, the kids will understand why I was so busy at work."*

But you know the truth, don't you? Even before I say it, you can say it better than I. Most "some days" never come! The price of practicality is often higher than the cost of extravagance. I should know. That boy standing there watching his friend mocked by the cool kids, that was me. That young husband buying the towels instead of the bracelet, that was me. That husband finding the unworn negligee, that was me.

The missed moment doesn't bring joy years later. The rewards of risky love are always greater than their cost. Go to the effort. Invest the time. Purchase the gift. Take them to lunch. Giver him a call, tell them. Just do it. The seized opportunity brings joy. The neglected brings regret. The reward was great for Simon. His gesture gave rest and refreshment to the Lord of the Universe. Mary's act will never be forgotten. Jesus promised, **"Wherever the Good News is preached, what this woman has done will be remembered."** And it is.

226

Which brings us back to Artful Eddie's son, Butch. Had he lived, Eddie would have been proud. He would have been proud of Butch's appointment to Annapolis and his commission as a WWII Navy fighter pilot. He would have been real proud when Butch downed five enemy bombers and saved the lives of hundreds aboard the carrier "Lexington." Sadly, Butch died fighting for his country, but he also won the Congressional Medal of Honor. When people in Chicago hear the name O'Hare, they don't think of gangsters, they think of an aviation hero, Butch O'Hare, son of Artful Eddie O'Hare, a father willing to give his life so his son would have it better.

Now the next time you hear that name you'll have something else to think about. "Risky Life, Risky Love" -- think of that the next time you fly into the airport named after the son of a bad gangster gone good, the son of Artful Eddie O'Hare. "Risky Love" Just do it. It's worth it!

LENT SERIES FIVE
"Living for the Lord"
Week Two

Matt. 21:21   "Courage to Dream"
"Jesus replied, "I tell you the truth, if you have faith and do not doubt, not only can you do what was done to the fig tree, but also you can say to this mountain, 'Go, throw yourself into the sea,' and it will be done."

✚ ✚ ✚

There is one kind of person I truly admire. He confuses and sometimes angers me, but I still admire him. That person is the dreamer, the visionary. He's the one who can look at a flat field and see a town. I see a few pieces of good wood and he sees a finished cabinet. I admire him and God rejoices in him. I often wish I were more of a dreamer.

Hans Babblinger was a dreamer. He lived in the city of Ulm, in Germany. Hans Babblinger wanted to fly. He wanted to soar like a bird. But he had a problem -- he lived in the sixteenth century, not long after Martin Luther died. There were no planes, no gliders, not even any hot air balloons. He was a dreamer born too soon. What he wanted was impossible. Yet Hans Babblinger made a career of helping people overcome the impossible. He made artificial limbs -- arms, legs. In his day, amputation was a common cure of disease and infection, so he kept busy. He helped handicapped people overcome big obstacles.

But he wanted to do the same for himself. In time, he used his skills to make a set of wings. He had watched the birds and made his wings like theirs. One day, he took his wings up onto the hills near his city to test them. The hills nearby were a good choice. Updrafts were common there, and one day, with friends watching, Hans jumped off a high hill and soared lightly down. His friends applauded, his heart raced and God rejoiced.

Why do I think God rejoiced? Because I believe God is always happy when His people reach beyond themselves. I believe He is pleased when we stretch out, when we use the talents He has given us to give Him glory. I believe He delights in seeing people do the impossible.

Want some examples from the Bible? Eighty-year old

229

shepherds didn't usually go head-to-head with Egyptian Pharoahs, but don't tell that to Moses. Teenage shepherds didn't normally have showdowns with giants, but don't tell that to David. Night-shift shepherds didn't normally see angels, but don't tell that to the Bethlehem bunch.

For sure don't tell that to God. He gives us wings, as Isaiah 40 says, **"Those who hope in the Lord will renew their strength. They will soar on wings like eagles. They will run and not grow weary. They will walk and not be faint."** God wants people to dream. Remember the passage Peter quoted at Pentecost? **"In the last days," God says, "I will pour out my spirit on all people. Your sons and daughters will prophesy. Your young men will see visions and your old men will dream dreams."** God wants people to dream. And I think He is angered when people's wings are clipped. That's the message of the fig tree, the fruitless fig tree Jesus cursed.

Jesus and His disciples were walking to Jerusalem after spending the night in Bethany. He was hungry and saw a fig tree. Going to it, He saw it had no fruit and was angered. Something about that tree reminded Him of what He saw among the religious people, so He denounced the tree, **"You'll never have fruit again!"** He didn't say it kindly, and His anger really showed.

The next day the disciples walked by that tree and saw it had completely dried up. **"What happened?" they said. "How could the tree dry up so quickly?"** Jesus gave them an answer. **"Truly, if you have faith and don't doubt, you can do what I did to this tree and much more. You can tell a mountain to go jump in the lake, and it will happen. If you have faith, you will receive whatever you ask for in prayer."**

You won't find the words *dream*, or *fly* or *wings* in that story, but maybe if you listen closely, you'll hear God telling the dreamers of this world to strap on their wings and jump off a cliff. And maybe you'll also hear God's anger with those who put dreamers into a cage and tell them what they want is impossible.

That tree symbolized much to Jesus. In that tree Jesus was reminded of something all too familiar in the church of His day. It was all promise and no performance. He was disgusted at the so-called believers that are all talk and no action. He was weary of lukewarm Christians who are have all the answers but take no action. He was tired of fruitless followers.

Remember the Laodicean Church of Revelation 3? That church was wealthy and self-sufficient. They could pay all their bills and still and had lots left over. They had plenty of people in the pews but little heart for the helpless. **"I know what you do," God said to the Laodiceans. "You're neither hot nor cold. But because you are lukewarm, I will spit you out of my mouth."** Graphic stuff!

You see, God can't stand a lukewarm faith. He is angered by religious people who put on a show but ignore people in need. Those were the religious people He faced in His day, and they are still around today.

When there was service to be done, they found fault. They complained His disciples gathered food on the wrong day. They complained He healed on the wrong day. They griped that He healed the wrong people and hung out with the wrong crowd and had the wrong influence on children. Worst of all, they saw He tried to free tied down by all sorts of foolish rules and regulations. When some courageous soul tried to do the impossible, they said it couldn't, or shouldn't, be done.

By the way, the same thing happened to Hans Babblinger in the late 18th century. Historians tell us the King was coming to Ulm and the citizens wanted to impress him. Word was out that Hans could fly, so they asked him to fly for the king. Hans agreed. One change, however. Since there would be a large crowd and the hills were hard to climb, they wanted him to fly at a lower place. Hans chose the high bluffs by the Danube river. He would jump off the high bluffs and float down to the river. Poor choice! The updraft common to the hills was nonexistent by the river. So in front of the king, his court, and half the city, Hans jumped and fell like a rock straight into the Danube. The king was disappointed, the Bishop was mortified, and next Sunday the Bishop preached on the topic, "Man was not mean to fly." And Hans believed him. Listening to the naye-sayers, he put his wings away and never tried to fly again. Shortly later, Hans died and his dreams of flying were buried with him.

Through the years, Christians have become all too good at telling others what they can't -- or shouldn't do. I'm not talking

231

here about morality. That never changes because that's God talking. But I am thinking here about how we serve people, or how we express our emotions, or what kind of songs we sing in church. And I am talking about how we rarely help people to think for themselves. Does the church give people wings, or lead weights for their feet?

What about that friend who offended you and needs your forgiveness? Or that co-worker burdened with guilt? Or that relative who carries a sack filled with yesterday's failures? Or that friend weighed down by anxiety? Or that church member who has a great idea he'd like to use? Tell them about Jesus. Forgive them. Encourage them. Turn them loose and watch them fly.

In a marriage I had last year the woman was from another country. When I asked her about repeating the vows, she said, *"I can do it, but it will be with an accent."* She spoke her vows beautifully! This is how God wants it from us, each of us to living our faith with our own accent. For some, the accent is on the sick. For others it is working for the imprisoned. For still others it is teaching, or working with children, or listening to the hurting or helping the poor.

One message of the fig tree is that not all of us have the same fruit. But the BIG message is that all of us must bear SOME kind of fruit. If we have faith, we must bear fruit. It's not easy, but it is necessary. We need to pray for it. As Jesus said, **"If you have faith, you will receive whatever you ask for in prayer."** And please remember it is faith in God, not in a religion. Being a Lutheran doesn't save us. Going to a Lutheran School, or sending your kids to one, or even teaching at one doesn't save us. Having faith in the Jesus of the Holy Bible, Jesus, the Son of God, that's the only thing that saves us.

Jesus is many things to us. He is the Shepherd in search of His lambs. He calls out the name of His lost lamb, and the name He calls is yours. He is the Housewife who sweeps the house in search of the lost coin, and the coin He seeks is you. He is the Father pacing the porch waiting for the son or daughter to come home. God wants his child home, and the child He wants is you and it is me.

He has told us, **"If you have faith, you will receive**

whatever you ask for in prayer." It's His promise. But don't limit this promise to perks or paychecks. His fruit is far greater than earthly goods or promotions. God wants us to fly, free from yesterday's guilt, free from yesterday's fears, free from tomorrow's grave. Trust in Him and get set to fly. One day all believers will fly home to Him.

One final word about the church at Ulm. It has the highest spire of any church in the world, over 500 feet high, which is a nice height for flying. But today it stands empty. On Sunday maybe 40-50 people are in worship while hundreds of visitors and tourists walk around and look the place over.

And how do most of those tourists get to the city of Ulm? They fly, on jet airplanes, not a few feet above the ground, but a few miles above the earth. So can we, when we trust the Lord for all our needs. Amen

LENT SERIES FIVE
"Living for the Lord"
Week Three

1 Peter 2:9-10   "The Family of God"

"But you are a chosen people, a royal priesthood, a holy nation, a people belonging to God, that you may declare the praises of Him who called you out of darkness into His wonderful light. Once you were not a people, but now you are the people of God; once you had not received mercy, but now you have received mercy."

✚ ✚ ✚

No man is an island, no man stands alone;
Each man's joy is joy to me,
Each man's grief is my own.
We need one another, so I will defend
Each man as my brother, each man as my friend.   (John Dunn)

Do you belong to a family? If so, how's your family life? Of course, we all belong to a family somewhere, but we may not always feel connected. We all need to belong. We all need the certainty of belonging, to those who love us, to an earthly family, and to a heavenly one, too. St. Peter once wrote:

"But you are a chosen people, a royal priesthood, a holy nation, a people belonging to God, that you may declare the praises of Him who called you out of darkness into His wonderful light. Once you were not a people, but now you are the people of God; once you had not received mercy, but now you have received mercy."

Today people often feel disconnected from family. Work, hobbies and other interests take people far away from family. I'm a bit that way. There were five children in my parent's family. We all got married and produced 20 grandchildren. Most of those grandchildren are now married, producing a total of 43 great grandchildren. And all but seven of those 20 families live in southern Minnesota, so I guess I'm one of the disconnected ones.

But being disconnected by miles doesn't mean separation. You and I can find a community wherever we are. That's why we join clubs, societies, and churches. We all need to belong somewhere. Even the technology of Electronic Mail - EMail - brings people into communities. We all need to belong to a community of God's faithful – that's our extended family.

Wherever we go, we can still belong to that family, God's people. Wherever we go, there are believers who need each other. God's family has characteristics. For example, God's Chosen People:

1. *Commit to Jesus Christ, then to each other.*
2. *Seek first the Kingdom and know the rest will be added to them.*
3. *Work to become more like Christ in word and deed.*
4. *Love and forgive like they have been loved and forgiven.*
5. *Are generous because they know who the Giver of All is.*
6. *Care for and do good to each other.*

St. Peter again: **"But you are a chosen people, a royal priesthood, a holy nation, a people belonging to God, that you may declare the praises of Him who called you out of darkness into His wonderful light. Once you were not a people, but now you are the people of God; once you had not received mercy, but now you have received mercy."**

God's family isn't perfect. We often fail each other. We get too busy seeking wrong things. We don't always care for others as we should. We don't always love or forgive. But still the family tries. God's chosen people don't throw in the towel and quit. They don't shoot themselves in the head and call it gallantry. God's people care for each other, or else they must ask if they really are God's people.

You and I are part of the Family of God. We may not like all that happens, but we know God is the one we all must trust, and so we try again. We try to work together, even though we know it won't always be right. A family supports its members.

A member asked why I hadn't been to see him for several months. I knew he had experienced troubled times and that many members had supported him and prayed for him. "But why haven't you been to see me in the past 2 months?" he asked. I said, "Have others been ministering to you?" "Oh, yes, many have called, and stopped by and sort of surrounded me with their caring, but you weren't with them." "That's true," I said, "but they were there. They were ministering to you."

You see, the church isn't just one pastor caring for 400 members, it's 400 people caring for each other. Sometimes the pastors can do it, but much of time family members must care for each other.

Does that make sense to you? Do you understand what I've just said? Does it bother you that you might not receive pastoral care from the pastor each time you need it? Might it not be that the most important work you and can do in the church, outside of sharing Jesus Christ, is to care for each other?

Jesus our Lord has given His life for each of us. He died on the cross of Calvary that we might live in eternity. He has called us together into this congregation. Epiphany is not just a collection of individuals, we are the family of God in this place. We aren't just spiritual consumers, we are God's workers.

I reported to our Elders last night that during the month of March Epiphany will become a church of 400 members. Each weekend from 220-250 men, women and children are in one of our worship services. 400 is the maximum that one pastor can effectively minister to. In fact, that's too many, as shown in that we're losing some members. We are now on the threshold of going either forward or backward. God has brought so any to our doors, and without another plan, maybe another worker, the only way to keep us together is to minister to each other.

During May, a team from Harvesters For Christ will come to Epiphany to train members in how to minister to each other. They will show us how we can grow together, and how we can assimilate new members in a better way than we've been doing. For three weeks, classes will be held under the topic, *"Church as Home, Media Evangelism, Outreach and Witnessing."* In the coming weeks you will be asked to attend one or more of those classes. I hope you will do so.

This is a rare opportunity. I pray we will not neglect this, but rather that make use of the gifts brought to us, and the gifts we have to help each other. It's not about money, there's no cost to this. We just need to invest our time. If we do, we'll see how John Dunne's words are true:

No man is an island, no man stands alone;
Each man's joy is joy to me, each man's grief is my own.

Easter is only a month away. May is just two months away. God will continue to bring new people to our doors each week. What will we do with them? I can't do it all any longer. God grant us grace to grow first in faith, then in knowledge, and last but now least in our caring for each other. We are not islands, we do not stand alone. May we reach out to each other as a family should. Amen

LENT SERIES FIVE
"Living for the Lord"
Week Four

Matt. 20:17-19   "Travelling the Road"
**"We are going to Jerusalem. The Son of Man will be
turned over to the rulers and they will say He must die. The
Son of Man will be handed over to be crucified. But on the
third day He will rise to life again."**

In my life I have visited several foreign countries. Things
are different there than in America. I've never been to Russia,
though a few years ago I heard of Father Borisov, a Russian
Orthodox Priest, who went on a mission that he figured would
be his last. It was August, 1991, and people seeking freedom in
Moscow were under siege. It looked as if the Russian bear
would stomp its communist foot on them again. Father Borisov
and a few members of the one-year-old Russian Bible Society
decided to battle tanks with New Testaments. They wanted to
give the soldiers a Bible and were ready to toss them into the
tank hatches if necessary.

Father Borisov said later, "I believed that soldiers with
Bibles in their pockets would not shoot their brothers and
sisters." They were ready to do battle with God's Word rather
than with mighty weapons.

Moscow was not the first time people tried to do that.
Consider the text for tonight. Jesus is talking, **"We are going to
Jerusalem. The Son of Man will be turned over to the rulers
and they will say He must die. The Son of Man will be
handed over to be crucified. But on the third day He will rise
to life again."**
The road from Jericho to Jerusalem is only 14 miles, a long
day's journey walking through a treacherous canyon. But it's
not the road we're interested in. Dangerous roads were
common back then and still are. No, it's not the road, but the
man who walks the road. Jesus was at the front if His band of
disciples. Usually He was surrounded by people but this time
Jesus was out in front. He was the "point man" of His platoon,

239

walking first into battle. If you want to know someone's heart, watch that person as He prepares for battle.

You can tell a lot about a person by the way he dies. Matthew Huffman was a 6-year-old son of missionaries in Brazil. One morning he complained of a headache. His temperature shot up and he began to lose his vision. His mother and father put him in a car and raced to a hospital. As they drove, he lay on his mother's lap, he reached his hand into the air. His mother took it away but he reached out again. Again, she took it down, and again he reached out his hand.

"What are you reaching for, Matthew?" she asked. "His hand – I'm reaching for His hand," he answered. And he closed his eyes and never woke up. Of all the things young Matthew had no chance to learn in his short life, he had learned the most important one of all, who to reach for in the hour of death.

You can tell a lot about a person by the way he dies. Consider Jim Bonham. Few would know him as a hero of the Alamo, but he was as great as any there. A young South Carolina lawyer, he had been in Texas only three months when he joined the army. Santa Anna's armies had begun to attack the Alamo. Jim broke through the ranks and rode through the enemy lines east to the city of Goliad for help. He rushed to closest army and pleaded with the commander, "Send us troops! We are only 150 and Santa Anna has thousands. Give us help! Start to march right now!" But the commander made no commitment. He said he would think it over. Young Jim Bonham knew what that meant, and yet he jumped on his horse and headed towards the Alamo.

Another soldier asked, "Now where are you going?" "Back to the Alamo," he shouted as he rode away. The soldier turned to another and said, "If things were so bad, why is he going back there?" Came the reply, "I doubt if he considered doing anything else." Young Jim Bonham rode into battle knowing it would be his last.

So did our Lord Jesus. With His final mission before Him, he told His disciples for the third and last time, **"We are going to Jerusalem. The Son of Man will be turned over to the rulers and they will say He must die. The Son of Man will be handed over to be crucified. But on the third day He will rise to life again."**

Some have held theories that Jesus died in Jerusalem because He was trapped there. Others believe He made a major miscalculation that got Him crucified. Some even believe it was

240

His last attempt to save a dying mission. I say forget such ideas. Jesus went to Jerusalem on purpose, God's purpose. There was no surprise, and no hesitation. He knew what He had to do and He went there to do it.

You can tell a lot about a person by the way he dies. And the way Jesus marched to His death leaves us no doubt. He had come to earth for this one moment. As the Apostle Peter said on Pentecost, **"Jesus was given to you, and with the help of those who didn't know the law, you put Him to death by nailing Him on a cross. But this was God's plan which he made a long ago. Jesus knew this would happen."** (Acts 2:23-24)

Your see, Jesus' journey to Jerusalem didn't begin at Jericho. It didn't begin in Galilee or even Bethlehem. Jesus' journey to Jerusalem began the moment the fruit was eaten in the Garden of Eden. The moment mankind fell into sin, Jesus began His journey to Calvary's holy mountain, where He removed the sins of the world.

Just as Father Borisov walked into battle with the Word of God in his hand, Jesus Christ stepped towards Jerusalem with the promise of God in His heart. Though He was true man, Jesus was also true God, and so He said, **"On the third day He will rise to life again."** Is there a Jerusalem journey on your horizon? Are you a few steps away from something painful? Are you near the walls of heartache? Then learn from the master. Don't march into battle without God's Word in your heart.

When you are confused, remember God's Word to Jeremiah 29, **"For I know the plans I have for you,"** declares the Lord, **"plans to prosper you and not to harm you, plans to give you hope and a future."** If you feel dragged down by failures, remember Paul's Word to us in Romans 8, **"There is no condemnation for those who are in Christ Jesus."** On those nights when you wonder where God is, remember God's promise in Hebrews 13, **"Never will I leave you, never will I forsake you."** If you think God can't love you, remember the words of Paul who had persecuted and even killed God's people, from Ephesians 3, **"That you may have power, together with all the saints, to grasp how wide and long and high and deep is the love of Jesus Christ."**

The next time you find yourself on a road marching towards trouble, take the promises of God with you. When the blackness of depression settles on you, think of Father Borisov who battled tanks with Bibles.

By the way, on August 20 of the Russian Communist resurgence, they offered one soldier a Children's Bible because they were out of small New Testaments. Needing to hide it from his superiors, he found only one pocket large enough, his ammunition pocket. A soldier went into battle with a Bible instead of bullets.

In many ways, we're all marching to Jerusalem with the promises of God in our hearts. It was for Father Borisov. It was for Matthew Huffman. And it is for you and me, too. May Jesus Christ lead us there on the way. Amen.

LENT SERIES FIVE
"Living for the Lord"
Week Five

2 Corinthians 5:21   "Our Righteousness"
"God made Him who had no sin to be sin for us, so that in Him we might become the righteousness of God."

✠ ✠ ✠

Our theme for Lent during these Wednesdays has been "Living for the Lord." We live in uncertain days, when we are not sure whom to trust or what to believe. Tonight I want to attempt to debunk a fact that we've all lived with for decades -- the supposed fact that 50% of all marriages end in divorce.

I've believed this statistic and, like many others, have even taught it as true. People all over openly talk about the 50% divorce rate as it were unchangeable truth. The other day I came across a book that proves the 50% divorce rate false. Louis Harris, the pollster, in his 1987 book, Inside America, *reported that our best numbers show that, in reality, that nearly 80% of all first marriages survive. He told how the myth got started by how people read the statistics. In 1981, the number of divorces in America hit a record high at 1.2 million. That year there were 2.4 million marriages (3% of American marriages). That year became a "Benchmark" for statistics, so commentators and much of the public ever since have used this data to prove that half of all marriages fail.*

But using just those two statistics to prove the divorce rate is faulty. Suppose, he writes, that in 1982, the year following, there were 2.4 million divorces and 2.4 million marriages. Does that mean 100% of marriages will fail? Of course not, it only talks about marriages and divorces in just one year. The stats don't take into consideration the other 97% of marriages that are still in force at the same time. Two other writers I read confirmed his conclusion. Using the data from the last several regular 10-year censuses, at any given time, nearly 80% of all American first marriages are working. In 1991, the National Center for Health Statistics reported that the divorce rate actually went down for the fifth consecutive year.

So in reality only about 20% of all marriages actually end in divorce. What's this world coming to when you can't even be certain of the 50% divorce rate? I guess that just proves the wisdom of the old axiom – "Figures don't lie, but liars figure." And you don't read about this in the evening papers, because it's accepted as fact. Even if you did, it would take us years for us to unlearn what we have come to accept as a fact of life -- while in reality it isn't fact at all.

Now you might find that fascinating bit of information strange and out of place here tonight. But it actually gives credence to the axiom, (1) *"If you repeat a lie long enough, it will be accepted as fact."* (2) *"Some prophesies are self-fulfilling."*

St. Paul says in tonight's Bible text, **"God made Him who had no sin to be sin for us, so that in Him we might become the righteousness of God."** Remember the story of David and Goliath? Two armies were fighting, the Israelites and the Philistines, God's people and the pagan enemy. One battle of champions would determine either victory or defeat for the two armies. We remember how the boy David defeated mighty Goliath with faith in God, using only a sling and a stone.

Some consider that this story is a forerunner of a far greater battle, between God and evil, between Jesus and Satan. Like Goliath, Satan seems invincible. We think he's gigantic and can do anything! Then consider Jesus, who, like David, was an unlikely opponent. He was a shepherd who came into Jerusalem meekly riding on a donkey, preaching love and forgiveness. The crowds and even his own friends did not consider He could win this battle.

But like David defeated Goliath with a weapon of stone, Jesus won over Satan by a grave of stone. Jesus went to the cross and died. He was buried in the grave, but the grave did not hold Him. He was the all-powerful Son of God who came to take away the sins of the world. Remember Luther's hymn?

With might of ours can naught be done, Soon were our loss effected;
But for us fights the Valiant One, Whom God Himself elected.
Ask ye, Who is this? Jesus Christ it is, Of Sabbaoth Lord,
And there's none other God; He holds the field forever.

The message is plain: Jesus, Son of God, took our place on the battlefield of life and He defeated Satan. That little scene from Matthew 3 in which Satan tried to tempt Jesus is the big battle, and Jesus prevailed. He did not succumb to Satan's temptations. He is our champion who wins the battle. He is the

244

"Lord our Righteousness," or as His name is in Hebrew, "Jehovah Jirah."

Things may seem bad in this world these days. Many people, including some Christians, think evil will prevail. But that's a lie. Evil is talked about as if it is invincible, as if nothing can overcome it. That, too, is a lie repeated so often we have come to believe it's true. But evil will not prevail in our world. Jesus already won the big battle long ago. Life is not the Big Battle against Satan. It's just a series of skirmishes that mop up on the field where the BIG ONE has already been fought - and it's been won - by Jesus, our Champion.

You and I have been brought up from birth to believe we must fight our own battles in life. We teach our children they must fend for themselves in this world. Some of us think we must also do all the fighting against Satan, and when we think that we feel overwhelmed.

But the battle has already been won, Jesus did it for us. He, like David, faced down the monstrous champion of evil and destroyed him. Our life is a bunch of little battles, and Jesus promises us power through the Holy Spirit to overcome them.

In many ways, Lent is like a re-run of David defeating Goliath, of seeing again that Jesus truly did defeat Satan. We already know the outcome, but we need to watch it again and again to be reminded what really happened and who really won. Otherwise, we'll just retreat into believing Satan is all-powerful and that we're helpless against him.

Paul wrote, **"God made Him who, had no sin, to be sin for us, so that in Him, we might become the righteousness of God."** This means that, in the battle, Jesus became like He was sinful, He took on Himself our sinfulness, so that all who trust in Him and His victory will have everlasting life.

So how should you and I react to life and its uncertainties? With fear and terror? No! With the attitude, *"I can do it myself, God?"* No! With the belief that God grades life on a curve, and so if I am better than most others, I'll get to heaven? Not that either! Should we sit back and let Jesus do everything? No again!

We should give Christ the honor and praise. He has won heaven all for us, so we can serve Him and honor Him by our words and deeds. We must tell the truth in Jesus, the truth that will set us free from sin and guilt. There is a whole world of people out there who believe a lot of lies. The truth will set them free.

The idea of having a champion fight the battle for us is not so foreign as we might think. Soon millions will gather to watch their champions do battle with the enemy. It's not so much the army as it is the NBA or the NCAA or wherever our favorite team does its battles.

May all of us, young or old, new Christians or seasoned veterans, will line up on the sidelines and sofas and cheer. This year, let's praise God that Jesus, our Champion, has won the Big One, the Super Bowl, the World Series, the Final Four, the Olympics of the big battle of good and evil. Jesus, God's Son, is our Champion. He won it all for us. Now let's spread the world for Him. Amen!

LENT SERIES FIVE
"Living for the Lord"
Week Six

John 13:4-5, Luke 22:19   "Served by the Best"

✠ ✠ ✠

You and I have come a long way in our journey to the cross. We have heard our Lord speak many things as we are "Living for the Lord." Tonight let's examine Maundy Thursday, the final day of Holy Week, the last night before our Lord Jesus died. Tonight we will look at a real man giving His real heart to His real friends, showing them the supreme example of what it means to serve.

Imagine for a moment an incredible event. Imagine you received a great invitation, an unexpected invitation, an invitation you never dreamed of. You are just getting ready to leave work when a man with a leather briefcase asks for you at the desk. You are tired and he looks refreshed. You are driving your old car home and he comes in a limousine. You need a change of clothes and he is dressed in a fine dark suit. You wonder if he's a salesman and what he wants to sell you.

He addresses you by name and hands you an envelope. It's from, of all places, Washington DC, the White House. It's an invitation to dinner with the President! After you've read it, the man asks, "Do you accept the invitation?" Folks, when the President invites you to dinner, it is more than a request. You change your plans. You re-arrange your schedule. It is not so much an invitation as it is an command to be present. Of course you accept his invitation, whether you voted for him or not.

When you arrive in Washington, a limousine picks you up at Reagan National Airport. The car drives you past monuments of heroes until you enter the secured gate at 1600 Pennsylvania Ave. This is a far cry from South Pennsylvania Avenue in your hometown. A servant opens your door and escorts you into a huge room.

But then you notice something strange. You are alone. You wonder where all the other guests are. Then you notice that hanging over the huge fireplace is a picture of you -- a huge painting of YOU. What's that doing there? As you stand there, a voice behind you speaks, "Good evening. May I show you to your chair"" You turn and it is none other than the President himself, and he is wearing an apron! The President of the United States in an apron! This is being served by the best!

He escorts you to the only chair with the only place setting. "Wait," you say, "Where are all the other guests?" "You are my guest tonight," he replies. "You are the only one I want to serve. Please have a seat and I will bring your first course. What would you like to drink this evening?" (You're tempted to ask for a glass of Whitewater, but you refrain.) You wonder if she is in the kitchen doing the cooking, but you don't ask. This evening is too strange to be true. What's going on here? No one as important as the President ever waits on just one common person like you.

NOT QUITE TRUE! As unusual as this scene might be, is this not what happens in Holy Communion? Jesus, Son of the Mighty God, Lord of all the universe, makes us a special meal. The main entrée is Himself, His body and His blood given under bread and wine. He speaks to each of us and tells us He forgives us. He comes to each one of us individually and offers us a new start. This is so much greater than the President. Here we are TRULY SERVED BY THE BEST!

How would you react if you receive such an invitation? Would you dare point out how it might be worded differently? Would you ask for one printed in a different color? Would you, in the face of such honor, ask to change the menu? Of course not! This is Jesus. This is the Lord and Master. No one would EVER think of such things!

Then the Lord does something even more strange. He stoops down and removes your shoes and socks. Your shoes aren't polished. You've been in those socks all day. Your feet probably smell! Yet He stoops down and starts to wash then. What's going on here? He shouldn't be doing that! That's a job for some staff member working for minimum wage.

In Jesus' day, to have one's feet washed was a sign of high honor. It might be similar to a gentle backrub or providing you with steaming, scented towels to freshen up. I once went to a restaurant that gave me a hot, moist towel after dinner. What a treat! What a pleasure to be treated so well.

Jesus' disciples were stunned. Some objected. Most didn't understand, even when He told them why. **"I have washed** your feet," He said. **"Now you should wash each other's feet."** When we realize what an incredible mess Jesus has to wash off us, our feet and our souls, then you realize why this is so hard, and why you and I are truly being served by the best.

I believe few of us truly understand what His foot washing represents. It's not as obvious as you think. You and I are Christians. We've studied our Bible well. You and I are Americans. We know our rights. You and I are members of this congregation, so we know what good service is. It is hard to wash each other's hands, let alone each other's feet. It is hard to be a humble servant when we drive here in fine cars from fine homes wearing fine clothes.

Foot washing is dirty work. It means we dig in. It means we take on tasks we'd rather avoid. It means we make sacrifices when we'd like to keep it all. It means laying aside differences that don't matter. It means taking up the cross of Jesus and risking being hurt as we help someone else. Foot washing means humility, and humility is another dirty word today. I want be served. I don't want to wash your feet! It's my human nature, and I think you are not much different from me.

On Holy Thursday night, Jesus showed us His heart. He came to serve, not be served, and He that night showed us His true colors. The Lord hosting His own meal. The King passing the bread. The Master of the Universe on His knees at your feet. God Himself washing off your dirt.

To me, dirty feet symbolize a dirty soul. Even nice feet are not pleasant. Dirty feet are nasty, and we all have them. And our Lord Jesus, the babe of Bethlehem now grown, the miracle worker, the healer of the unwell, lover of the low, patron of the poor, the accepter of the unaccepted, our Savior washes our feet and our whole bodies clean and pure. He removes our sinful stains and cleanses our corrosive guilt. He cares not what others think. He just stoops to His task and washes us clean.

Jesus does what none of us can, and few of us would attempt. He forgives us of eternal punishment. He accepts each of us as we are, unconditionally, without criticism, without reservation. He waits on us so we might wait on each other. He washes our feet so we might be clean, that we might wash each other's feet. He loves us so we will love each other, not just with words, but with actions. He is the Best, and you and I are served by the Best.

This might be a good time to end with a political joke or some comment that would show my political stripes. But that would demean the presidency and it would also demean our Lord. Just be content in knowing there is an engraved invitation with your name on it. To an incomparable meal, served by the best. What an honor! AMEN!

LENT SERIES SIX
(8 weeks)
"The Lord's Prayer"
Week One

Matthew 6:9: **"This, then, is how you should pray. 'Our father who art in heaven...'"**

✠ ✠ ✠

Of this petition, Martin Luther writes in his Small Catechism, "God would by these words tenderly invite us to believe that He is our true Father and that we are His true children; so that we may with all boldness and confidence ask Him as dear children ask their dear father." (Luther's explanation of the Lord's Prayer)

"Father" is God's favorite name. Jesus called God "Father" over two hundred times. His first recorded words were, **"Didn't you know I had to be in my Father's house?"** (Luke 2:49), and His last words from the cross were, **"Father, into your hands I commit my spirit."** (Luke 23:46) In the Gospel of John alone Jesus repeats this familiar name of God over 150 times. God loves to be called Father. That's why His Son Jesus taught us to pray, **"Our father who art in heaven..."**

It's hard for us to understand how revolutionary it was for Jesus to address God in this way. Though today we take this title for granted, and we assume an intimacy with God, in Jesus' day it was almost blasphemous to do so. The Old Testament traditions were still in effect; they demanded no one dare even speak the name of God aloud, let alone call Him Father. No good Jew would have dared address God in this manner, and yet Jesus did it and taught others to do the same.

When Jesus teaches us to pray "Our Father," He is telling us the status He wants to give us. He wants us as His children. By nature, we are not *"Children of the Heavenly Father,"* but **"children of wrath."** (Ephesians 2:3) and **"enemies of God."** (Romans 5:10) "Our Father" is not prayed because of our natural condition, but it is the position in life God wants to give us. He wants to give us His own name.

In 1864, the night President Abraham Lincoln was shot, Dr. Samuel Mudd set the broken leg of John Wilkes Booth. He didn't know
251

what Booth had done, so he did his duty as any doctor would have. Because of it, Dr. Mudd was arrested and imprisoned several years for aiding the president's murderer, giving rise to the accusative term, "Your name is mud!" Although he was released after only a few terrible years in a filthy prison, and although he spent nearly a year of his sentence helping quell an outbreak of the plague there, and although his personal health was broken and he had broken no law, his name has never been exonerated. Because he aided Lincoln's killer, the United States government has never allowed his name to be cleared. Even as late as in the 1990's, descendants of Dr. Mudd have tried once again to clear his name, and always unsuccessfully.

Thanks be to God that when we are forgiven, our names are cleared. When we trust in Christ, we are considered sinners no more. It would be enough if God just did that, to clear our name. But He wants to do more. He wants to give us His name. It would be enough if God just set us free. But He wants to do more. He wants to take us home as His own dear children. He wants to adopt us into His family.

St. Paul knew this, and so he wrote, "**For you did not receive a spirit of slavery that leads you again to fear, but you received the spirit of adoption as sons by which we cry, 'Abba, Father.'**" (Romans 8:15 NASV) God wants to adopt us as His children. He wants to make us His own, and He makes us His own by faith in Jesus Christ.

We're all pretty well aware that Epiphany is in the midst of a sustained baby boom. Twenty-two baptisms in the past year proves this! Just when we thought we knew all our expectant mothers, another one made her announcement. We thought there would be about half dozen, but now it's a dozen and ten more! Biological parents well know the earnest longing to have a child, but in most cases, our cribs are easily filled. We decide to have a baby, and soon a baby is born! In fact, sometimes the child came along without being planned.

But with adoptive parents, it's a different story. They have to get ready. They must be determined. Adopting a child almost becomes a passion. I've heard of many unplanned pregnancies, but I've never heard of an unplanned adoption. That's why most adoptive parents can understand God's passion to adopt us. As the Bible says, "**When the fullness of**

252

time came, God sent forth his Son, born of a woman, born under the law, in order to redeem those under law, that we might receive the adoption of sons." (Galatians 4:4-5 NASV)

On a Utah spring morning in 1984, Mrs. Peterson called me with the frantic news they could pick up their adoptive baby that Friday. I didn't even know they wanted to adopt! They'd done all the work long ago - passed the tests, endured the screenings, spent the money. They'd gotten their hopes up, but then came the waiting and waiting. And in the years of disappointment they'd nearly forgotten what they were waiting for. Until the phone call came, that is. Then their world was turned upside down. I went to see her and brought them our old crib. I helped her call a few friends, but she was a basket case for days. But when their beautiful little black-haired, dark-eyed girl was placed in her arms later that week, she became a real Mom. She and her husband loved that little girl and also the next girl they adopted a few years later. It was an emotional experience for them and our whole church that I'll always remember.

Adoptive parents know what it is to go through this. They know what it is to set out on a mission, to go through all the testing, to sit through the waiting, and hopefully also - finally - to get the phone call. They know what it is to take responsibility for a child with a shaky past and a flimsy future. They, probably better than anyone else, understand God's love for His adopted children.

And it's also true for one who's been adopted. When you've been an orphan rescued from despair and given parents who love you, you know better than anyone what it is that God has done for us. He has sought us, and found us. He has spent the effort and signed the papers to take us home. God has become Our Father.

Adoption is received; it is not earned. It's a gift, not a right. It's a privilege of being loved. Like parents, God does the adopting. Like the parents, He does all the work. Adoption agencies don't find children for parents who want them, they find parents for children who need them.

God wants to adopt us because we have eternal needs. Parents will adopt the child for what he needs, not what he has. They don't ask first if the child has money or clothing or is smart. They don't ask if he can wash his clothes or make his meals. They adopt him because of what he needs, a home and love and security.

The same is true of God. He doesn't adopt us because of what we have. He doesn't give us His name because we are good looking or live good lives. Adoption is something God gives us, something great from His grace and mercy.

Yes, we may rebel against God, even when we know He loves us. Sometimes even adopted children try to run away from home. But God will welcome us back when we stray. He is the father of the Prodigal Son, waiting, welcoming him home. Nothing can separate us from the love of god. He is "Our Father" in heaven and on earth. He will never turn us away when we come to Him.

And so we pray, **"Our Father, who art in heaven."** This wonderful prayer has been the comfort of Christians through the ages. It has brought us peace where there was strife and strength when we were weak. This prayer has brought courage during our wars and has given life in the midst of death. May these days of turmoil be make us return from the desert of our worries to drink from the sweet fountain of God's mercy. And may we rejoice that we can come to God as our dear Father. Amen!

LENT SERIES SIX
"The Lord's Prayer"
Week Two

Matthew 6:9: **"Our Father in heaven, hallowed be Your name."**

"God's name is indeed holy in itself, but we pray in this petition that it may be kept holy among us also. God's name is kept holy when the Word of God is taught in its truth and purity, and we, as the children of God, also lead holy lives according to it. Help us to do this, dear Father in heaven! But anyone who teaches or lives contrary to God's Word profanes the name of God among us. Protect us from this, heavenly Father!" (from Martin Luther' explanation of the Lord's Prayer)

A son was taking his mother to see an immense waterfalls, and as they walked the long path to get there, he began to describe it to her. He'd seen it before and had read about it in National Geographic, and so he attempted to impress his mother by lecturing about it to her as they walked. So full of information was he that he began speaking louder and louder, forced to raise his voice by a noise in the background that also grew louder and louder. He was almost getting perturbed at this noise when finally his mother, said, "Hush now, son, and look at that!" Then she pointed to the what he'd been trying to describe. She didn't need to hear his description, just to see the majesty of the great waterfalls and bask in its grandeur.

I've tried many times to preach on the name of God, but always it's fallen so far short to the name itself. To presume to describe something so powerful and majestic as the name of almighty God is almost a waste of time. You just can't do it justice. *"You can't get there from here."* So God is saying to us, "Hush now, and look at that!" Let God's name speak for itself.

To preach on this petition is to fall far short of the mark, because this petition points the finger of condemnation even as we speak it. Martin Luther wrote, *"I know of no teaching in all the Scriptures that so mightily diminishes and destroys our life as does this petition."* He goes on to say God's name is constantly being diminished and maligned by what we say and do in our lives.

We use God's name profanely in cursing, and we use it casually and carelessly in our oaths. Every time we pray the Lord's Prayer, under our breaths we should utter a prayer of repentance, a confession that we fail miserably in hallowing His name. A better petition for us might be, *"Thank You, O God, that You let us miserable sinners even speak Your holy name."* The Old Testament people didn't feel worthy to speak His name. At times I believe we should follow their example.

Besides faith, there are two requirements for any prayer to be valid. First is that we must know to whom we are praying. We are praying to God, our holy and heavenly father. We speak to Him as dear children speak to their dear father.

The second requirement is that we realize who is speaking as we speak to Him. No one can truly pray, *"Our Father"* who does not realize that he or she is the prodigal son or the wayward daughter, coming back from the far country where he or she has strayed and squandered the Father's fortune in riotous living. We do not hallow God's name, but usually profane and betray it a hundred times. Thus, our prayers may actually condemn us rather than help us.

Truthfully, the name of God plays a pitifully small part in our lives. The name of our employer, or our children, or our spouse or even our friends plays a much larger part. When we pray, we must always must repent, for each petition reminds us that we have not lived as we ought, nor loved as we ought, nor had faith as we ought. *"Hallowed by Your name,"* must be spoken in utter humility.

Yet we must continue to pray, *"Hallowed be Your name."* His name is holy in itself, but we His people must hallow it by how we live. That includes in our business, even if people might think us a religious fanatic. And also in our bedroom, for even there His name must be kept holy. We cannot think this is a problem others have, but not us. We all must pray for the strength to hallow His name.

Sometimes in this prayer, I feel the Lord pointing at me and saying, **"You are the man!"** (2 Samuel 12:7) Remember that verse from the life of King David? Nathan the prophet had told him the story of a wicked man with thousands of sheep who had stolen the only lamb of a poor man. Hearing the story,

256

David ranted, *"Where is this man? Bring him here and he will pay!"* But Nathan pointed at him and said, **"You are the man!** *You, with all your possessions, have stolen the precious wife of Uriah, your faithful soldier, and even sent him to his death to cover up your sin."*

When we pray, *"Hallowed be your name,"* we should feel the hand of God pointing at us, showing us our failures to make His name holy by how we live and what we say. We who know the sanctity of God's name must do all we can to make sure His name is not profaned by how we live.

There are always certain parts of our lives that we want to keep secret from God, areas we refuse to surrender to Him. These are areas of life we know God would never agree with or sign His name to, the little pigeonholes of sin known only to ourselves, or so we think. It could be our anger, or lust, or greed, or gluttony, or sloth, or envy, or pride. Such sins are deadly because they try to lead us to further sin.

But our Father in heaven stands at the gate watching for us to return. When He sees us coming back, tattered and dirty from our venture into life, He runs to us with joy and welcomes us back into the family. He places on us a new robe, calls together all His family and gives us a banquet. We who should have the lowest of all places, sweeping the street or shining boots or washing dishes, are given the place of honor.

So then, when we again pray *"Hallowed by Your name,"* we do so as forgiven children, restored to our Father by His love. We are no longer troubled about our personal failures, but soothed by our Father's success in His Son Jesus Christ.

The Lord's Prayer is made up of seven petitions, six about the heavenly concerns and one about the earthly things. Only the one about daily bread deals with earthly needs. The rest are all about the heavenly. That means this prayer is to help us grow in our faith, in our being more like Christ. It's not so much about making sure we have all we need, as to make sure we need what we already have. We need to grow in our faith. We need to hallow God's name. We need to forgive as we have been forgiven. We need help to do His will, here on earth as it is done in heaven.

But this will only happen if we live near to God and cling to His Word. People who live and work in dark places need light. Without it, they become listless. They lose energy and are weary. To make up for the light, they drink stimulants or pop pills.

When we run from the light of God's Son and live in the dark, we'll try to get our "kicks" from artificial means, whether by pills, or an orderly life, or doing our duty, or by ambition. Living by the letter of the law is an artificial stimulant that will never satisfy. Only trusting in Christ can. Only knowing we are forgiven can help us hallow God's name. We must be pushed out of the dark room of self-righteousness and into the light of God's grace. There we see ourselves and our God as we really are. Hallowed be the name of God for doing all this for you and for me! Amen.

LENT SERIES SIX
"The Lord's Prayer"
Week Three

Matthew 6:10   **"Your Kingdom come"**

✠ ✠ ✠

To hear about the kingdom of God during wartime is a blessing. Helmut Thielicke, Lutheran pastor in Stuttgart, Germany during WWII, preached a series of sermons on the Lord's Prayer, and on the Sunday he was to speak on "Your Kingdom Come," his ragtag flock had to meet in the choir, a small room of the cathedral, because allied bombs had reduced the rest of his church to rubble.

Thielicke said to his people that Sunday, *"Isn't there a comfort, a peculiar message in the fact that, after all the conflagrations that have swept through our wounded city, we can continue our study of the Lord's Prayer? We don't need to interrupt and search the Bible for texts appropriate for catastrophe. The Words of the Lord's Prayer are immediate to every situation of life. The farmer can pray it at close of day's work, the mother can pray it with her children in the air-raid shelter, the little child seeking fatherly protection or the aged person in the trials and pangs of his last hour, both can pray it. It can be prayed by everybody in every situation, without exception."*

We can suppose this beloved prayer is being prayed this very hour in tanks and tents, planes and ships in the Middle East, by devout believers and earnest seekers. It's being prayed by soldiers who know their lives are in the hands of God, not just their fellow comrades. It's also being prayed by their families who want simply their loved ones to be brought safely home again. And we're praying it, too.

The facts of life have a way of reminding us of the End Times. In an age where the facts of death stare at us from our video screens, where our sophisticated ways of living are brought to a halt by a huge spring snowstorm, we need more than ever to pray, *"Our Father..."* **"Your Kingdom come!"**

Luther explained this petition this way: *"The kingdom of God certainly comes by itself without our prayer, but we pray in this petition that it may come to us also. God's kingdom comes when our heavenly Father gives us His Holy Spirit, so that by His grace we believe His holy Word and lead godly lives here in time and there in eternity."* (from Martin Luther's Small Catechism)

The kingdom of God would seem to be part of the heights of life, being adopted into the King's family, being made royalty despite our sin and rebellion. The kingdom of God comes when we have the grace to believe the Word of God about Jesus Christ. The kingdom is ours by God's grace and the working of the Holy Spirit. Christ is with us in the heights of joy in God's kingdom.

But the kingdom is also ours in the depths of life's troubles because Christ is there in those depths, also. He is there in the hospital recovery room and beside the deathbed. One can never draw God too deeply into humanity, and one can never draw the kingdom of God too deeply into the misery of this world.

As I prepare to write sermons, I am often drawn to the television screen for the latest news, hoping for some really good news, hoping to hear that good has triumphed over evil. But all I see is sand blowing, and all I hear are more predictions. The news isn't all bad, but it's not as good as we'd like it to be.

The kingdom of God is where God reigns supreme. In the midst of the kingdom the news is always good. There is no bad news there, for all events happen by His plan and His time-table. In the kingdom of Christ there are no sneak attacks, there are no vicious cruelties, and no wise people second-guessing the plans of those who wish to keep the world free.

"Your Kingdom come!" Our Lord Jesus spent most of his ministry speaking about the kingdom. He once told His disciples that the kingdom of God is a matter of the heart, not of a map or Day-timer. It cannot be located outside the heart of the believer, because the Kingdom of God is within us (Luke 17:21). He said the kingdom is united, not divided (Matthew 12:25). The kingdom will never end (Luke 1:33). The kingdom of heaven is nearer than we think (Matthew 10:7). Therefore, to live as subjects in this kingdom, Jesus challenges us to seek first His kingdom and His righteousness, and all these things will be given to us as well (Matthew 6:33).

If you want to learn about the kingdom, read the parables. The Gospel of Matthew is filled with these stories about the nature of the kingdom of God. Matthew chapter 13 contains seven separate parables: the Sower and Seed, the Weeds among the Wheat, the Mustard Seed, the Yeast in the Flour, the Net and Fishes, The Hidden Treasure, and the Pearl of Great Price. Each one of these precious gold nuggets tells us another facet of the kingdom. His parables tell us the kingdom starts small and grows large, that it grows in the hearts of those who are receptive, and how both believers and unbelievers will live in it until they are separated in the end. Jesus tells us the kingdom is so precious that some people will forsake everything just to be part of it.

Christ instructed us to seek the kingdom, to be part of it. *"May Your kingdom come to us,"* we pray in this prayer, asking our Father to make us part of that kingdom. **"Your Kingdom come!"** is closely linked to the first words, "Our Father." We ask Him as dear children ask their dear father to be in that holy gathering before God's throne.

Seven-year-old Sarah asked her father for a desk. She was proud to be in school and wanted a special place for her books and papers, and so they went shopping. They found two nice desks that were affordable, one of unfinished wood at a furniture store and the other of imitation wood desk at Wal-Mart. She loved the shape of the unfinished desk and so her Dad said he'd buy it. The salesman said they would have someone paint it in just the colors she wanted, but it would take several days. This was disturbing news! "But Daddy," said Sarah, "I want to take it home today." Fortunately she didn't stomp her feet or demand her way, but she did set out to change her father's mind. "Daddy, do you think we could paint it ourselves?" "No Sarah, I don't have time to do that right now." "But Daddy, can't I just take good care of it until you have time to paint it?" "No Sarah, we'd better wait till it's painted." "Guess what, Daddy, it'll fit in the back of our car!" Her father had no comeback for that one. And finally the clincher, "Daddy, can't we P-L-E-A-S-E take it home?" Her new desk came home in the car that very day!

The father didn't know it, but it was probably just one word that changed his mind, "Daddy." Hearing those heartfelt pleas, what father wouldn't want his child to spend more time writing or reading? We parents often want what our children want, but they always want it sooner.

When we plead to the Lord for the things we want, our Heavenly Father hears us too. 1 John 5:14 tells us if we ask anything according to His will, God hears us. The prayer of a righteous person has great power, said James 5:14, written by the brother of Jesus. But when we go to the Father like a pleading child, calling Him "Daddy,"

In Galatians 4:6 Paul says we can cry out to God, **"Abba, Father!"** That is calling Him "Daddy!" God loves to hear that word. He is really moved to hear us. He not hears us, He wants to answer us. And so, with all His children we pray, **"Your kingdom come."**

"Your Kingdom come!" A Christian's life does not start with birth, but with death, Christ's death and our death to sin. If we spend our whole life in pursuit of selfish gain, what's left? An eternity of anguish and sadness, of pain and separation! But life lived with faith in Christ results in an eternal kingdom and eternity in the presence of our dear Father. **"And so, when these things begin to take place, stand up and lift up your heads, for your redemption is drawing near."** (Luke 21:29)

"Your Kingdom come, O Father!" Amen!

LENT SERIES SIX
"The Lord's Prayer"
Week Four

Matthew 6:10 **"Your will be done on earth as it is in heaven."**

✠ ✠ ✠

Of this petition, Martin Luther writes in his Small Catechism, *"The good and gracious will of God is done even without our prayer, but we pray in this petition that it may be done among us also. God's will is done when He breaks and hinders every evil plan and purpose of the devil, the world, and our sinful nature, which do not want us to hallow God's name or let His kingdom come, and also when He strengthens and keeps us firm in His Word and faith until we die. This is His good and gracious will."* (Martin Luther, 1530)

Every Christian, no matter how weak or strong his faith may be, has had to struggle with knowing God's will. *"What is God"s will for my life?"* we ask, pleading for some kind of revelation and faith. That question may be the wrong one to ask. We may want to know, but the answer is part of something bigger than any one of us.

The newspapers once told of three nuns who were arrested for trespassing and trying to destroy military property. *"For the sake of Christ, we are doing God's will,"* they said as they are escourted off to jail. At about the same time a chaplain, assigned to the Army's Third Infantry Division, was giving counsel and hope to soldiers doing their duty in battle and facing the enemy. *"For the sake of Christ, I am doing God's will,"* he says. So who is right? One is protesting for peace and the other is aiding people in war. Are both right, or are both in some way missing the point of knowing God's will?

Years ago I stepped inside the huge doors of a new large church in Germany. There was a crowd, so I walked along the back wall about fifty feet and noticed a strange light behind me. I turned around and a rather ugly light caught me in the face. It was the sun shining through a piece of brown glass a foot or two in diameter. It was a cold, nasty color and there were several pieces of pink and amber glass next to it. I tried looking up, but was too close to see what it meant. Only when the crowd dispersed and I was able to step back did I realize that piece of glass was part of the sandal on the foot of Christ on the cross. Up close it made no sense, but when seen as part of the bigger picture, I saw it was part of Jesus.

If we never step back from seeing our life close up, if we only think of God's will in terms of ourselves and our needs, we will never see the "Big Picture," the wonderful story of God's love for us, the plan of salvation for all, earned by our Lord and Savior Jesus Christ. Trouble is, most of us prefer to concentrate and worry about on our tiny piece of life rather than step back and see that it's part of something bigger.

In a Bible Class I was asked, *"Is God always in control of the world?"* He said someone at work had openly challenged him whether God could be in control of everything, including war. I said God is in control of the Big Picture, the details of plan of which only He fully knows and the outcome which He fully understands. He will allow things within that plan we may not like, and some of it may make no sense, but He knows the outcome.

Consider Job of the Old Testament. God let Him go through hell. His life was so rotten that he wanted to die, but there was a purpose. But God wasn't playing games with him or "jerking his chain," as we say. He was bringing Job to an eternal realization of what was important in life. It was terrible in the middle, but the end was worth it.

When you're in the midst of life-changing struggles, remember, this is all a part of a bigger picture, the story of your salvation. We are important, but we are not center stage here. It involves much more than just us.

A little girl was given her part in a Christmas program. Being named Mary, she assumed she'd get the part of Mary. When they told her she would be in the angel choir, she cried. "Why can't I be Mary?" The pagent director soothed her and said, "This story is not about you, Mary. This story is about something much bigger than you and I. It's bigger than me or all of us put together. It's a story about God and about His son Jesus. We're here to tell His story, not our own. Every small part is just as important as the biggest. And the biggest part is no better than the smallest. Being an angel is exactly as important as being Mary."

264

When we struggle with difficult times and difficult decisions, with what we should or shouldn't do in life, we must keep in mind it's all part of something bigger than us. God doesn't love us less because we feel ours in a minor part. God doesn't forget any of His people in need. The trials of life toughen us, strengthen us for the better. But if we concentrate only on our small piece of rough, ugly, stained glass, we'll forget it's all part of the Big Picture.

The will of God is His desire for our eternal welfare, His eternal wishes that we live with Him in eternity. His will is part and parcel of our existence on earth, but we don't have to agree with it. We can thwart His will. We can give up and break down. We can vaunt our human pride and rage against God. We can go against His will because we stubbornly want our own way. We can get drunk or curse the government or even God. But when we do, we will pay a price. Job could have cursed God, but then he would never have seen the prize God had for him in mind.

In the depths of WWII, when Pastor Helmut Thielicke preached on the Lord's Prayer, his first two sermons to his small flock were uninterrupted. His third sermon was preached in a small room because most of his church had been bombed by the Allies. But his sermon on this petition, the will of God, was interrupted by air raid sirens, and everyone was forced into an air raid shelter. As he spoke, Allied bombers destroyed the last standing walls of his precious old church. Yet he did not quit preaching in anger or despair. He finished his message on God's will down there in that air raid shelter. He told his people, "Not until we realize we are encircled by the powers of satan, do we realize the tremendous liberating power that comes from being able to pray, 'Our Father.' Not until we realize that we live in a world in which men kill and die, a world in which we can fall into terrible hands of men, a world in which only dim traces remain of the glory of God intended for his creation, not until all we remember all this can we really begin to pray, 'Your will be done.'"

Like Thielicke's little flock, we live in a world where the will of God is obscured. Bombs of trouble and heartache explode all around us. The bombs of humanism and idolatry and sickness and unemployment will threaten to blow up our relationship with God. But we must not give in! We are God's children by faith in Jesus Christ. We are loved by the eternal Creator. We are destined for heaven.

God's will is always done, on earth as it is in heaven, and His will is that we be saved. Don't despair, my friends. Don't immerse yourself in anger or self-pity. All of us at some time go through hell, but we come out again. One man loses his job and another man loses his wife. One has bills, the other has cancer. But the same God answers our troubles. This, too, shall pass. In Jesus, He will bring us to heaven.

By the way, that church I stepped inside of? It was quite new, built near the place where Pastor Thielicke once preached. Newness out of the rubble! God's will be done! Amen

LENT SERIES SIX
"The Lord's Prayer"
Week Five

Matthew 6:11   **"Give Us Today Our Daily Bread."**
✠ ✠ ✠

Of this petition, Martin Luther writes, *"God gives daily bread to everyone even without our prayers, also to evil people, but we pray in this petition that God would lead us to realize this, and to receive our daily bread with thanksgiving. Daily bread includes everything that has to do with the support and needs of the body, such as food, drink, clothing, shoes, house, home, land, animals, money, goods, a devout husband or wife, lawful government, good weather, peace, health, self-control, good reputation, good friends, faithful neighbors, and the like."* (Luther's Small Catechism, 1530)

Of the seven petitions Jesus teaches us in the Lord's Prayer, this is the only one that asks for physical blessings. All the rest are petitions for spiritual blessings: *"May Your name be holy,... may your kingdom come,... may your will be done,... forgive us our sins,... lead us not into temptation,... deliver us from evil..."* All these are about spiritual matters. Only these six words in the middle on the Lord's Prayer are about physical needs. We spend most of our prayer time asking God to provide our physical needs, but Jesus spends just six words. All the rest is for the spiritual.

Most of us in the United States have trouble relating to the phrase. **"Give Us Today Our Daily Bread."** should ring hollow for our pantries are so packed and our bellies so full. We rarely pray, *"God help me eat."* more often we pray, *"God help me not eat so much."* You won't find books in our stores on surviving starvation, but you'll find the shelves loaded with books about losing weight.

Daily bread is about more than food. It's about everything to keep us alive, all our needs and, yes, even all our wants. He may not give us all the luxuries, but He will make sure we have all the necessities. Psalm 37:3-4 says it so well: **"Trust in the Lord and do good; dwell in the land and enjoy safe pasture. Delight yourself in the Lord and he will give you the desires of your heart."** God is committed to providing our needs. We can count on it, because God is good. *"**His mercy is everlasting**

267

and His faithfulness endures to all generations." (Psalm 100:5)

"**Give us today our daily bread.**" we pray. Luther explains, "*God certainly gives daily bread to everyone even without our prayers, also to evil people.*" We pray these words so quickly, not realizing how richly He has already answered them. We pray this petition only to find our prayer is already answered. We're like the High School senior who decides to go to college and then learns the high cost of tuition. He runs to his father and pleads, "*I'm sorry to ask so much, Dad, but I have nowhere else to go. I want to go to college and don't have a penny.*" The father puts his arm around the boy and says, "*Don't worry, son, the day you were born I began saving for your education. The money's already there.*" Some parents may disagree with providing all their child's college money, but God isn't concerned about providing for all our needs. He's already set aside all we need to support this body and life. He did it before we were born or even conceived.

Most children grow up thinking food and clothing just appear, that they're always just there. They never wonder where it came from or that it took money or work. Food comes in the refrigerator and clothes come in the closet, immediately and abundantly. One day it occurs to them someone else has put it there, and they usually become aware of this when they have to earn the money to buy things themselves.

It's the same with most Christians. One day we realize all this stuff we depend on comes from God. We may work for the money, but someone else developed the company. Someone else made the clothes in some factory, packaged the food or developed the transportation. We may momentarily think we are independent and self-sufficient, but then we get sick or the car breaks down. We're not a doctor and we don't fix cars. We didn't sew the jacket or refine the gasoline. It's just there and we've bought it. But we certainly gripe if the price is too high!

Rarely does the day pass when our very existence is not completely dependent on the work and ingenuity of others. And it all comes, ultimately, from the providence of God. He provides our daily bread through industry, technology, and economics. Our daily bread could include much more trouble or tears, but more often than not our bread comes in peace and far more abundantly than we'll ever need. You and I can only imagine what it must be like to live in a nation at war, or under a vicious dictatorship or living in abject poverty. Grumble about all those laws and politicians if you must, but it's still vastly better than the lawlessness so many must endure.

Asking for daily bread requires great faith. It's not faith that the food will be good, but faith that the cook will provide it. Now and then Carol and I enjoy watching period movies about life in old England, you know, stories about people who live in the big country houses and never work. They sit around doing needlepoint or talking and worrying and crying or playing the piano, but always and without fail, someone else brings them their tea and biscuits. You never see them in the kitchen, and you never see them with dirty hands. Even when working the garden they're in a white dress, and even if they're poor, they seem to have a maid and a cook. How can they always have a maid and a cook? They never do any meaningful work, and yet they always seem to have money to pay others to work for them.

Well, friends, we have our maids and cooks too. Who makes all the food we buy at King Soopers? Who sews all the clothes we get at Dillards? Who manufactures all those tools we get at Home Depot? And how come even the most poor in our society always seem to have enough to buy cigarettes? Yes, indeed, *"God gives daily bread to everyone, even without our prayers, also to evil people, but we pray in this petition that God would lead us to realize this and to receive our daily bread with thanksgiving."* Yes, by God's grace, we have our maids and cooks too.

Asking for daily bread requires great faith. God is the provider. He gives us work so we can have our daily bread, and He forgives us our sins as well. In Jesus Christ, God loves us with an everlasting love, and that means He provides for all our needs, earthly and eternal. He does not forsake His children, and He does not forget what they enjoy in life.

Think of your life as a plate with food on it. It's rarely the empty plate that makes us unhappy, but rather what's on the full one. The veggies are healthy but dull, and fruit is good but not filling. There's roast beef but it is overcooked. And right there in the center of the plate sit some Oreo cookies - yum!

They may be fattening, but they do wonders for our attitude. Our plate is never empty. It's filled with good things from God. We might not like what's on it, but it's never empty. We always have daily bread.

The next time your plate contains more broccoli than apple pie, remember who prepared the meal. The next time you find a portion hard to swallow, remember that Jesus did too. His suffering on the cross for you and me was very hard to swallow. But with His Father's help He was able to do so, and so are we. Thank you, dear God, for our daily bread. Amen!

LENT SERIES SIX
"The Lord's Prayer"
Week Six

Matthew 6:12   **"Forgive us our debts, as we forgive our debtors."**

✦ ✦ ✦

Of this petition, Martin Luther writes, *"We pray in this petition that our Father in heaven would not look at our sins, or deny our prayer because of them. We are neither worthy of the things for which we pray, nor have we deserved them, but we ask that He would give them all to us by grace, for we daily sin much and surely deserve nothing but punishment. So we, too, will sincerely forgive and gladly do good to those who sin against us."* (Small Catechism, 1530)

Is life really different when you become a Christian? Does it make any difference when we experience God's forgiveness? *Victor Hugo's classic, "Les Miserables," is the story of how a man's life is changed by forgiveness. Jean Valjean, embittered by nineteen years in prison for stealing a loaf of bread, is shown mercy by a priest who saves him from jail and even gives him silver candlesticks so he can start a new life. Valjean is humbled, almost devastated by this act of kindness, so that his life is changed forever. The forgiveness he's granted moves him to be merciful to others, even to Javert, his archenemy who had imprisoned him and hunted him all his life. The story of this novel is the contrast between Valjean, empowered by mercy, and Javert, embittered by the law.*

So, does it make a difference when people become Christian? Absolutely! When we come to know Christ and experience His forgiveness it's like coming out of darkness and into light. Being forgiven is like being born again. Every day is new with promise and hope and joy, like beginning all over again. That's what happens to all people who can say with sincerity and commitment the words of the Apostle's Creed, *"I believe in the Holy Christian Church, the communion of saints, the forgiveness of sin."*

I believe in the forgiveness, and I believe in forgiving. Jesus taught us all to pray, **"And forgive us our sins as we forgive those who sin against us."** Forgiven and forgiving! The

271

two go together. You can't have one without the other.

Our Lord was blunt about forgiving. He told a great story about a servant who owed his master more than he could possibly pay back in a lifetime. The indebted servant pleaded, **"Be patient with me and I will repay you everything!"** So the master forgave him his debt, because that was the only way the poor man could live. Without forgiveness, he might as well die, so great his debt.

But this forgiven servant then went out and found a fellow servant who owed him a few dollars. He grabbed him by the neck and demanded he repay every penny. This second man now pleaded with the same words, **"Be patient with me and I will repay you everything!"** But he wasn't patient and he wasn't forgiving. Instead, he had him thrown in jail until he should pay every penny. And who can repay anything in jail?

Those who saw it told the man's master, and he took predictable action. He jailed the unforgiving servant, and told him he could forget about any more mercy. Jesus concluded the story with chilling words: **"This is how my Father in heaven will treat you if you do not forgive your brother, every one of you, from your hearts."**

That's blunt language, but you and I need blunt language about forgiveness. We either ignore what Jesus says on this or we explain it away. *"I have a right to be angry, I have a right not to forgive!"* we say. True, others may have done terrible things to us, but still God forgives them. He loves all people out of the goodness of His heart. That's the way God is, for even His Son prayed from the cross, **"Father forgive them, for they know now what they do."** As the saying goes, *"To forgive is to set a prisoner free, and to discover the prisoner was you."*

Some will say they can't forgive another person until he or she says they're sorry. That's not the way of God. He forgives first. Forgiveness is not a matter of feelings, but a decision of the will. It does not depend on actions of the one who has harmed us, but upon us.

Forgiveness is viewed by many as weakness. To them payback is strength. *"I don't get mad -- I get even!"* Forgiveness may seem a small and weak thing, but it's the greatest thing of all. It's what our world needs most of all, yet as the world rationalizes its hatred and resentment. *"I have a right to be angry!"* But as another wise saying goes, *"He who cannot forgive, burns the bridge over which he himself must pass."*

We live in a world that is not at peace with God nor with itself. People are at war with one another, husbands war against wives, children war against parents, companies against employees and the rich against the poor. To help deal with this, you and I must learn to forgive. He forgives and so must we. When our Lord taught us to pray, **"Forgive us our trespasses as we forgive those who trespass against us,"** He further clarified that statement: **"For if you forgive men when they sin against you, your heavenly Father will also forgive you. But if you do not forgive men their sins, your Father will not forgive your sins."** Forgiveness is not optional – it's required! Refusing to forgive is throwing God's precious gift back in His face.

Forgiveness isn't easy, and if it's hard for us, think how hard it must be for Jesus. He went to Calvary's cross knowing most of the world would reject Him. He walked the way of sorrows knowing people would hate Him. How easy would that be? No, forgiveness is not easy for God. It takes His whole heart and strength to love those who don't care about Him. It took the life of His only Son to forgive you and me.

There are a lot of people who treat God as someone to blame, a dog to be kicked around when things don't go right. Yet the Father does not kick us around. He gave His only Son because of love. The only Son forgives because of His love. **"While were still enemies, Christ died for us."** That's the amazing quality of God's grace. His love is for us, the undeserving ones. His love is for us, the unkind ones. His love is for us, the resentful, angry, stubborn and unforgiving people we so often are.

Christians today wonder why the church has lost its power. Friends, forgiveness IS its power. An unforgiving church is no church at all, and an unforgiving Christian is on the verge of being no Christian at all. When Christians cannot forgive, it's no wonder non-Christians laugh at us. Perhaps it's why so many just ignore us. But the world is watching to see if it does make a difference to be a believer. What we do will show them whether or not being a believer makes a difference in life.

As our Lord once said, **"If you are bringing your gift to the altar, and remember that a brother has something against you, leave your gift. Go first and make peace with your brother. Then come and offer your gift."** (Matthew 5:24-25) You and I can't be right with God if we are unwilling to be right with others. When we come to the altar tonight or any time, we must be willing to make peace with our brothers and sisters.

That's God's way. It is not just church talk, it is God's talk. God is for real, and you and I are for real. The grudges we hold are for real, but Calvary was the most real of all. The death and resurrection of Christ gives freedom to us real people. God grant us all the grace to forgive as we have been forgiven. Amen.

LENT SERIES SIX
"The Lord's Prayer"
Week Seven

Matthew 6:13   **"Lead us not into temptation, but deliver us from the evil one."**

✛ ✛ ✛

The last petitions of the Lord's Prayer encompass most all the concerns of our life. **"Give us our daily bread"** is about the present, **"Forgive us our sins"** is about the past, but **"Lead us not into temptation, but deliver us from evil"** is about the future. It's amazing how God can reduce all our needs to such simple statements.

Martin Luther also had a way of simplifying these words. He said, *"God tempts no one to sin, but we pray in this petition that God would guard and keep us so that the devil, the world, and our sinful nature may not deceive us or mislead us into false belief, despair, and other great shame and vice. Although we are attacked by these things, we pray that we may finally overcome them and win the victory. We further pray that our Father in heaven would rescue us from every evil of body and soul, possessions and reputation, and finally, when our last hour comes, give us a blessed end, and graciously take us from this valley of sorrow to Himself in heaven."* (Luther's Small Catechism, 1530)

Temptation is very real to adults and youth alike. Evil is very real. Satan, the deceiver, is the Evil One. He is the source and power behind all the world's evil. He tempts us to evil and he shows us the evil side of mankind. *"If you want to keep from slipping, avoid slippery places,"* we say. Only Jesus can keep us from falling to temptation.

Jesus Himself does not lead us not into temptation, but when we are tempted, He gives us the power to resist it. The Apostle Paul makes this plain: **"No temptation has seized you except what is common to man. And God is faithful; he will not let you be tempted beyond what you can bear. But when you are tempted, he will also provide a way out so that you can stand up under it."** (1 Corinthians 10:13)

275

C .S. Lewis wrote Screwtape Letters, a fascinating book that shows how Satan leads us into temptation. Screwtape, Satan's experienced agent in hell, writes letters to his nephew Wormwood, a junior demon in the world, and coaches him in ways of handling Christians and casting aspersions on their God. Here's some of the "advice" he gives: *"Get his mind off the eternal and on to the present. Make him fearful, mix fear with hatred, because fear is your greatest power. Get his mind off prayer all together and get him to believe you don't exist. Then you've really got him!"*

Simply being in the world is temptation enough for humans to pervert a good relationship with God. The devil, the world and our sinful self continually pull us away from God.

Wm. Golding wrote his classic novel, Lord of the Flies, about the evil and natural depravity of sin in people. In this book a dozen boys are marooned on island by a plane crash. The adults have died, so they are on their own, and soon they become cruel and oppressive. The mob kills one boy just for sport, and chases another. When at last the fleeing boy is rescued by adult, ironically the adult is a naval officer currently on patrol to kill the enemy in war. Lord of the Flies is a parable about original sin, the sinful nature we have from our birth that causes us to do evil.

St. Paul once warned young pastor Timothy about the evil in the world. He wrote, **"But mark this: There will be terrible times in the last days. People will be lovers of themselves, lovers of money, boastful, proud, abusive, disobedient to their parents, ungrateful, unholy, without love, unforgiving, slanderous, without self-control, brutal, not lovers of the good, treacherous, rash, conceited, lovers of pleasure rather than lovers of God--having a form of godliness but denying its power. Have nothing to do with them."** (2 Timothy 3:1-5).

"Lead us not into temptation, but deliver us from the evil one." said Jesus. The good news of these petitions is that Christ has overcome the evil one. He does not lead us into temptation, but He does deliver us from evil. When Jesus met Satan in battle, He was victorious. Christ won that battle! Matthew 4 is an account of Christ's temptation in the wilderness. Three times Satan tried to tempt Christ, and three times Christ overcame temptation with the Word of God. His certain victory assures us that we, also, can and will overcome evil and temptation when we rely on God's Word.

Jesus' greatest temptation was on the Mount of Olives in the Garden of Gethsemane. There He easily could have stepped aside, have quit the fight and let us fight the battle alone. But Jesus chose to remain in the fight. There was a war going on and the crucial battle was at hand. The war against the Evil One climaxed in the events of Calvary. The disciples ran away, the crowds mocked Him, and the enemies got their way. All creation seemed against Him, the world was in darkness, the earth quaked and shook. Everything and everyone showed the battle scars of war.

But Jesus Christ overcame the powers of evil in His resurrection. When we live by faith in Christ, we, too, have power to overcome evil. Having faith in Jesus Christ means confidence that Christ will win the victory for us. Having faith means knowing and trusting His Word. It means partaking of His Sacraments and loving His people. Having faith means praying and believing God will answer your prayers.

To believe in Jesus is to trust Him, to know His almighty power is with us in all our times of temptation, trouble or evil. Whether evil comes at us at home, at work, at church, or school or in the neighborhood, we do not face it alone.

We Christians live on the Easter side of life. Good Friday is a memory, but it is not where we live. It reminds us what Christ had to endure, but it is in our past. It's only the troubles of today that make us think evil is winning the battle. This current war our soldiers have fought in the Middle East shows the presence of evil, but not its victory. Whether the dictators of the world may enslave small boys, viciously beat women, or poison their followers, evil is not winning the day.

Living on the Easter side of life means we have hope for salvation. We need not fear that evil people or evil events will win the day. They will not, for Christ has won the victory. On Good Friday He took our places in the great battle of good and evil. He faced the enemy on the front lines and died in our places. He faced the fear and He took our sin upon Himself. And though the outcome, His death, looked grim for us, we know the final outcome. Though the chapter seemed evil, we know the end of the book. Because of Him we are the victors. So we need not fear, for He has won the day for us. Good Friday and Easter are God's "Fear Not!" for the world.

When the angels first announced the birth of the Savior, they said, **"Fear not!"** When the angels came to Joseph they said, **"Fear not!"** They said the same to the shepherds, and also to the disciples at the open tomb. **"Fear not, for He whom you seek is not here; He is risen from the dead."** (Mark 16:6)

Regardless of what we may face in the world, "Fear not!" We need not be afraid. It is finished! Christ has delivered us from the Evil One. He faces all struggles with us and gives us the strength to overcome temptation. He gives us the hope that we are delivered from all evil. May this Friday truly be good, because we trust the One who has made it good. Amen

LENT SERIES SIX
"The Lord's Prayer"
Week Eight

Revelation 1:6   **"To Him be glory and power, forever and ever, AMEN!"**   (An Easter Message)

Christ is risen! He is risen indeed! Easter, the ancient Christian festival to commemorate Christ's resurrection is here, and so we say AMEN! The calendar has come full circle once again, and so we say AMEN! The only Son of God has completed God's plan of salvation for us and so we say AMEN! Christ is God's great AMEN to the world, His word of affirmation and assent, His word of hope and joy. AMEN is His word of approval for all mankind.

When the angels sang **"Glory to God in the highest!"** in the fields of Bethlehem, it was God the Father who said His great AMEN! When Jesus defeated Satan, turning away his temptations in the wilderness, the Father said AMEN! When Jesus hung on the cross and said, **"It is finished!"** His Father said AMEN!

To everything God has done for mankind, Jesus Christ is God's great AMEN for all people of all cultures and all ages. There is no human being who has not been given life, no human being who has not been blessed by the Lord. Every person of every age of every clime and race is the beneficiary of God's redemption in Christ Jesus.

This past Lent during our services, we've been considering the petitions and parts of the Lord's Prayer. Except for one snow day, each week we've had opportunity to ponder the greatness and majesty of this magnificent prayer which Christ gave to the twelve.

Surprisingly, over the ages, the Christian community has chosen to conclude that prayer with words our Lord did not say. We pray (say it with me), *"For Thine is the kingdom, and the power and the glory, forever and ever, amen"* But the only part of those words Jesus said was AMEN. Those familiar words were added by Christians at worship, probably come from the words

279

of David in 1 Chronicles 29:11, **"Yours, O Lord, is the greatness and the power and the glory and the majesty and the splendor, for everything in heaven and earth is yours. Yours, O Lord, is the kingdom; you are exalted as head over all."**

It's highly probable that somewhere in the first five centuries the people of the church wanted to add something, a conclusion, a finality to the great words of our great Lord. They'd heard the words of the priest and wanted something more, so they added *"For yours is the kingdom, and the power and the glory forever, amen."*

They said AMEN because our Lord had commanded them to. In the original Greek language, Jesus used the word over and over. **"Truly, truly I say to you..."** Maybe you learned it from the King James version like I did, **"Verily, verily I say unto thee..."** That's Jesus saying AMEN. **"Truly, truly"** or **"Verily, verily'** in the Greek language is **"AMEN, AMEN..."** **"To Him be glory and power, forever and ever, AMEN!"**

Martin Luther taught his students what this word means. He wrote, *"Amen! This means that I should be certain that these petitions are pleasing to our Father in heaven, and are heard by Him; for He Himself has commanded us to pray in this way and has promised to hear us. Amen, Amen, means Yes, Yes, it shall be so."* (The Small Catechism, 1530)

A man named Nicodemus came to Jesus one night. He was a member of the Jewish Council and didn't want to be seen with Him. He told Jesus, **"Rabbi, we know you are teacher from God, for no one can do the miracles you do if God was not with him."** Jesus answered him, **"Truly, truly I say to you, no one can see God unless he is born again."** (John 3) **"Truly, truly"** – **"Amen, amen,"** said Jesus, and He still says it today.

Saying **"Amen, amen"** was the customary way Jews emphasized what they were saying. It's a minor oath. What followed **"Amen, amen"** was sure to be true, you could count on it. You could take it to the bank, and it'll be there when you came back.

Nicodemus never forgot that night. He became a follower of Christ who later shed his cloak of secrecy on Good Friday when he brought spices to help another member of the Sanhedrin named Joseph of Aramithea bury the body of Jesus in a new grave. His coming out of secrecy was his way of saying "Amen" to Jesus.

Amen is the word of approval. If you worship at some Christian churches, during the sermon you'll hear "Amen!" repeated often by the worshippers. It's their way of agreeing with the speaker. It's saying, *"Right on! We agree with you, pastor."* I like to hear approval, but "Amen!" doesn't happen often during my church services.

I suppose if we started that custom here, some wouldn't appreciate it. It would surely take awhile to get used to. Not just because we don't talk out loud in church. We say lots of things out loud, so long as they're printed in the hymnal or bulletin. And not just because we like only formal worship – we're fairly informal here compared to some Lutheran churches who don't vary a note from what's printed in the hymnal liturgy.

But you know what I think? I think it would be hard to get used to because we'd have to agree with the pastor, and to affirm what he's saying right there on the spot. Lutherans aren't sure they want to do that on the spot, and certainly not out loud. We want to think about it awhile before we agree publicly. We may agree silently, so maybe we'll agree with a little wink or a nod of the head and a slight pursing of the lips. But this is much different from the nodding of the head by tired people. We want a nod of approval, not the nodding neck of the sleepy head. But whatever our custom, "AMEN" is still truly a word of agreement.

Jesus said, **"Amen, amen"** often in the Bible, 78 times, to be exact. **"I tell you the truth, heaven and earth shall pass away, but My words will not pass away."** (Matthew 5:18) **"I tell you the truth, the Pharisees have received their reward in full..."** (Matthew 6) **"...It will be more tolerable on Judgment Day for Sodom and Gomorrah than for those hypocrites."** (Matthew 10) **"...You will see the Son of man coming in glory."** (Matthew 16) **"...If you have the faith of a mustard seed, you can move a mountain."** (Matthew 17) **"...Unless you become like little children, you won't enter the kingdom of God."** (Matthew 18) Each time, Jesus began with, "Amen!"

And God says AMEN every time He brings a child into His kingdom by the waters of Holy Baptism. He forgives our original sin in baptism, He accepts poor miserable sinners in baptism, and He loves us with an everlasting love that never dies in baptism. Baptism is one of His many AMENs to us people.

Holy Communion is another AMEN from God. In bread and wine we're given His holy Body and Blood and reminded of His love and forgiveness for all. Marriage is another AMEN. It was not good for man to be alone, so God made him a companion. Men and women are God's AMEN to each other. The church is another AMEN from God. The Holy Spirit knew believers needed to belong, so He created the church. Here we hear Good News preached, here we serve and here we fellowship.

I believe we can say that life itself is God's AMEN to us. He allows us to live, and He gives us pleasure and love. Yes, there is pain and struggle, but there's usually more good than bad in life. And heaven is God's greatest AMEN to us. There we'll know no pain, no heartache, no tears, no rejection. There in eternity, we'll sing and live out God's great AMEN forever.

But it all started with an open grave on the first Easter, the empty tomb of the resurrection. We don't know whether the angels said "AMEN" but when they saw Jesus, the disciples surely did. The women who saw the open grave did. A week later a doubting Thomas surely did.

May God give us all, every person here this morning, the joy and peace to say with joy and delight, **"Amen!"** He's done all for us in Jesus. Christ is risen! He is risen indeed. **"To Him be glory and power, forever and ever, AMEN!"**

+ *FINE* +

Rev. Robert L. Tasler

The author is a native of Windom, Minnesota, and a career ordained pastor in the Lutheran Church-Missouri Synod. A 1971 graduate of Concordia Seminary, St. Louis, Missouri, he has served parishes in North Dakota, California, Utah and Colorado. Now retired, he and his wife Carol divide their time between Colorado, and Arizona. He has authored several other works, electronically and/or in print, including his highly successful first devotional, DAILY WALK WITH JESUS, all of which can be seen on his website: http://www.bobtasler.com/. Thank you for reading this book. If you liked it, please tell others about it.

Made in the USA
San Bernardino, CA
02 June 2015